New Paths in Criminology

New Paths in Criminology

Interdisciplinary and Intercultural Explorations

Edited by

Sarnoff A. Mednick
University of Southern California, and
Psykologisk Institut, Copenhagen

S. Giora Shoham
University of Tel-Aviv

with the assistance of
Barbara Phillips

Lexington Books
D.C. Heath and Company
Lexington, Massachusetts

Library of Congress Cataloging in Publication Data

Main entry under title:

New paths in criminology.

1. Crime and criminals—Addresses, essays, lectures. I. Mednick, Sarnoff A. II. Shoham, S. Giora
HV6028.N4   364   77-25739
ISBN 0-669-01510-5

Published simultaneously in Canada

Printed in the United States of America

International Standard Book Number: 0-669-01510-5

Library of Congress Catalog Card Number: 77-25739

Contents

v

Acknowledgments

The leaders of the international community of scholars in criminology responded enthusiastically to the opportunity to further the cause of interdisciplinary and intercultural research and thinking in this field. The fact that they could at the same time honor Karl Otto Christiansen, a beloved, highly respected senior colleague made their acceptance of our invitation even more ready.

We wish to thank the authors of the articles in this volume for their help at all stages of this manuscript.

Barbara Phillips, a psychologist by training, coordinated the complex series of intercommunications between the editors, the authors, and the publisher. She carried out an initial editing of every manuscript and corresponded with authors regarding possible additions, omissions, and alterations. From her work in typing and proofreading to her help with decisions relating to choice of manuscripts, content, and titles, Barbara's work was indispensable and of uniformly professional quality.

Mednick's work on this volume was supported in part by NIMH research grant MH 25311 "Interactional factors in antisocial behavior" from The Center for Studies of Crime and Delinquency and by a contract (Number 81733-8-CA-NI) with the Law Enforcement Assistance Administration, "Longitudinal Research in the United States."

Introduction

Sociocultural factors have been criminology's dominant explanatory variables since Goring's study gave empirical justification to social science's distaste with nineteenth century Lombroso-type biological determinism. In the ensuing years, the importance of these sociocultural factors for understanding crime has been exhaustively elaborated both empirically and theoretically. Unfortunately, the vigorous assertion of social determinism seemed to require the almost total exclusion of consideration of biological factors.

We think we can detect some stirrings of change. The 1978 meetings of the American Society for Criminology included a section on biological determinants. Marvin Wolfgang, in his January 2, 1978, testimony to a congressional committee studying violence, listed biological factors among the potentially influential variables worth exploring. Perhaps now that sociology has won its place as criminology's establishment, it can maturely retrace its steps and attempt to integrate relevant and useful biological approaches. The field seems to be moving in the direction of a growing accomodation.

One important factor which has contributed to this accommodation has been research on the genetics of criminality. If a genetic influence exists it will have one important meaning: a biological factor (or factors) exists which interacts with social forces in the etiology of some criminals' antisocial behavior or some subtype of criminal behavior (e.g., violence). Positive genetic findings should imply an acceptance of research including biological variables.

Genetic studies of crime began with Johannes Lange's 1929 report *Verbrechen als Schicksal* (*Crime as Destiny*). Lange stated that of thirteen monozygotic twins, ten were concordant for criminality; of seventeen dizygotic pairs only two were concordant. He concluded "that heredity plays a quite preponderant part among the causes of crime" (p. 41). Legras (1933), Rosanoff (1934), Stumpfl (1936), Kranz (1935), Borgström (1939), Yoshimasu (1947), and Tienari (1963) followed with twin studies which on the whole supported Lange's statement. (See Karl Otto Christiansen's thorough review, 1977b.)

What is remarkable is the lack of interest this research evoked among criminologists. Most likely this was due to the serious methodological flaws of these early studies and the weakness of their efforts to integrate their findings with sociological theory and data.

Karl Otto Christiansen (1977a) reported on the criminality of a total population of 7,172 Danish twins. His study overcame the methodological failings of the earlier work. He found that identical twins were concordant for criminality in 35 percent of the pairs, while fraternal twins were concordant in only 13 percent of the pairs (pairwise concordance). This work was solid and compelling; the apparent strength of the genetic effect was considerably more moderate than had been claimed in the earlier work.

Christiansen's research became known and accepted by leading criminologists; his research is probably the most critical single factor which is responsible for what may become a "new look" in criminology, a new look distinguished by its interdisciplinary, interactionist approach. Two factors may explain the pivotal influence of Christiansen's work. First, he was primarily a sociologist; he was personally a man of unimpeachable integrity, sobriety, and moderation. He was the major Scandinavian criminologist, having introduced his Nordic colleagues to sociological thinking. His mature, thoughtful, humorous, and warm human influence was sought and heard in the world councils of learned societies. These personal characteristics induced many to carefully and positively evaluate his work and ideas.

An additional critical reason for the pivotal influence of Karl Otto Christiansen's work was his attempt to teach us how genetic factors interacted with sociocultural forces. Taking his inspiration from Sellin's theory of culture conflict (1938), Christiansen demonstrated that the genetic-biological factors express themselves most clearly where cultural factors suppress the likelihood of criminal behavior. In people or situations in which anticriminal cultural forces are weaker, the expression of the genetic factors is less apparent. "Offenders who have overcome the greatest and most comprehensive group resistance probably disclose more clearly than others the type of personalities which are important" (Sellin, 1938). Karl Otto Christiansen (1968) postulated: "An increase of group resistance within a given population will involve an increase in the relative frequency of mentally and/or socially deviating persons among the criminals recruited from this population. A strong group resistance is more easily overcome by persons who because of *mental* deviations feel the resistance less strongly, or by persons who due to unfortunate *social* conditions are living under special pressure" (p. 113).

For example, Christiansen's twin study demonstrated that the genetic effect expressed itself more strongly in the middle classes than in the lower classes. In the middle classes the group pressure against criminality is relatively high. Some of those who become criminal may be more influenced by genetic-biological forces. He demonstrated analogous relationships for seriousness of crime, rural-urban residence, and sex. The genetic effect expressed itself more clearly in rural areas, for more serious criminals, and for women.

The genius of Karl Otto Christiansen was in his firm leading of criminology to understand and be excited by his vision of interdisciplinary interactionism. He died in 1976; the editors and authors of this volume have been inspired by his ideas and research and hope to honor his memory with this volume.

Hod-Hasharon, Israel   *Sarnoff A. Mednick*
March, 1978   *S. Giora Shoham*

1

Real and Perceived Changes of Crime and Punishment

Marvin E. Wolfgang

Deviance and Crime

The definition of crime is culturally subjective. So is society's response to persons who commit crimes.[1] Crime is an act that is believed to be socially harmful by a group that has power to enforce its beliefs and that provides negative sanctions to be applied to persons who commit these acts.[2] Although crime, like pornography, may be in the eye of the beholder, subjective perceptions about crime are closer to universality and retain a more temporal stability than do definitions of obscenity and pornography.

At least this generalization applies to serious crime and the meaning of seriousness. Acts that are defined in American culture as crimes which contain no personal victims and which do not involve physical injury, theft, or damage to property have a wider range of perceived seriousness; acts that involve injury, theft, or damage have a narrow range of seriousness and considerable stability over time in their rank order of gravity (Sellin and Wolfgang, 1969).

It is commonplace to refer to the cultural relativity of crime and to mention that the crime of yesteryear is noncriminal today. What is less trite and certainly not trivial is Emile Durkheim's notion that crime is normal, not pathological (Durkheim, 1938, p. 67-71). Durkheim said that even in a society of saints there would still be crime, by which he meant that if all acts we know as crime were eliminated, small differences in behavior that now appear to have no moral significance would take on a new and important meaning. Slight breaches of manners and good taste could become serious crimes. In his terms, crime involves acts that offend strong collective moral sentiments. If these sentiments weaken, then what were formerly considered to be serious offenses would be considered less serious; when the sentiments grow stronger, less serious offenses are promoted to a more serious category. The degrees of enforcement and severity of sanctions are correlated with the intensity and degree of commitment to the collective moral sentiments.

Even though deviance may have both inevitability and elasticity, we are currently experiencing in America, perhaps in Western society, an expansion of acceptability of deviance and a corresponding contraction of what we define as

We gratefully acknowledge the permission of *Daedalus* to reprint this article from their December 1977 issue.

1

crime. The total quantity of criminal and noncriminal deviance may be constant, both in value definitions and in statistical frequency; but the line of demarcation between criminal and noncriminal deviance is being positioned at a different point in the total line segment we call deviance.

By a contraction of what is deemed delinquent, the criminal law will be made more enforceable. The more narrow range of behavior considered criminal will mean a stronger link of consistency with history, for the persistently serious offenses like homicide, rape, and thefts, which have almost everywhere and always been viewed as criminal, will constitute the hard core of criminality, and the actors will continue to be viewed as criminals.

The Increase and Decrease of Crimes of Violence

Since 1930, the major method for determining the amount of crime in the United States has been the Uniform Crime Reports (UCR) of the Federal Bureau of Investigation. These annual reports are produced from the collection of police reports in departments of cities and county jurisdictions across the country. There are twenty-nine categories of offenses, but only the first seven are used for what is known as a crime index, a classification analogous to the consumer price index, the cost of living index, and the index of economic productivity. These seven include criminal homicide, forcible rape, robbery, aggravated assault, burglary, larceny of $50 and over, and automobile theft, and are referred to as "offenses known to the police." All the remaining twenty-two offense categories are reported only in terms of the number of persons arrested.

There has been much critical commentary over the past forty-five years about the validity of the crime index, both from traditional scholars who use the crime index reports and from Marxists who deride the data and deny the validity of a capitalist system that fails to take into account the criminogenic forces of the economic and political power of the state. Putting aside those issues and admitting that except for the new series of data known as "victimization rates," collected by the Bureau of the Census cooperation with the Law Enforcement Assistance Administration, there is little other basis upon which scholars or public officials have for determining whether crime rates are increasing, decreasing, or remaining stable.

Using the UCR data (Uniform Crime Reports, 1975), it can be said that since 1960 crimes of violence have increased 180 percent. The fear of crime, as indicated in a variety of localized studies, has probably increased in even greater proportions than the recorded reality of crime. That many crimes are unrecorded, that reporting procedures have varied over this time, and that more crimes may be reported now—particularly rape—than in earlier days are issues that are difficult to test empirically.

Nonetheless, there appears to be some consensus among the community of criminologists who examine criminal statistics that the amount of real criminality has considerably and significantly increased during the past fifteen years. That there have been equally high rates of crime and crimes of violence recorded in earlier eras of the history of the United States has been asserted by using such long-time series data as Buffalo and Boston provide and as are recorded in the Task Force Reports of the National Commission on the Causes and Prevention of Violence (Mulvihill et al. 1969). Crimes of violence in the latter part of the nineteenth century were as high or higher than even the currently reported rates of crimes of violence.

The issue, however, is that within the memories of the current living population of the United States, since the early 1960s, there has been such an upsurge in crimes of violence, or street crimes, that social concern, governmental budgets, and public policy are increasingly affected.

Explanations for the assumed increase are varied but usually embrace such issues as unemployment, broken homes, inadequate education, housing, racial injustice, relative deprivation, lack of law enforcement, and leniency in the courts. Our purpose here is not to be explicative, but descriptively analytical.

We do know that there have been significant demographic changes directly related to the changing crime rates. High fertility rates immediately after World War II, known as the "baby boom," produced a significant alteration in the age composition of the United States population, such that a swelling of the age group between 15 and 24 years occurred in the early 1960s.

For example, in 1940 and 1950, 15-24-year-olds constituted 14.7 percent of the total population. By 1960, 1965, and 1970, the proportions of the same age group were respectively 13.6, 15.7, and 17.8 percent (Census of Population, 1970). Because this age group is the most "criminogenic," meaning that this age-specific group contributes more than any other to the rates of crimes of violence for the total population, it has been asserted that the sheer increase in this age group has been the major contributor to the increase in crimes of violence. Studies designed to factor out statistically the contribution of this demographic change have generally supported the assertion that no matter what social interventions may have been made to control, prevent, or deter crime, the changing age composition of the population has been importantly responsible for the increase in crimes of violence.

In an econometric-type model of crime rates over time in the United States, James Fox has shown how the 14-21 year age group has significantly contributed to the rising rates of crimes of violence in the United States (Fox, 1976). But he has also shown with carefully controlled demographic projections to the year 2000 what changes are most likely to occur (figure 1-1). In the United States we are now at our lowest rates of fertility, and the reduction of fertility has already begun to be reflected in the reduced increase in crimes of violence. In 1976 we began to notice both relative and absolute decreases in crimes of violence. The rate of increase dropped, and in many major cities across the

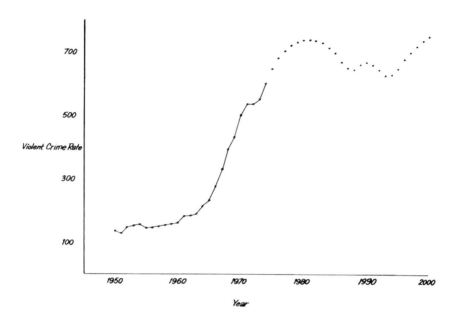

Source: James Alan Fox, *Forecasting Crime Data*, (Lexington, Mass.: Lexington Books, D.C. Heath and Co., 1978) p. 57. Reprinted with permission.

Figure 1-1. Prediction of Violent Crime Rate

country there was an absolute decrease in crimes of violence. The proportion of the youthful group in the total population has decreased and the earlier "baby boom" generation is in the late twenties and early thirties, ages at which the commission of violent crime normally decreases. We should be witnessing from now through the mid-1980s a decline or stability in the amount of crimes of violence.

However, the postwar "baby boom" children, now grown, are getting married and will produce high fertility rates again despite the relative decline in the number of children per couple. Consequently, the 15-24 year age group will rise again in the 1990s, producing once more a rise in the amounts of violence. These claims are made without reference to any effect which greater amounts of law enforcement activity or changes in the criminal justice system may have on the reduction of crime. As a matter of fact, the weight of empirical evidence indicates that no current preventative, deterrent, or rehabilitative intervention scheme has the desired effect of reducing crime.

Two other points need to be made about the changing rates of crimes of violence. One is related to the increase in violent crimes since the early 1960s, and the other is related to the expected decrease in crimes of violence from the late 1970s to the 1990s. First, it is not simply the increase in crimes of violence that has promoted public fear and increased expenditure of public funds to combat crime; it is the expansion of crimes of violence to groups that have "the power to enforce their beliefs," namely, the large middle class and the upper class in American society who have increasingly become victims of crimes of violence.

The major crime control system in Western civilization has traditionally been that of residential segregation. From the time of the ancient Greeks in Athens through classical Rome, the Middle Ages on the continent of Europe, and in the United States, the slaves, the "criminal classes," the beggars of society, and the lower socioeconomic classes—to use the more current traditional phrasing of social scientists—are the groups attributed with being the major crime committers of theft and physical injury; they have always been residentially kept within their own densely populated, propinquitous areas. Kept on the other side of the river, the canal, or the railroad tracks, the "criminal classes" have been segregated, and crime committed among these groups has either not been well recorded or reported, or it has been considered to be of relative inconsequence to the social structure that has been politically and economically powered by the aristocrats, nobility, or bourgeoisie.

In the United States, the under class, which has always included a high proportion of blacks since the days of slavery, has conveniently been residentially segregated from the middle class. Rapes, robberies, and homicides committed intragroup among the lower classes have been relatively unimportant to those groups in legislative, executive, and judicial power. With the increasing importance attributed to equality of opportunity, the breakdown of racially restrictive covenants in 1949 by a Supreme Court decision and the value placed upon political equality, the traditional residential segregation crime control system has been altered. Moreover, technological changes affording greater opportunities for physical as well as social mobility and interaction among groups have contributed to the breakdown of barriers that formerly existed. Consequently, even as there has been an increase in the amount of social interaction among social and ethnic classes and groups, there has been an increase in the amount of intergroup and interclass crime which has contributed to the greater victimization of middle and upper classes. Burglaries, muggings, rapes, and killings among the groups that define and rate the seriousness of crime and that have the power to enforce sanctions have increased their concern with crimes of violence.

So long as the poor and the blacks were raping, robbing, and killing one another, the general majority public concern with crimes of violence was minimal. Public visibility of concern with such crimes has been related to the more generalized victimization as well as to the rise in the rates of such crimes.

The second point dealing with the expected stability or decrease in crimes of violence concerns the change in public perspectives about seriousness of other kinds of crimes. For example, crimes of violence caused by what some of us call a "subculture of violence" (Wolfgang and Ferracuti, 1967) may be replaced by cunning and corruption. Lombroso foresaw some of this condition as he compared societies in the nineteenth century: "Civilization introduces every day new crimes, less atrocious perhaps than the old ones but nonetheless injurious. Thus in London the thief substitutes cunning for violence" (Lombroso, 1912). Georges Sorel's *Réflexions sur la Violence*, which first appeared in 1906, was in a similar vein (Sorel, 1936). Speaking for the revolutionary syndicalist wing of the labor movement, Sorel focused on the struggle for social power and suggested that reduction of overt acts of violence in social relations is correlated with an increase in fraud and corruption; fraud comes to replace violence as the means to success and privilege. Manipulation of persons and things, especially through economic institutions and the impersonalized relationships represented by money, increasingly is substituted for force. Men become interchangeable, alienation accumulates, minds are raped in subtle ways.[3]

With reduction in crimes of violence, major public concern about crime will probably shift to organized and white-collar varieties. In this transitional stage we will make the trade-off of violence with fraud. In the 1970s organized crime uses less violence than thirty or forty years ago. Monopolies of power in service industries are gained by legal purchase or fraudulent conversion. Accounting practices and legal services constitute the backbone of organized criminal business. Loopholes in regulatory law, purposefully retained, are exploited by legitimate and illegitimate business. Violent liquidation of competitive persons in organized crime gives way to incorporation of the adversary by buying him out or burying him in bankruptcy.

When professional and business crime is finally viewed as corporate dysfunctionality, as an attack on the body politic, such crime will then be more carefully scrutinized and placed under the focus of stringent governmental control and public appeal for action. The change is already occurring and will continue. The rise in the number and political and economic power of consumer interest groups, the increased perceived seriousness of political corruption, corporate criminality, and multinational bribery are already reflections of the changing emphasis in our society from crimes of violence to fraud and corruption. Pollution, bribery of public officials, and Medicaid and Medicare fraud may yet be viewed as being as serious as burglary or sexual assault.

Nam et Ipsa Scientia Potestas Est

Part of this change is already being reflected in a new form of information or knowledge theft that is becoming a major type of criminality. Computer tape theft, computer program theft, and corporate information burglary are styles of crime that are already prominent. The theft of information in order to obtain positions of power will increase. The Pentagon Papers, the attempt to steal information from Daniel Ellsberg's psychiatrist, the entire Watergate scandal are among the more dramatic illustrations of this kind of theft.

But there are many others. Recently six persons were arrested in California in what is described as a "multimillion-dollar industrial espionage case" perpetrated against the International Business Machines Corporation (The New York Times, June 30, 1973). An IBM engineer was arrested and charged with ten felony counts: four of conspiracy, three of theft of trade secrets, two of offering or accepting inducements to steal trade secrets, and one of receiving stolen property. The principal subject of the theft was an IBM-developed direct-access-storage device known as the Merlin, which comprises the data-storage portion of many computer systems.

This is not an isolated case, for many similar ones are coming to light. These, combined with consumer fraud, securities thefts, and political corruption constitute a growing form of major crime in our postindustrial era (Whiteside, 1977).

The penal codes of socialist countries may more nearly represent this future condition in the United States. No inference is made that the socialist countries represent a further step in social evolution; whether the change suggested is upward, downward, or horizontal is irrelevant. The point is that economic crime—embezzlement, theft of corporate money and property—is considered in socialist countries as more serious than many, or most, crimes against personalized victims. The sanctions for the former are more severe; the frequency of committing either is apparently lower than in capitalist countries.

Explaining Crime

System Shifts

Talcott Parsons (1949, 1951)[4] has provided a useful analytic model of three major systems: culture, society, personality. The culture system refers to values and norms, the social system to the structure or group and individual interaction, and the personality system to the biopsychological and psychiatric forces within the individual. These are interesting systems, idealized and isolated for analytic purposes. Each individual is a biological organism, a vessel of culturally transmitted values, a member of some social groups who thereby interacts with others. The three systems are, in reality, meshed and merged, but disciplines of knowledge and of science focus on different aspects of each system.

Both in academic criminology and in the public mind, shifting system emphases can be noted. If the modern scientific analysis of crime and the criminal can be said to be dated from the writings of Cesare Lombroso in the last quarter of the nineteenth century, then the emphasis in the early stage may surely be said to have been on the personality system. He wrote, for example, about the atavistic, or born, criminal, who was a biological throwback to an earlier stage of evolution, a genetic anomaly characterized by marked physical traits like the prognathous jaw, long arms, and sloping forehead (Lombroso, 1912, p. 34-35).

Psychological studies, such as those from William Healy in 1915 to contemporary ones, have emphasized the mental condition of the *individual*. The main task of such studies was to devise a typology of personalities, with one or more types susceptible to deviance in general, or to some specific type of deviance. Mental aberration was a central point in Healy's eclecticism.

A move toward the *social system* emerged in the writings of W.I. Thomas in the 1920s: " 'Environment' is no longer regarded as a scene of action for the person, but as material out of which the personality itself is built."[5] Thomas's emphasis on social psychology as the "subjective side of social culture" places him in the interactionist approach to personality and culture. People have attitudes, or propensities to act; values are external to the individual and the objects toward which people have attitudes. Certain social drives, such as the desire for security, response, recognition, and new experience are universal, but in varying strengths and weaknesses in different personalities. Thomas's explanation of prostitution took this social-psychological form which required use of the learning process to explain behavior (Thomas, 1923).

With the notion that learning is part of a response pattern leading to deviance, Edwin Sutherland's (1934) differential association, which further emphasized the social system and interaction between the individual and his group, found fertile intellectual soil for growth in 1924. One now became criminal because of frequent, long, intense, or early associations with others who were criminal, compared to those who were not criminal. Differential association indeed shifted American criminology from a focus on the personality system to the social system. There developed a variety of psychodynamic theories of criminality, of deviance in general, that brought to the fore such concepts as sex-role identifications, ego strength, dependency needs, defense mechanisms, and other psychoanalytic notions of individual response to social interaction. The learning process emphasized the way that external values were differentially ingested into the personality by means of the social system.

But there was yet a further shift to come, one that firmly placed the burden of explanation on the larger ambience, that drew upon macroforces and made the individual offender more a captive of historical, political, and economic determinism than of his biology or personal interaction with others.

Clifford Shaw and Henry McKay, in the early 1930s (Shaw and McKay, 1931, 1942), exemplify the "cultural transmission" approach and the changing focus from how criminogenic forces get inside individuals to what those forces are and the gradient degree of their appearance in the environment outside the individual. We are told, for example, that "delinquent behavior is related dynamically to the community" and that "all community characteristics, including delinquency, are products of the operation of general processes. . . ." Delinquent conduct of children in a city is surely due not to a personality maladjustment but to a much larger social disorganization. The "differential rates of delinquents," Shaw and McKay (1969, p. 315-316) asserted, "reflect the differences in social values, norms, and attitudes to which the children are exposed." And, "from the point of view of the delinquent's immediate social world, he is not necessarily disorganized, maladjusted, or antisocial. Within the limits of his social world and in terms of its norms and expectations, he may be a highly organized and well-adjusted person."

Emile Durkheim (1951, 1950, p. 65-73) had much earlier (1895) provided a *culture system* emphasis. His social "facts" possessed an exteriority to the personality and social systems that influenced generations of scholars. Sociological inquiry, suicide, and other phenomena were to be explained in a style reminiscent of the earlier work in social physics. Anomie was borrowed from medical literature to describe norm conflict, normlessness, and general social states of anxiety. Robert Merton (1957) expanded the notion of anomie in the 1950s and introduced a means-end schema that emphasized structured social strain and stress, the disparities between what was wanted and how it could be achieved. Aspirations and achievement gaps and variations were viewed not from the point of individual frustration but from a higher level that saw cultural systems with conflicts.

Thorsten Sellin (1938) drew attention to this emphasis when he spoke of "conflicts between the norms of *cultural systems* or areas," and in this phrasing itself helped to transform research interests to the current focus.

The link to contemporary sociological thoughts about crime and delinquency that push the culture system approach further is fairly obvious. Albert Cohen (1955) introduced a kind of Hegelian antithesis with his description of the delinquent subculture: "The delinquent subculture is not only a set of rules, a design for living which is different from or indifferent to or even in conflict with the norms of the 'respectable' adult society. It would appear at least plausible that it is defined by its 'negative polarity' to these norms." With this note on a delinquent subculture, Cohen took us beyond the point of raising questions about an emphasis on personality or on a social or cultural system. The culture system was assumed from the outset as the generation of forces producing delinquency, or at least the predominant mode of delinquency.

Cohen argued that a delinquent subculture arose because of conflict with middle class culture and was oriented to deliberate violation of middle class norms. Walter Miller (1958) took the position that gang delinquency emerged directly from, and in response to, a set of norms in the lower social-economic class, which constituted a culture system of its own, an idea similar to that of Oscar Lewis. Delinquency was not a directed negativistic and malicious attack on the middle class. "In the case of 'gang' delinquency," Miller said, "the *cultural system* which exerts the most direct influence on behavior is that of the lower class community itself. . . ." (Miller, 1958, p. 5, emphasis added).

Richard Cloward and Lloyd Ohlin (1960) differentiated three subcultures—criminal, conflict, and retreatist—with the vector of illegitimate opportunities. Combining anomie, role theory, and cultural transmission traditions, they asserted that not only are legitimate opportunities (access to normatively acceptable means) differentially distributed in the social structure, but so are opportunities to achieve cultural goals by illegitimate means. Deviant responses were in subcultural forms depending on the types of opportunities available in various communities.

Wolfgang and Ferracuti (1967) emphasized the culture system approach with their contention that a clustering of individuals who have allegiance to and share in the resort to violence in many situations of interaction constitute a subculture of violence. The major thrust of their position is that a subcultural system tolerates, encourages, and even requires the use of violence under prescribed circumstances, and that high rates of aggressive offensivity are due to the value system, not to instinctual aggressive drives or to idiosyncratic motivations or drives.

The recent basic assumptions of the "labeling school," or the symbolic interactionists, take the culture system approach even further. At the same time, emphasis is placed on the dynamics of social psychology by the claim that the definers implant a conception of the self in the self. Criminal deviance occurs, says Kai Erikson (1962), by reason of the assignment of labels by the "social audience." As he claims: ". . . deviance is not a property *inherent* in certain forms of behavior; it is a property conferred upon these forms by the audiences which directly or indirectly witness them. The critical variable in the study of deviance, then, is the social audience rather than the individual actor, since it is the audience which eventually determines whether or not any episode of behavior or any class of episodes is labeled deviant" (Erikson, 1962, p. 308).

One of the chief elements in the manufacturing of criminal deviance is the official labeling by the public response agents—police, court agents, correctional personnel, the guild of therapists. The social organization of the criminal justice system also imposes behavioral restraints that support and confirm the conferred label of deviance. There are many more important features of labeling, but each reaffirms the passivity of the deviant who is defined and processed, who is stamped with social stigma. The act or actor is dethroned from importance and a position of initiation; the reactors and the reaction process are paramount.

The major thrust of social thought has thus been from the personality to the social to the cultural system in an effort to explain. No set of explanations of social phenomena moves in phalanx style; there is usually some overlapping. The claim here is only that these have been the dominant modes of explanation represented in the sequence described.

Neoclassic Revival

New Wine in an Old Bottle

The major purposes of punishment historically have been retribution, expiation, deterrence, reformation, and social defense. Throughout history, an eye for an eye, the payment of one's debt to society by expiation, general deterrence of crime by exemplary punishment and specific or special deterrence of an individual offender, reformation of the individual so that he will not commit further crime, and protection of society against criminality by detaining or imprisoning offenders have been the principal rationales for disposition of criminal offenders.

In 1764 Cesare Beccaria, in his classic book *Dei delitti e della pena (On Crime and Punishment)*, wrote that there should be a scale of the seriousness of crime with a corresponding scale of the severity of sanctions. In the Age of Reason in the eighteenth century, with an emphasis upon the rationality of man, deterrence was the principal purpose of punishment. And Beccaria wrote poignantly about this rationale. One of his major statements—which surely has contemporary value—was that it is not the severity but the certainty of punishment that deters.

Since that time and through the nineteenth century, Western civilization encountered a different and new rationale for disposing of criminal offenders: rehabilitation. In the nineteenth century there was an increase in psychiatric concern with criminality. Isaac Ray (1838) wrote in his famous treatise on medical jurisprudence about insanity and criminal responsibility. Following him were the writings of Sigmund Freud and others that increased the psychiatrization of the criminal law. The medical guild linked with the legal guild in criminal justice and convinced the administrators of criminal law that offenders could be reformed, rehabilitated, remolded, resocialized, and thereby produce a decrease in criminality. In 1870, the American Prison Association met in Cincinnati, Ohio, and declared that the principal purpose of punishment was reformation. From that time on, through six decades of the twentieth century, criminal justice was primarily oriented toward this rationale.

Around 1960, careful studies began to evaluate the efficacy of the rehabilitation model. As these studies increased in statistical sophistication, they increasingly reported negative conclusions, namely, that intervention techniques from individual to group therapy, reduced case loads for probation and parole officers, and other intervention models had no significant effect in reducing recidivism (Bailey, 1966; Hood, 1967; Ward, 1967). In 1975, a major report of 289 studies of rehabilitation and intervention was made showing that no therapy significantly contributed to the reduction of recidivism (Lipton et al., 1975). Since that report and Robert Martinson's (1974) article in the *Journal of Public Interest* entitled "What Works?" there has been an increasing disillusion with the rehabilitation model.

The Struggle for Justice (1971) was a major report by the American Friends Service Committee that had earlier questioned the rehabilitation model and was primarily concerned with the enormous disparities in criminal sentencing and suggested greater uniformity. Since that time, and with the impact of articles by distinguished authors like Francis Allen (1959) and Herbert Packer (1968), there has grown a social policy assertion that the uniformity of sentencing and a decrease in judicial discretion are necessary attributes for promoting greater justice in our criminal policy. The Goodell Committee for the Study of Incarceration, whose report was recently published by Andrew von Hirsch (1976) under the title *Doing Justice*, has expressed explicitly the growing public concern and disillusion with rehabilitation and a desire to produce a criminal justice system based upon the "just deserts" model, which means that criminals should be punished not for what they might do in the future but for what they have done in the past. This "just deserts" model is in much conformity with the eighteenth-century writings of Cesare Beccaria and the later works of Jeremy Bentham and his felicific calculus regarding risks, rewards, and punishments.

Current thinking among many jurists, police, legislators, well articulated by James Q. Wilson (1975), is that we cannot do much about the "root causes" of crime, nor that government at any level can legislate love or affect the rate of broken homes. Unemployment, low levels of education, poor housing, and similar social problems among the working classes are issues that the government can and should try to change sui generis with only secondary reference to crime and only because they are major issues concerned with social welfare.

On another level, the criminal justice system is capable of direct manipulation, and federal and state governments should make efforts to effect change. These changes involve the following: increase in the probability of arrest and conviction and a positive sanction of incarceration for offenders who have committed offenses of injury, theft, or damage; elimination of the indeterminate or indefinite sentence by judges and reduction of judicial discretion at the point of sentencing; inclusion of the juvenile record for adults who are convicted and about to be sentenced so that the seriousness of crimes committed as juveniles will be considered in the sentencing discretion; decrease of judicial discretion, which should be substituted by a uniform sentencing process based upon the seriousness of the crime committed rather than on characteristics of the offender.

A new bill submitted to the Congress by Senators Gary Hart and Jacob Javits is in agreement with many of these suggestions. The bill recommends the establishment of a Federal Sentencing Commission which would base its guidelines for sentencing on the seriousness of the crime alone.

A relatively small cadre of persons is responsible for most of the crimes of violence in America. In one study (Wolfgang et al., 1972) it was noted that only about 6 percent of an entire birth cohort of 10,000 boys born in 1945 and followed through their years from 10 to 18 were responsible for the many street crimes about which the public is so fearful. It follows that a social criminal policy designed to incapacitate for three to five years persons upon conviction of their second or third violent assaultive offense could have a significant effect upon the total rate of crimes of violence.

Under the "just deserts" conceptualization there is no expectation of rehabilitation. In fact, David Rothman (1971), who gave us one of our best histories of asylums, refers to the concept of a failure rather than a success model as being more appropriate to punishment. However, under the current mode of thinking, therapy and service programs should continue to be available but on an optional basis, and participation in those programs should have no effect on the time of release for any convicted offender. Because of the excessive and intolerable number of false positives, the prediction of dangerousness would remain as an academic exercise only and should not be included in a criminal justice system. Even if we were able to predict future violent behavior, it would be inappropriate for us to determine the length of a sentence or the degree of restraint based upon future expectations. Offenders should be punished for what they have done, not what they might do.

Punishment, even retribution, now becomes acceptable as a basis for justice. The Durkheimian conceptualization is reintroduced as a reinforcement of the community moral sentiments and not necessarily as a vengeful reaction by the madding crowd. Humane treatment in and out of prison is highly emphasized, as is the likelihood of fewer prison sentences, and then only or mainly for violent, assaultive offenders. The use of fines such as "income days," restitution to victims, and the right to be treated as well as the right not to be treated would be fundamental principles of the system. Definite sentences rather than indefinite or indeterminate sentences constitute a core item in the agenda, whereas parole or aftercare from an institution would be eliminated as an institutional procedure and a part of the criminal justice bureaucracy. Helping agencies that currently exist could be augmented for assistance to persons released from prison, but not under coercion.

The deprivation of liberty is a punishment sufficient unto itself in a democratic society that places high value on liberty and freedom of movement. Such a proposition implies that capital punishment is an unnecessary and unjust sanction. Retribution does not require it; neither proportional sentencing nor just deserts suggests the death penalty.

We should recall that throughout most of the history of Western civilization, jails, prisons, and detention quarters were used for purposes of detaining suspects awaiting trial or convicted offenders awaiting some form of corporal punishment, exile, or banishment. The use of prisons as penitentiaries, as loci of restraint, as a punishment per se, is a relatively new invention. The Eastern State Penitentiary in Philadelphia (1829) was not the first prison to be used as punishment, but it had few antecedents and few that resulted in the cultural diffusion of the idea of imprisonment as a form of punishment.

Triumph of the Public Mind

Vilfredo Pareto (1935), the Italian sociologist, spoke about culture imitation and the diffusion of folkways, mores, and social inventions from the leaders of society downward through social classes to the masses. Ideas generated by the nobility, intellectuals, and the powerful migrate downward and broaden their base until they strike the lower classes. Pareto's sociological theorizing may have been more appropriate in earlier periods of history, for we have witnessed, particularly in America with the technology of mass media, many examples of reverse diffusion. What has happened is that concepts of crime, criminality, and justice that have existed in the general public mind have had stability over the centuries and are now merging with the current thinking of the social scientific community, criminal justice analyzers, and administrators.

When Beccaria wrote his famous essay 200 years ago, he exemplified an elite rationalism that quickly spread among the leaders of Western society, including Benjamin Franklin and Thomas Jefferson, who were well aware of his writing when they were working on their own independence and creation of a new government (Maestro, 1975). This classical school of criminology and criminal justice took hold among the less learned primarily because the ideas were expressions of the grievances of most people. Whimsical, arbitrary, capricious administration of criminal law benefited the wealthy and the nobility; the poor were punished and tortured severely.

But early in the nineteenth century the Philadelphia Quakers, the elite leaders, introduced at the old prison in Cherry Hill what came to be known as the Pennsylvania, or separate, system. In that prison all inmates, all convicts were kept in solitary confinement from the moment they arrived until the moment they left the institution. With humanitarian intentions to promote self-reformation and to eliminate the effects of social contamination from other convicts, this philosophy and correctional movement were imposed on the criminal justice system and enforced, as Rousseau would force men to be free, on the unfortunates caught in a network of the administration of criminal law.

Charles Dickens visited the famous Philadelphia prison in 1842. At first he was complimentary, but when he put his impressions into writing he was very critical, and his perspective is as current as the critics of today who are opposed to coercive therapy: "In its intention I am well convinced that it is kind, humane and meant for reformation; but I am persuaded that those who devised the system and those benevolent gentlemen who carry it into execution, do not know what it is they are doing. . . . I hold this slow and daily tampering with the mysteries of the brain to be immeasurably worse than any torture of the body; and because its ghastly signs and tokens are not so palpable to the eye and sense of touch as scars upon the flesh, because its wounds are not on the surface, and it extorts few cries that human ears can hear; therefore I denounce it as a secret punishment which slumbering humanity is not roused to stay" (Dickens, 1842, pp. 119-120).

Coercive reformation thus began and later changed its language but not its style. The invasion by medicine, especially psychiatry, of the philosophy of responsibility and of the "reasonable man" changed sin and evil to sickness and disease. The subconscious and unconscious came to dominate cognitive reasoning, and offenders were to be treated rather than punished. It was not the sin in the soul but the disease in the mind that needed to be changed, and mind-altering mechanisms were invented to remold, refashion, and reform the offender for his own good as well as for the protection of society.

It is doubtful that this model and these messages of reform were ever fully accepted in the popular culture. But when the heavy weight of authority from the well-respected academies of medicine and law joined to promote policies of criminal justice, the voices of punishment and retribution from the folk culture remained hushed for over a century.

Only now, with the revival of the eighteenth-century classical position, are these muted tones being heard and articulated by leaders in social science, criminal law, and public policy. Neoclassicism was born from the popular culture and is now nourished by sophisticated research. Deterrence, retribution, and punishment, never abandoned by the populace, have once again become acceptable to those "with power to enforce their beliefs." Reformation, although still accepted as desirable, is dethroned from its position of dominance and is subordinated within a more retributive penology.

Rehabilitation will surely continue and will be researched but in a noncoercive style. Imprisonment should be used as infrequently as justice can design, and humane concern for involuntary victims, by means of such programs as victim compensation and counseling, as well as concern for captured criminals, should govern our democratic justice system. The public, the police, the judiciary, and legislators are now joined by many social scientists in an ethical stance that requests retribution, not revenge, as the definition of justice; that requires an emphasis on stability rather than law and order; that looks to certainty rather than severity of punishment. California, Indiana, and Maine have already passed legislation reflecting these views, and many more states and the federal government can be expected to follow these changes in the perceptions of crime control and the meaning of justice.

Notes

1. This section includes some remarks presented at the Fifth National Conference at the Institute of Criminology, University of Cambridge, England, on July 5, 1973.

2. This is essentially John Louis Gillin's definition of crime in his *Criminology and Penology* (New York: Appleton-Century, 1945).

3. See my earlier comments on this topic in "A Preface to Violence," *The Annals of the American Academy of Political and Social Science* 364 (1966): 1-3.

4. Portions of this section are drawn from an earlier paper entitled, "The Viable Future of Criminology," *Criminology in Action* (Montreal: University of Montreal, 1968), pp. 109-134.

5. W.I. Thomas, "The Relation of the Individual to the Group," *American Journal of Sociology* 33 (1927):814. The statement quoted is embodied in a notice to the American Sociological Society, of which he was then president. The notice was designed to justify his selection of the general topic to be discussed at the next meeting of the Society.

2 The Multidisciplinary Approach to Theory Evaluation

Katja Vodopivec

It is the object of criminology to describe and explain criminality, not to condemn it or to defend it. –   Karl Otto Christiansen

The analytical divergence of knowledge today enables us to give partial answers to problems related to partial social phenomena; it hinders, however, the synthetic and all-encompassing approach to essences of these phenomena. Individuals try to compensate for that by applying knowledge from different areas of science. Karl Otto Christiansen, for example, was versed in sociology, psychology, and law. Others attempt to achieve the same by working in multidisciplinary teams. Still others strive to create new, synthetic scientific disciplines out of modern particularized branches of science.

In the social sciences these attempts are particularly obvious within the empirical pursuits, whereas the formation and evaluation of concepts remains the domain of individuals, or of teams having a common preeducation. It is the intent of this chapter to examine whether the formation and evaluation of theories should be the domain of individuals or of teams with the same professional orientation.

I shall employ the following definition of theory: A theory is a coherent set of general concepts, which explain a particular phenomenon (Filipović, 1965), in this case criminality, or deviance, that is, *what* it is and *why* it exists. On the level of presently attained knowledge, these general concepts may well be hypotheses needing further verification.

A Historical Evaluation of Criminological Theories

In most criminological systems (outlines, textbooks, doctrines), we are presented with past criminological theoretical generalizations and their evaluation in view of the present state of knowledge. There is often a search for an understanding of the theory with regard to its potential impact today. However, such an approach tends to neglect the question of why people thought as they did, how their creations reflect the time in which the theories were brought to light

Translated by Boštjan Zupancic

(Kosik, 1967), and what role they played in the particular historical setting in which their creators lived: Did they lag behind their own time? Did they out-distance it? Or did they perhaps anticipate the future? In short, what were the economic, social, political, and cultural conditions of the time, and what was the theoretical knowledge available? Perhaps not all of the theories should be defined in terms of their birth, but for social theories this is obviously essential. This is all the more true of criminological theories, for they deal with particular forms of deviance in particular social settings.

Less important for evaluation perhaps are the psychological motives which contributed to the establishment of a particular theory by a particular theorist. One should not neglect the importance of the writer's social role in his time since it is that which enables him to transcend the conditions of his own time. Consequently, what is essential are the possibilities of a particular period of time, on the one hand, and the theorist's ability to take advantage of the onto-logical potential, on the other hand.

Such evaluations are rare in the criminological literature because they re-quire too much effort and knowledge on the part of their evaluator even if he works in a multidisciplinary team whose members have similar backgrounds. The final stimulus for this chapter was supplied by the *New Criminology* by Ian Taylor, Paul Walton, and Jack Young (1973)—a work dedicated primarily to the evaluation of different criminological theories, present and past.

The methodological achievement of Taylor, Walton, and Young is primarily that they have shown how impossible and misleading it is to interpret a partic-ular author on the basis of quotations torn out of their context. They have shown for Karl Marx's theory, for example, how important it is to take into account the integral text and the basic underlying thread of thought if one is to interpret particular passages. The evaluation of William Bonger in Taylor et al. is a good illustration of this. I should like to emphasize that Bonger's work and his theoretical approach have been transcended, but the theories which have evolved contain some of his ideas. Taylor et al. admit that "in terms of the social positivism of his time—[Bonger's] work surpasses much that was, and is, available" (p. 228), and that in certain areas of his work "Bonger seems far ahead of [his] time" (p. 232). Their reproach is, however, to "the lack of scepticism about the social content of the law" (p. 229), about "his correctional perspective of deviance" (p. 232) and his indeterminism (p. 234).

The very vocabulary of these reproaches is modern, but the question is whether it was possible to expect this theoretical awareness by the end of the nineteenth century. In the nineteenth and early twentieth centuries the deter-ministic interpretation of human beings and their social interactions was a progressive postulate of philosophical thought, something that emerged under the influence of the development of the natural sciences even before that period.

Indeed, Marx wrote about the intentional and creative activity of man in the mid-nineteenth century, as did Dietzgen and Labriola (cited by Vranicki, 1971), but Engels tended to interpret him more deterministically than Marx himself would have liked (Vranicki, 1971; Mike, 1976), and thus today we are discovering the young Marx again. According to Taylor et al. (1973), "The continuing debates over Marxism in sociology and philosophy (as well as within socialist movements) in the twentieth century, therefore, have to do with problems of consciousness, contradictions and social change" (p. 220).

Something similar applies to the skepticism concerning the social content of legislation. Such a skepticism had been expressed by Marx before Bonger (Marx, 1859); however, this skepticism had not entered the consciousness of contemporary writers until the second half of the twentieth century. The intellectual discovery per se is one thing, but its incorporation in the social consciousness of those who are exposed to it and who should expand it is something quite different. This usually happens only later when the social conditions are such as to foster understanding.

Thus Mike (1976) is justified in saying, "To engage oneself in Bonger's massive work is to enter into the cultural milieu of the late nineteenth and early twentieth century" (p. 236). In spite of his successful effort to understand what Bonger knew about Marxism, Mike blames Bonger from the point of view of the modern problem repertoir. Thus, he says, for example, "The logical extension of Marx's understanding of the world would be to develop a 'social psychology' to mediate between the individual and the social and economical world of which he is an acting part" (p. 220). The question is whether this is a logical consequence to be extrapolated from the interpretations of Marx in the nineteenth century, or merely after World War I in the twentieth century. According to Mike, "Bonger has attempted to combine two incompatible systems, his social determinism and his biological determinism" (p. 227). Was it really so clear in the nineteenth century that these two were incompatible systems of thought? And, finally, Mike reproaches Bonger's statistical conclusions as causal and primitive. But were they generally different in that time at all?

I do not mean to imply that my knowledge of the intellectual atmosphere of the nineteenth century is better than that of the writers I refer to; it is only my perception that is different. Nevertheless, to evaluate a writer and his role in the intellectual atmosphere of a particular period in history should be predicated upon a thorough knowledge not merely of the writer himself and his creations but also of the sociohistorical conditions and philosophical streams of thought of that particular period. Knowledge of the writer and his work, as well as of related writers and their work, should complement the following generalization: Such an undertaking is probably more than an individual, or even a team with a similar professional background, can hope to achieve.

Evaluation of Modern Theories of Deviance

Historical distance acts as a strainer to separate the relevant from the less relevant. Thus it is not possible to evaluate the present in the same way as we evaluate the past because we live it, we cocreate it, and we have no way of knowing how relevant our own contributions will be to the future. For an appraisal of the pertinence of present theories, consequently, it is necessary to assess the social and political climate in which they are generated and applied (Moedikdo, 1976; Fromm, 1973) with the view that these assessments tend to be characteristic of the assessed theory, as well as of the assessor himself. More important, in my opinion, however, is the practical appraisal of the theory in view of its explanatory power for contemporary, modern problems and happenings, that is, for an understanding of the whole of the social interaction and for an application of these theories.

According to Kosik (1967) the intellectual conquest of the world is a permanent process of concretization, a continuous movement from the whole to its parts, and from the parts to their whole, from substance to manifestations and from manifestations to substance. There is a mutual illumination by the selected parts of reality of the whole of social interaction. Pečuljić (1976) says, "We are therefore concerned to discover how a particular phenomenon emerges from the whole of social framework, and to see how this particular manifestation supports the whole as it is or affects its change" (p. 48).

For evaluation of the applicability of theories, Sagarin (1975) enumerates eight criteria, among them, for example, "how much [the theory] can explain . . . , how profoundly it can explain the activities under study . . . , how successfully it can be employed for predictive purposes . . . , the extent to which the theory is compatible with a variety of theories that explain other areas of human behavior . . . , the minimal number of exceptions" (p. 68).

Theories to be submitted to such a verification are numerous, and the verification itself can only be applied to a particular mode of behavior, to a particular social setting with its specific social circumstances.

If past theories concerned themselves with crime and it was then fairly obvious what crime was, then modern theories can focus their attention upon the problem of deviance, a concept much harder to define. This finds its repercussions in divergent and not very useful definitions and unavoidable misunderstandings on the level of theory. Thus, Sagarin (1975) defines deviance as "disvaluated people and disvaluated behavior that provoke hostile reactions." In my view, however, such a definition could be misleading since the "hostile reaction" itself may well be deviant. In my attempt to find another one which would encompass the value criterion, I used the following reasoning:

If it is true that creativity is a basic and specifically human characteristic, then destructiveness should be a basic and essential element of deviance (Vodopivec, 1971). Thus we have:

The destruction of the personal and spiritual integrity of the victim.

The destruction of the industrial, social, and spiritual creations of people.

The destruction of oneself.

I will admit, of course, that such an interpretation has its exceptions, especially since the destruction itself may have a defensive nature or it may be necessary for paving the way for a new and greater creativity. On the other hand it is probably impossible to render a definition of deviance today which would hold true for all cases. Yet the above definition does narrow the scope of deviance, since it does eliminate the modes of behavior included by some authors into the spectrum of deviance, such as homosexuality and the use of the so-called soft drugs; it is questionable whether, for example, prostitution should be defined as self-destruction.

But even such a narrow concept of deviance encompasses many kinds, each of which can be subsumed under different theoretical explanations. As an example, let me take Fromm's *Anatomy of Human Destructiveness* (1973) which refers exclusively to the destruction of the personal and spiritual integrity of the victims. Fromm cites the instinctivist theories (Freud and Lorenz), as well as the theories of behaviorism (Skinner), and environmentalist theories (theories of frustration) (Dollard), and theories of learning (Alee, Nissen, Nimkoff). Fromm is trying to develop his own theory, partly on the basis of a reinterpretation of Freud, and partly on the basis of the thesis—apparent in all of Fromm's works—that man is a specific being with a specific psyche with its own idiosyncratic structure and regularities. According to Fromm there are two essential features of man—his character and his passions. His *"character* constitutes the main motivation of human behavior, but restricted and modified by the demands of self-interest under varying conditions . . . and his *passions*, his meanest and his noblest. [The man] is often willing—and able to risk his self-interest, his fortune, his freedom, and his life in pursuit of love, truth, and integrity—or for hate, greed, sadism, and destructiveness" (p. 83). Fromm does not conceive of destructiveness as an innate characteristic of man, and he passionately attacks the theories of instinct, applying knowledge derived from neurophysiology, animal behavior, paleontology, and anthropology. He also offers a social and political evaluation of these theories.

His rejection of human destructiveness as a consequence of human drives and instincts, however, does not make him insensitive to all those forces which stretch man between good and evil: "However, even if a better understanding of many instances of destructive and cruel behavior will reduce the incidence of destructiveness and cruelty as psychical motivations, the fact remains that enough instances remain to suggest that man, in contrast to virtually all mammals, is the only primate who can feel intense pleasure in killing and torturing. I believe I have demonstrated . . . that this destructiveness is neither innate, nor part of 'human nature' and that it is not common to all men" (pp. 180-181). According to Fromm, man became destructive "with the increasing productivity and division of labor, the formation of a large surplus, and the building of states with hierarchies and elites" (p. 435). It is for that reason that he advocates humanistic radicalism "which goes to the roots, and thus to the causes; [it] seeks to liberate man from the chains of illusions; it postulates that fundamental changes are necessary, not only in our economic and political structure but also in our values, in our concept of man's aims, and in our personal conduct" (p. 438).

Fromm's first goal was to render his own theory well founded, and it was through that prism that he chose and criticized other theories he touched upon. Thus, for example, he does not even mention the theory of conflict except insofar as it is implicitly present in analyzing different kinds of destructiveness. I would like to emphasize that in spite of the tremendous work he accomplished, he simply was not able to overview the whole field of knowledge. This adds to our doubt whether it is indeed possible to evaluate all the pertinent theoretical knowledge, especially because this multifaceted and enormous knowledge must be put together by one person who starts from his own professional orientation.

Formation of New Theories

Formation of new theories requires at least a good knowledge of all existing accomplishments in order not to "discover" what has already been unraveled. A new theory is neither a sum total of empirical discoveries nor a synthesis of existent theories on the basis of verification by means of empirical testing.

According to Adorno (1969), the establishment of the description of things is not the same as the establishment of their essences. Social theory derives from philosophy; positivism and empiricism, from natural sciences. The synthesis of both aspects has so far not been established. A reified method only gives a footprint, a reified perception of the object. To Adorno an object-event can be understood only in its social framework (see also Kosik, 1967). Thus Adorno writes that even if we could statistically establish that workers no longer conceived themselves as a working class and thus that the proletariat no longer existed, this would still not be in accordance with reality. The subjective perceptions of the workers ought to have been compared with their position in the process of production, with the possibility of their disposing with the means of production, and with an assessment of their social power. In the meantime the task of establishing the essences of phenomena is the postulate of philosophy.

To attempt to synthesize all those elements of existent theories which were empirically tested would be to fall prey to eclecticism. Even though Hardman believes that "an eclectic approach is not only possible, but advantageous," I agree with Sagarin (1975) "that what [Hardman] suggests by his eclecticism is what could be better termed a low-level-of-abstraction theory" (p. 76). An essentially new synthesis is possible exclusively in terms of a qualitative leap which in turn requires a totally new relationship to the essence of the matter and, therefore, implies a transcendence of eclecticism. One has to agree with Datta that "one cannot take the best of many disciplines, mix them, and emerge with 'theory, eclectic' " (Sagarin, 1975, p. 75).

With this we have already touched upon the problem of many disciplines, all related to the attempt to explain human behavior in society (for example, philosophy, sociology, psychology, social psychology, psychiatry, neurophysiology, anthropology). Whether it will ever be possible to synthesize all these aspects remains to be seen. When Fromm talks of neurophysiology, he says: "It would seem that each science should proceed in its own way and solve its own problems, until one day, one must assume, they both have developed to the point where they can approach the same problems with their different methods and can interrelate their findings" (1973, p. 90). Is it possible to catalyze this process in the present?

Thus it seems that even the formation of new concepts and theories will no longer be a domain of individuals. Since the formulation of a new theory is a qualitative leap from the existent into the new, intuition is required. Intuition can derive from the insight of an individual, or it can be a product of collaboration and mutual influence among several individuals.

But even for these accomplishments in the field of the social sciences it will still hold true that they will depend on the dimensions of time and place in which they are generated, and will not necessarily be valid for a different historical setting.

The Pitfalls of the Multidisciplinary Approach

Although I advocate a multidisciplinary approach even in the realm of evaluation and theoretical generalization, I am aware that such a collaboration of specialists with different basic orientations is not without problems.

I have been working in an institute of criminology associated with the Ljubljana University Law School for twenty-two years. Some time ago the institute employed four permanent staff lawyers, one psychologist, and five part-time associates, all lawyers. The ratio, therefore, was nine lawyers to one psychologist. The present ratio is ten lawyers to one psychologist. The institute has completed many studies, most of them by multidisciplinary collaboration with professionals and specialists from different branches of science: physicians, psychiatrists, psychologists, sociologists, social workers, statisticians, education specialists, and practicioners. All have been employed ad hoc for the particular study in question; we have not attempted to tackle the theoretical problems in this manner.

My general evaluation is that the "outsiders" have not identified intensely with particular projects. Their work on a study remains secondary, in contrast to full-time employees who identify strongly with their projects, have themselves structured them, and have thus been committed to them from their inception. The products of such cooperation have often remained compilations of individual, independent, and—to the rest of the study—unrelated monographs. One exception is a long-term study in one of the reform schools, which lasted over eight years. But the team still experienced great internal crises, which are described in Vodopivec (1974).

The full-time psychologist has, as others have, intensely identified with the projects in which he has engaged. Yet throughout his ten-year association with the institute he has remained a psychologist, not a criminologist. The psychologist provided the following evaluation of his own cooperation in several different research teams:

> If there is one dominant field of knowledge which characterizes a particular institute, the specialist of another field will feel lonesome and insecure, since he knows too little about this field.
>
> Teamwork requires cooperation, rather than competition, whereas our cultural orientation, because of education and schooling, remains competitive.
>
> There is much competition for prestige. Some team leaders tend to ascribe to themselves ideas proposed by others.
>
> The teamwork enables some to live parasitically, that is, to appropriate other's ideas and present them as their own.
>
> A special problem is the cooperation between theorists and practicioners: the latter do have ideas, although they often do not know how to express them, and thus theorists tend to formulate these ideas, whereas the practicioners do not receive the appropriate satisfaction.

A different situation seems to be prevalent at the University of Ljubljana Institute of Sociology, which, however, I can only evaluate from the outside. In the Republic of Slovenia until 1960 sociology was not a separate field; thus the Institute of Sociology employed as full-time associates people with different backgrounds. Slowly they were becoming sociologists. The full-time employees intensely identified with the institution. Sociology thus became of primary importance to them, whereas their different backgrounds tended to become of secondary importance.

Alonso (1971) offered his own objections against interdisciplinary cooperation in the field of regional planning. He concluded that "the interdisciplinary approach is of limited validity and that [it] hides many pitfalls" (p. 169). Among others he enumerates the following problems:

> Every scientific discipline is a conglomerate of numerous specialties. A university degree does not guarantee the qualifications of a particular specialty.

All disciplines are subject to fast advancement. The specialist desires to improve in his specialty yet besides the fact that his commitment to the team project hinders this desire, the commitment itself is not particularly appreciated among other specialists of the particular discipline.

Good specialists are difficult to attract to team work, because they tend to be too engaged in their own specialty.

If it proves to be possible to engage older experts from different disciplines, since they became bored by their own specialties, they will as a rule tend to play the role of wise men, rather than experts.

The problem itself, in view of its development, will with time perhaps require a greater participation of the specialists of one branch on account of the specialists of other branches, the consequence being that some will be too burdened with work, whereas others will lose their interest in the matter. With the development of the project, these roles may change, thus fostering conflicts within the team.

The specialists tend to use concepts which have different meanings in different specialties (p. 169).

As a positive alternative to the interdisciplinary approach Alonso advocates that "urban and regional problems and plans be attacked by one or more professionals who are first and foremost scholars in urban and regional problems and secondarily members of traditional disciplines" (p. 171). However, Alonso, still believes that the ad hoc interdisciplinary approach is useful in solving totally new problems since it fosters a confrontation of different opinions and ideas. But, according to him, there are few such problems.

The range of knowledge and its interrelatedness has become so immense and so complex as to make the individual, with his limited intellectual and energy resources, incapable of encompassing and mastering it. The multidisciplinary approach makes it possible to analyze the particularized bits of knowledge and to synthesize them. Until now we have tried two different paths: (1) the formation of interdisciplinary teams ad hoc, and (2) the formation of new synthetic disciplines at the postgraduate level. Both attempts have their negative sides, the first approach in the heterogeneity of the people constituting the team, the second in the prolongation of the education and in the danger of creating still new specializations. But the cooperation of people competent in different fields of knowledge is becoming a modern necessity, and the search for future paths for cooperation should be pursued. This could be complemented by the gradual change of competitive cultural tradition into a culture of cooperation on different levels of social life (Skalar, personal communication).

3

An Alternative Approach to the Etiology of Crime

Wouter Buikhuisen

It is sometimes said that the roots of many sciences can be found in the work of Aristotle. It is difficult to say whether this holds true for criminology. If we look at criminology as an empirical science, it might be more correct to locate its beginnings with the famous Italian criminologist Lombroso, who made a considerable effort to increase our understanding of the origins of crime.

In his early years Lombroso tried to explain crime by referring almost exclusively to the physical traits of the offenders. Only in his later publications did he pay more attention to the possible relevance of social factors. Since Lombroso, many scholars have approached the crime problem, be it from different angles; this has led to the creation of different schools of criminology, such as the anthropological, sociological, ecological, psychoanalytical, biological, and, more recently, Marxist schools.

The common factor in most of these schools is that they look at the crime problem in a unidisciplinary way. This is not to say of course that there have been no attempts to study crime in a multidisciplinary manner. Studies like those of the Gluecks (1950), Cohen's theory (1956) to explain lower-class gang behavior, and the research carried out by Ferracuti, Dinitz, and Acosta de Brenes in Puerto Rico (1975) are just a few examples to the contrary. Unfortunately, however, the multidisciplinary approach is more the exception than than the rule.

Crime as Behavior

All theories of criminology should proceed from the assumption that crime is behavior. Two important consequences result from this supposition: (1) there is a need for a differential criminology, and (2) to explain criminality, the criminologist must adopt a behavioral approach. In what follows, I shall consider both these points.

The Need for a Differential Criminology

The criminologist has to deal with such diverse behavior as drug abuse, drunken driving, shoplifting, white-collar crime, burglary, vandalism, armed robbery, sexual offenses, murder, bribery, and violence. In view of this, it is surprising to

27

see that crime is discussed in such general terms. This approach is reflected in many of the existing theories of criminology, which are often nonspecific and claim thereby to have a general validity. Eysenck (1964), for instance, considers that criminality is the result of bad conditioning, while Merton (1957) finds the explanation for criminal behavior in the fact that our society creates all sorts of needs but does not provide everyone with equal means of satisfying these needs within the law. Others such as Cohen (1956) look for the answer in the class system, Taylor et al. (1973), in the structure of society.

Although all these theories differ from each other, they have two things in common: (1) each of them claims to explain criminality—that is, *all* criminality—neglecting the fact that crime is a heterogeneous phenomenon, and (2) usually hardly any empirical evidence is presented to support the theory. To obtain a better understanding of criminal behavior, it is essential to study more homogeneous groups.

What criteria should be used to arrive at more homogeneous subcategories of offenders? One criterion should, of course, be the kind of offense committed. Although this would certainly help to achieve greater homogeneity, a group selected in this way would still be too heterogeneous in my opinion to allow an adequate theory to be built up.

For example, suppose that we are studying a group of violent delinquents. The significance of their behavior will vary according to a number of factors:

> The social class of the criminal. The lower social classes have different opinions, after all, on the acceptability of violence as a means of settling disputes than the higher social classes.

> The age of the criminal. The use of violence is more "normal" during adolescence than, for example, after the age of thirty.

> The sex of the criminal. Violence by women is more likely to require a different explanation than violence by men.

> Whether the act was committed alone or with others. It is an accepted fact that the causes underlying group violence are different from those underlying individual violence.

If no account is taken of these factors when studying violent delinquents, one runs the risk that the highest common denominator which can be found to explain their behavior will be a far from accurate reflection of the true state of affairs. What is true of crimes of violence is true of other crimes as well. Clearly, the greater the variety of crimes studied the vaguer and more generalized will be any cause that is common to all. It is only possible to identify more specific causes when one works with a more homogeneous group.

According to Karl Otto Christiansen (1968, 1974) the impact of genetic factors is greater in more serious crimes, in women, and in the higher social classes. In practice this means that subgroups must be formed as already indicated. The variables listed above (age, social class, sex, number of offenders) are important in this respect. Each of them can be applied as a criterion to increase the homogeneity of the group being studied and thereby to improve the accuracy of the theory. Other possible criteria are the degree of recidivism and the extent of urbanization. Quite obviously, there may be other criteria that are important, such as the degree of professionalism of the offender, and these should be selected in accordance with the type of crime being studied.

Relevance of the Proposed Criteria

In the previous paragraph the importance of working with more homogeneous groups was stressed. In this section I will present some evidence to support the relevance of the proposed criteria. Before doing so I would like to emphasize that creating subcategories of offenders is not the same as proposing a typology of delinquents. Typologies imply a theory. What I propose is to *classify* offenders in order to arrive at more valid theories about the origins of crime. In this respect classifying should be seen as a means to an end. Its relevance depends on the extent to which we are successful in reaching our aim: developing theories which are better able to explain the behavior of the offenders concerned. As such it is a pragmatic approach—some classifications might prove to be useful, others not. Here too the proof of the pudding is in the eating. Unfortunately, up to now there has been little willingness among criminologists either to "cook" or to "taste." By presenting some relevant data it is hoped to increase the appetite of criminologists for this.

Criminal Behavior as a Criterion. Probably one of the most disputed criteria for classifying offenders is the kind of offense committed. Many respectable criminologists like Korn and McCorkle (1959) and Clinard and Quinney (1967) are opposed to this method of classification. Arguments brought forward against legal classifications are, according to the latter writers:

1. They tell us nothing about the person and the circumstances associated with the offense, nor do they consider the social context of the criminal.
2. They create a false impression of specialization by implying that criminals confine themselves to the kind of crime for which they happen to be caught or convicted.
3. Because the legal definition of a criminal act varies according to time and place, the legal classification of crime presents problems for comparative analyses.
4. Legal classifications do not identify theoretically significant types.

In another article (Buikuisen and Jongman, 1970a) I showed that these objections are open to criticism. The results of a comprehensive study were presented to show that, contrary to Clinard's and Quinney's opinion, juvenile delinquents indeed exhibit a statistically significant tendency to confine themselves to specific offenses. It was found, for example, that among recidivists the observed distribution of subsequent offenses differed significantly from a chance distribution. Or to put it in a more concrete way, if a juvenile delinquent "started" his criminal career with a violent offense, the observed number of subsequent violent offenses on his criminal record differed significantly from the number that would be expected. This does not mean of course that juvenile recidivists have completely homogeneous criminal records, or that there are no juveniles with heterogeneous criminal records. On the contrary, it was found that 5 percent of the offenders studied had committed a completely heterogeneous set of offenses. In view of our pragmatic approach to the classification problem there is nothing against regarding these as a specific group or type, worthy of separate study.

There is another comment I would like to make about legal classifications. For our purpose criminal records should not be examined too rigidly. Two possible approaches can be distinguished. First, on the basis of probability statistics we ascertain whether the criminal record of a recidivist allows us to label him as a specific type of offender. It is important here to determine the probability of each offense's occurrence. For instance, if an offender has committed two sexual offenses and three economic offenses, we will call him a sexual offender, as the probability of finding two sexual offenses in a list of five offenses is considerably lower than that of finding three cases of theft in such a list.

The second approach to identifying types of offenders on the basis of a legal classification is the clinical one. This approach is characterized by a kind of psychocriminological analysis of criminal records. If, for instance, a list of offenses of a recidivist consists of two convictions for drug abuse and three for theft we should label the offender concerned as a drug abuser, since we should assume that the thefts probably have to be explained as a way of getting money to buy drugs. For similar reasons a combination of drug abuse and prostitution would be identified as representing the drug abuse type. Of course this way of classifying offenders is a rather subjective one, certainly compared to the first approach we suggested. However, for our purposes it might be useful.

One of the objections of Clinard and Quinney to legalistic classifications does not apply to the situation in the Netherlands: in our research we were able to identify a kind of specialization among juvenile recidivists. A second objection of Clinard and Quinney was that legal classifications do not identify theoretically significant types. Research in the Netherlands also contradicts this statement. For instance, I found many statistically significant differences in an empirical study in which juveniles repeatedly convicted for theft were compared with juveniles involved in violence. This study illustrates that classifying offenders according to their behavior can be revealing from a theoretical point of view and can be useful for prevention (Buikhuisen, 1969).

Age as a criterion. Offenders form a heterogeneous group not only with regard to the crimes committed; heterogeneity is also caused by a difference in the ages of offenders. This well-known fact has led to a distinction between juvenile criminology and the criminology of adult offenders.

Unfortunately this distinction has not been worked out systematically. Yet we believe that from an etiological point of view age is an important factor. In this respect it might be interesting to report the results of a study of unreported crime, carried out in the Netherlands (Buikhuisen and Jongman, 1970b). In this project the relationship between age and crime nuisance in seven different types of offenses was examined. The sample consisted of subjects aged from sixteen to twenty-eight, each age group containing 100 subjects. All subjects were asked to report to what extent they had committed shoplifting, violence, vandalism, or sexual offenses, during the past year. Among other things it was found that the percentage of subjects in each age group committing offenses like shoplifting and vandalism decreased steadily after reaching its maximum at about seventeen years. This means that, while it is quite normal from the statistical point of view to commit shoplifting at seventeen, it is abnormal to behave in that way at the age of twenty-eight. This makes it all the more likely that we could increase our understanding of shoplifting by taking into consideration the age of the offender. The same applies to offenses like vandalism, violence, and drunken driving.

That it is important indeed to differentiate between age groups has been shown by the Canadian psychiatrist Bruno Cormier (1965). He compared offenders in their twenties with those in their thirties, forties, and fifties and found great differences. For instance, those in their twenties were rarely "lone operators," many of them showing serious personal and social problems and an antisocial attitude, committing crime as an act of rebellion against society. Those who became first offenders in their thirties were rarely rebels with basic antisocial attitudes. Their problems were often connected with unhappy marriages or with sexual disappointments. Finally, loneliness and physical and emotional deterioration are characteristics of those who become first offenders in their fifties. In short, since changes take place in the social position of the human being as in his biological system as he grows older, it is important in explaining crime to differentiate between age groups.

Social Class as a Criterion. The concept of social class plays an important role in the etiology of crime. Many criminological theories are basically rooted in factors associated with this factor, be it subcultural elements, different value systems, different opportunity structures, economic and housing conditions, or lack of leisure facilities. Many outstanding criminologists have explained crime by referring to the underprivileged position of the lower class. Such arguments do not apply to offenders from the middle and upper classes; their behavior, therefore, cannot be explained by most of the existing social theories. It is surprising to see that hardly any theory exists to explain middle-class criminal behavior. To arrive at theories of this kind it is necessary to classify offenders according to their socioeconomic status.

The Group Factor as a Criterion. Crimes can be committed by groups or by individuals. Research in group dynamics has clearly shown that the pressure imposed on members of a group make it difficult for them not to participate in group activities. Moreover, acting collectively—especially in gang behavior—reduces the feeling of personal responsibility for what takes place. We therefore may expect that subjects involved in criminal group activities (group violence, shoplifting with a group) will differ from offenders who commit these offenses by themselves.

Illustration of the Classification Model

The foregoing is illustrated in figure 3-1. For the sake of convenience, I have represented the total criminal population as a rectangular block whose sides are formed by the variables: type of crime committed, social class to which the criminal belongs, and age of the criminal. By taking into consideration the sub-categories which can be distinguished within each of these variables, subblocks can be formed. These subblocks are then divided in turn by the dimensions: male/female, whether the crime was committed with others, or committed alone. In this way, the whole block may be subdivided into subblocks each in the form of a triangle, representing a subgroup of criminals which is homogeneous with regard to the crime committed, the social class to which the criminal belongs, the criminal's age and sex, and whether the crime was committed with others or alone. (It is probably unnecessary to point out that: (1) the above-mentioned criteria may not always be applicable and that (2) with regard to certain crimes other criteria may be more appropriate. This does not affect the principle, however, that if more reliable theories are to be formulated they will have to be based on the study of more homogeneous groups.)

By comparing a subcategory with criminals from other subblocks and with matched control groups of noncriminals, one can gain an understanding of what is characteristic of this particular group. A differential criminology of this kind is essential. In principle, the results of this approach can be threefold.

First, it may appear that, whatever the crime, criminals do not differ from noncriminals. A result of this kind would substantially confirm the theories of those criminologists who hold that the only difference between criminals and noncriminals is that the former were caught and the latter were not.

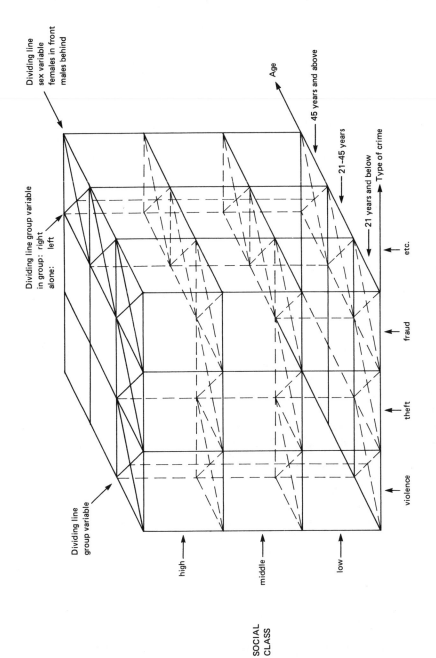

Figure 3-1. Illustration of the Classification Model

Second, the research might show that criminals, while differing from control groups of noncriminals, do not exhibit any differences among themselves. Such a result would call for the formulation of one general explanatory model for criminality.

Third, it may transpire that the various categories of criminals not only differ from the control group of noncriminals but also differ among themselves. Should this be the case, it will be necessary to devise more specific explanatory theories. My own feelings are that this will be the case. This is not to say, of course, that subgroups of criminals will not exhibit the same characteristics in certain cases. To allow for such exceptions, it would make sense to develop a more general theory. Whatever the result may prove to be, comparative studies of this sort must form the basis of criminological theories from now on. Anyone who omits this step is, in fact, courting disaster.

The Need for a Behavioral Approach

I stated above that two consequences result from the supposition that criminology is directed toward, among other things, the study of criminal behavior. I have already examined the first. My conclusion was that the diversity of both criminal behavior and criminal groups requires a differential criminology. There is no room within such a criminology for attempts to explain the origins of criminality in general. Differential criminology sets itself a more modest target. It searches for an answer to the question why certain categories of people (boys, women, members of a given social class), exhibit a certain type of what may be classified as criminal behavior. In practice, it is likely that this will result in the formulation of a multiplicity of criminological subtheories. This does not mean, of course, that they would have nothing in common. Some of the variables would definitely crop up in more than one theory, but they might then, for example, receive different emphasis or occur in different combinations. The second consequence of this behavioral approach is that any explanation of criminal behavior must be based upon behavioral principles. The point of departure is that all behavior is a function of the personal characteristics of the individual concerned and of the situation in which he finds himself. There can be great differences between the two sorts of characteristics. Below, I give a formula to express criminal behavior (which is, of course, also a form of behavior) in terms of these characteristics:

$$C f (P_i, S_i)$$

in which

C = criminal behavior

P_i = the collective expression of all the personal characteristics relevant to an explanation of the criminal behavior; the personal characteristics are:

P_1 = genetic factors
P_2 = endocrinological variables
P_3 = biological factors relating to the brain
P_4 = neurophysiological variables
P_5 = biochemical factors
P_6 = psychophysiological factors
P_7 = organic factors

P_k = psychiatric factors
P_l = psychological factors
P_m = sociological variables
P_n = attitudes, norms, and values

S_i = the circumstances or situation of the individual concerned, both past and present. A further distinction can be made between:

S_1 = *The situation at micro level.* The situation and circumstances in which the criminal behavior took place. In the case of shoplifting, for instance, this would be the shop. The victim's role may be another factor to be taken into account here.

S_2 = *The situation at meso level.* Situations where there is or has been some element of fundamental interaction between the individual concerned and third parties. This would include, for instance, not only events that occurred in the parental home, at school or at work, in the neighborhood where he lives and in contact with friends and others of his age, but also his experiences with the police, the courts, probation and aftercare services, child care and protection authorities.

S_3 = *The situation at macro level.* The social system and climate in which the individual lives. Important factors falling into this category are, for instance, the social and political climate, the economic situation, employment, educational facilities, housing, recreational facilities, the level of urbanization, and the social climate within a community (attitudes toward minority groups, the degree of tolerance present, and mutual solidarity).

The formula $C f (P_i, S_i)$ is the premise on which the theory of differential criminology is based. It functions, as it were, as a checklist enabling one to determine which variables may be relevant to any particular subject of criminological research. What is perhaps more important is that at the same time it makes clear to us which variables the researcher emphasizes and which are ignored in an attempt to explain the causes of criminal behavior. A cursory look at the existing theories quickly shows that they are not conspicuous for their variety.

Criminology as an Interdisciplinary Science

The formula given above expressing criminal behavior as a function of the person and the situation is not intended as an explanatory model. It is no more than an attempt to reduce the variables which may be relevant to criminal behavior to a single denominator. As such it could be called a sort of regulatory principle. The various criminogenic factors which may be relevant are expressed in the formula. The model is multidisciplinary, or if you like, multifactorial. In itself this is still insufficient to arrive at an adequate explanation of criminal behavior. To achieve that, an interdisciplinary approach is necessary which will in the long run be able to lead only to interdisciplinary models. Such an interdisciplinary orientation, however, should not be directed only toward supplementing views derived from one's own discipline. What is also important is that this approach should penetrate into the concepts applied in accordance with one's "own" science, so that multidisciplinary concepts can be established.

In my opinion, the lack of such concepts is an important reason why criminological research—which after all relies on these concepts—has until now produced so little criminological theory that will stand up to critical examination. For instance, many sociological theories concerned with class, unemployment, and separation from parents would be more valuable if, when applying and interpreting them, criminologists gave some consideration to views derived from other disciplines such as psychology, pedagogy, and cultural anthropology. To illustrate this, let us take the concept of unemployment. From the sociographic point of view, this is a static concept. It indicates that someone is out of work. For other sciences, however, it is a dynamic concept which may have extremely varied consequences for the person concerned. Psychology, for instance, is interested in how people out of work react to being unemployed; psychiatry is interested in how the experience affects their personalities; and social psychology is concerned with how neighbors and society in general treat the unemployed and what this means to the unemployed themselves. The answers can vary, both in the positive as well as the negative sense, depending on the personality of the individual concerned, the sort of work he had, the situation in which he finds himself, the neighborhood where he lives, the length of time he has been unemployed, the opportunities he has of occupying himself during this period, his financial situation and so forth.

Many criminologists would pay little attention to these sorts of deliberations. To them, the unemployed are all alike for the purposes of any relation between unemployment and criminality. They work only with the statistical concept: employed or unemployed. This is then correlated with criminality. The result of this calculation is then supposed to provide us with an understanding of what significance unemployment has as a cause of criminality. It can be seen that similar approaches have been used to deal with variables such as class, separation from parents, and religion.

Again and again, one finds that factors which may vary considerably in their significance to the individuals concerned have been treated as static magnitudes having only one meaning. This sort of undesirable interpretation and application can be prevented if an interdisciplinary approach is used to throw light on criminological concepts. An approach of this kind is an important condition governing the further development of criminology.

Another reason why we should adopt an interdisciplinary approach is that, as shown by research, the various individual disciplines are only able to explain the origin of criminal behavior to a very limited extent. Statistically speaking, each discipline is able to explain only a small proportion of the variance. This is partially attributable to the complex nature of the problem of criminality, which cannot be treated as a straightforward sociological, psychological, or biological question, to name but a few disciplines. Progress can be made, therefore, only by means of a multidisciplinary approach. Criminologists who, nevertheless, continue to favor a unidisciplinary approach might profitably consider how it is that the great majority of the population to which their theory is applicable (for instance, the lower classes, the unemployed, the mentally unstable) are not normally criminals.

In my opinion, there is yet another reason why we have so far not succeeded in producing a proper explanation of the phenomenon of criminality. We are still unable to determine in a reliable manner whether an individual is criminal, and if so, to what extent. This is another area in which political and ideological factors may sometimes play a role. History provides a fascinating example. Whereas every criminal was for long (far too long) thought of as abnormal, the balance has not tilted to the other extreme as a result of research into unreported crime. Self-reporting studies showed clearly that everyone actually commits crimes and that, statistically at any rate, the perpetration of crimes should be regarded as normal. As is often the case in such situations, this reaction is also extreme. Equilibrium must, therefore, be restored. For the present, I would consider this as achieved when it is accepted that criminality is as much a personal variable as is intelligence. Just as there are less intelligent, normally intelligent, and extremely intelligent people, so it should be recognized that people can be classified to form a continuum from the person who is barely criminal, at one extreme, to the serious criminal, at the other. If criminology is to develop further, means will have to be found which will enable us to determine the place every individual occupies on this continuum. True, that is no easy task, neither technically nor psychologically. We shall first have to surmount the ideological barrier that not everyone is equal in this respect—an unpopular task in a period in which the removal of inequalities is held to be progressive as a political objective.

A Model for the Formulation of Interdisciplinary Theories

Comparative research is in principle the basis of any interdisciplinary study. Comparisons of criminals with noncriminals will be based on the formula $C f (P_i, S_i)$, showing criminal behavior as a function of the person and the situation.

In carrying out these comparisons, the principles of differential criminology described above will need to be applied as much as possible. Any such comparative study will reveal a number of differences between the two groups. For example, a study of violent criminals might produce the following data: Violent delinquents are usually young and generally from the lower class. Their home life is characterized by a lack of affection and the children are often beaten by their parents. Their achievements at school are minimal. They have no hobbies, and they do not belong to any clubs, spending most of their leisure time outdoors, visiting pubs, and so forth. They have a low frustration tolerance and a quick temper. They are also found to have a deficiency of thiamin and an excess of dopamine, and their psychophysiological reaction level is said to be low. A preliminary analysis shows clearly that what is presented here as a collection of isolated variables consists in fact of a number of interrelated parts. Their composition can be changed to suit the approach one chooses to adopt.

A number of different regulatory principles can be distinguished. For instance, the variables I have listed could be classified under heads such as: the parental home, leisure activities, personal characteristics, education and school, organic charactersitics. Once again, this produces a multidisciplinary classification. However, what we want is an interdisciplinary approach. How can we set about developing such an approach? In my opinion we should start with a kind of phenomenological analysis, looking for mechanisms and general principles which might enable us to gain an understanding of the way crimes are committed.

The assumptions we use should not be overly biased by our discipline of training. Also, we should not be so naive as to look for real causal factors. Taking this into consideration it might be useful to distinguish three kinds of factors which each have some relevance to the cause of crime: predisposing factors, facilitating factors, and inhibitory factors. In the etiology of crime it should be possible to identify factors which make people likely to commit crimes. These are what I call the predisposing factors. Their presence increases the likelihood of criminal behavior.

Whether one or more predisposing variables will actually lead to crime depends on:

The number and strength of these predisposing factors.

The presence of factors which, in combination or interaction with predisposing factors, favor the commission of crimes. These we have called facilitating factors.

The presence of factors which in combination or interaction with predisposing variables remove the cause of crime: the inhibitory factors.

It can be easily seen that what we favor is a probabilistic model for the explanation of crime, approximately as follows: given the existence of predisposing factors A and B, the presence of facilitating factors a, b, and c, and the absence of inhibitory factors such as d and e, the probability that a specific crime will be committed is y. In this non-discipline-biased model each discipline can contribute any factor, be it predisposing, facilitating, or inhibitory.

Having arrived at this point the more empirically oriented reader might be a little puzzled. He might wish to know what is actually meant by concepts such as predisposing factors, facilitating factors, and inhibitory factors and what the differences are among them. He might wonder for instance whether facilitating factors and inhibitory factors should not be considered to be extremes of the same continuum. At this moment it would not be easy to give clear-cut definitions of these concepts. It is certainly true that they can overlap in meaning. It could be argued, for instance, that the difference between predisposing and facilitating factors is in some cases more quantitative than qualitative. For our purpose these concepts are nothing more than a means to an end. I think it will suffice to give the following descriptions.

Predisposing factors are variables which are able to explain by themselves a significant part of the variance in criminal behavior. This means that there is a kind of direct—although not necessarily compelling—relation between these variables and the phenomena studied. Therefore, when studying a certain type of offender, we must be able to show the presence of these factors. However, if we examined the general population of subjects characterized by predisposing factors, we would find that only some of them have actually been involved in the criminal behavior concerned. This is because the presence of predisposing factors in itself does not necessarily entail the occurrence of criminal behavior. We need either the absence of inhibitory factors or the presence of facilitating ones. For example, in cases of maltreatment it should be possible to show the presence of frustrations. However, of the population of frustrated subjects only some will actually behave violently. This is because it takes more to go from frustration to violence. This "more" is what is meant by either the presence of facilitating factors (for example, alcohol consumption, fatigue, a lack of verbal skills) or the absence of inhibitory factors (middle-class ideas about solving conflicts, low physical strength, attitudes about nonviolence based on religion).

By now it should be clear what is meant by *facilitating factors*. Initially they only have an indirect relation to crime. In order to be effective, they need the presence of a predisposing factor; by themselves they cannot cause crime. What they do is speed up delinquent processes, favor criminal solutions, and so forth. In this way they are to a certain extent comparable to the catalysts in chemistry. It is much more difficult to establish the presence of facilitating factors than of predisposing factors as there are so many factors which can facilitate crime.

In the case of some offenders, crime might have been promoted by certain variables; with others, different factors might have been crucial. The result is that it can be very difficult to identify a specific facilitating factor. The traditional approach, in which the significance of a variable is established by comparing its prevalence in delinquent and nondelinquent groups, is too crude an approach.

As already stated, *inhibitory factors* are of the utmost importance; they are able to rule out the potentially detrimental influence of predisposing factors. As such they are of tremendous importance in any crime prevention program.

One question remains to be answered: Are facilitating and inhibitory factors opposite extremes? In some cases they will be, but it is easy to show that they cannot be regarded simply as the extreme ends of the same variable. For instance, alcohol consumption can be considered a facilitating factor; nondrinking, however, cannot be perceived as inhibiting. The presence of strong religious feelings can act as an inhibitory factor; their absence, on the other hand, cannot be seen to favor crime.

Turning Theory into Practice

Now that we have put forward the concepts of a method of understanding crime, the crucial question is how to proceed from here. From the above it should be clear that this is no easy question to answer. Crime is, as we have seen, a function of the offender $[C f (P_i, S_i)]$. All disciplines dealing with human behavior could therefore, in principle, provide criminologists with what we have called predisposing, facilitating, or inhibitory factors. Unfortunately, criminology is not organized the way a behavioral science should be. Its frame of reference is predominantly confined to what could be labeled social sciences, supplemented by some psychiatry. The biological sciences are almost completely lacking. This means that the existing infrastructure of criminology does not allow a real biosocial approach.

In order to make such an approach possible the first thing to do is to increase the number of disciplines involved in criminology. This can be done in two ways. First the traditional staffs of criminological institutes could be supplemented with neurobiologists, psychophysiologists, endocrinologists, and so forth. A second, less drastic way, is to try to get representatives of biological disciplines interested in the crime problem. Let us assume that we have succeeded in the latter. Then, as a start, a kind of fishing expedition will have to take place. That is, variables that might be able to differentiate between delinquents and nondelinquents must be brought in from each discipline. Whether they actually have this power should be established by comparing offenders with control groups of nonoffenders according to the principles of differential criminology. Comparative study of this kind should provide us with a list of variables with which we can distinguish the two groups. In the case of violent offenders it could, for example, produce the following results: violent delinquents are young, generally from the lower classes; they are often beaten in their early years; their parents use violence as a means of settling arguments and do little to stimulate their children's development; there is lack of affection at home; the children are rarely at home; they frequently visit pubs, they drink a lot, have no hobbies and do not belong to any clubs; their achievements at school are minimal, they express themselves badly and have a low frustration-tolerance together with a quick temper and poor powers of concentration; they are also physically strong. In addition, they are found to have a deficiency of thiamin and niacin, an excess of dopamine and a low psychophysiological reaction level. Keeping in mind our probabilistic model of explaining crime, the first thing to be done is to fill in these data in the proposed formula. This requires the following steps:

1. Identify potential predisposing factors. In the case cited low frustration tolerance, lack of empathy and absence of any alternative means of achieving goals could be labeled as such.

2. Ascertain which of the remaining variables are related to the predisposing factors. Here a distinction should be made between causal relations (a low frustration tolerance can be caused by a thiamin deficiency) and functional relations. The latter are of a different order from statistical relations, and are therefore determined not by using correlational calculations—these would be completely out of place here—but by what I would call a chain construction, an inductive process. Given A, B, C, then Y will result. To put it in more concrete terms, given someone who is physically strong (A), has little opportunity to gain status by other means (B), and is a member of the lower class where violence is considered more normal (C), then he will be more ready to use violence to achieve status (Y).

In the example cited low frustration tolerance might be related to thiamin and niacin deficiency. Lack of empathy might be related to lack of parental affection and low psychophysiological reaction level.

In establishing relationships with the third predisposing factor, absence of any alternative means of achieving a goal, the situation might be different according to the goal. Where the aim is to relieve frustration, the following variables might be relevant: inability to communicate, ignorance of any other ways of resolving disputes, strong physique and beatings at home.

Should the objective be to gain status by behaving violently, factors like membership of the lower social class, strong physique, and an absence of other ways of gaining status could be important. It should be clear by now that variables displaying functional relations with predisposing factors are in fact facilitating factors.

3. Check which variables are left after steps 1 and 2 have been accomplished. In the case cited these appear to be the fact that the juveniles are

heavy drinkers, they frequently visit pubs, and they have an excess of dopamine.

Being a heavy drinker could be seen as another predisposing factor in addition to the existing three. That leaves us with the difficult question of what to do with the dopamine variable. A new line of research has to be carried out to see what the relevance of this variable could be to violence.

Having completed these three steps we have not yet finished our research cycle. An important question still has to be answered: which variables could, in their turn, be responsible for the presence of the predisposing factors identified? For example, having discovered a lack of empathy, we ask how this came about. Such research enables us to add new variables to our research model. What is more important, however, is that it also provides the basis for a preventive program or a course of treatment. I should like to illustrate this using the factor "absence of any alternative means of achieving goal (status)." Which variables could be responsible for this? Some which come to mind are: received little encouragement at home; lack of leisure facilities in the neighborhood; the deficiencies of the educational system, which is not directed sufficiently toward stimulating leisure interests and hobbies; a society which puts too little effort into improving the position of people from the lower socioeconomic classes and which accords too much significance to status.

Finally, one important step remains to be taken: to find out how it is that there are still so many people to whom these predisposing factors are applicable, but who show no violence. An analysis of this kind puts us on the track of inhibitory factors. A knowledge of these factors is essential, not only to increase theoretical knowledge but also to aid in prevention.

Back to Lombroso?

In this chapter we have approached the crime problem from the behavioral viewpoint. We emphasized the fact that crime is behavior and as such a function of the personal characteristics of the individuals concerned and of the situations in which they find themselves $[C \: f \: (P_i, S_i)]$. Among the personal characteristics, biological traits might play an important role (Mednick, et al. 1974; Mednick, 1975; Schacter and Latané, 1964; Shah and Roth, 1974). Unfortunately, as has been said before, the infrastructure of criminology does not make it easy to verify this assumption. In criminology the main emphasis is still on the social sciences, and hardly any attention is paid to biological factors. New schools of criminology concentrate even more on macro-level factors such as the social and political climate we live in (Taylor et al., 1973). For several reasons it will not be easy to change this frame of reference. In this respect too criminology displays all the characteristics of any subculture. By applying "pressure" to its members the subculture "determines" the direction in which the profession will develop, which subjects should be studied (for instance social factors) and which should not (heredity). This approach works like a self-fulfilling prophecy. By concentrating on social factors—leaving aside the amount of variance explained—criminologists seem to be right in stating that crime is predominantly a social problem. If biological traits are neglected their potential relevance cannot be established. In this respect too it is time the balance was restored. *Restoring* here does not mean going back to Lombroso, it means looking for a new equilibrium. In practice this means that due attention must be paid to social as well as biological factors. May the criminology of the future be a biosocial one!

4 Biosocial Factors and Primary Prevention of Antisocial Behavior

Sarnoff A. Mednick

Methods of Primary Prevention

There are parallels which can be drawn between science's struggles to control disease and its struggles to control crime. The two approaches share failures which stem in part from a similarity of approach. A good point in case is science's triumph in dealing with pneumonia. As Gruenberg (1977) has pointed out, before 1936 individuals who suffered from chronic incurable ailments typically did not die of those ailments. Instead they died of secondary terminal infections, chiefly pneumonia. In 1936 the mortality rate for pneumonia was 65 per 100,000. But in 1936 sulfanilamide was discovered. By 1940 the mortality rate from pneumonia had dropped to 20 per 100,000, and by 1949 to 10 per 100,000. Science had triumphed. But in the days before sulfanilamide, physicians typically called pneumonia "the old man's friend" because it frequently mercifully carried off a sufferer from an incurable chronic illness. Today these sufferers live on so that in effect the advent of sulfanilamide (followed by penicillin, aureomycin, and terramycin) has increased the number of sufferers and the amount of suffering. The wonder drugs did nothing to cure the chronic illnesses that existed or to prevent them in others. Today society is paying a huge and ever-growing bill caring for those survivors who are incurably ill. Of course this care must continue and the effort must continue to further develop the astounding technology which is being mobilized to maintain life in these incurably ill. I would argue that, in addition to this stupendous effort and investment, society's resources should also be channeled into research on the primary prevention of these incurable ailments. The benefits of primary prevention, in terms of suffering, greater productivity of the population, and a lessening of the burden on society, are obvious.

The picture regarding crime is not totally different. We are proud of our new jails, we are proud of our rehabilitation programs, we are proud of our development of mace. It is clearly important that we continue to do research studying the operation of the criminal justice system. But all of these attempts are technological patches. As in the field of medicine, primary prevention of

The research reported in this chapter has been supported by grants from the Center for Studies of Crime and Delinquency, NIMH (MH 19225, 24872, 25311).

crime is not eagerly studied. I would urge again, as in the field of medicine, that primary prevention become our critical objective.

How might we best effect primary prevention of crime? One approach suggested by many criminologists is societal manipulation. This is the logical approach of the sociocultural etiological view of criminal behavior. This etiological view has basically maintained that the criminal is a normal individual who has been socialized in a deviant manner. Clearly, if we change the socialization for the better, this normal individual will not commit crimes. This point of view has been the dominant one in the twentieth century.

If there are, however, individual characteristics (such as intelligence or the XYY chromosome anomaly) which increase an individual's chances of behaving antisocially, then societal change may not be the only feasible approach. We may need to consider methods of primary prevention which take into account the individual characteristics of the potential offender. Is there evidence that the criminal has distinctive individual characteristics with etiological implications?

I will relate five sets of facts which persuade me that societal manipulation, alone, will not be enough to prevent manifestations of antisocial behavior.

Fact Number One: Twin Studies

There have been a series of studies of criminality in twins which seem to have demonstrated that genetic factors in criminality can not be ruled out. The studies began with the 1929 report of Johannes Lange which suggested that identical twins evidence far more concordance for criminal behavior than do fraternal twins. Lange's study shared a number of methodological problems with most of the early research in this area. More recently Karl Otto Christiansen (1977a) studied a total population of 7,172 Danish twins; he observed 35 percent concordance for criminality in identical twins, while fraternal twins evidenced only 13 percent pairwise concordance. Christiansen's work is solid and compelling. His results suggest that the possibility of genetic factors in criminality cannot be ruled out.

Fact Number Two: Adoption Studies

In three separate studies of adoptees and their biological and adoptive parents, it has become clear that if a child who was adopted at birth later becomes criminal, it is an extremely good bet that his biological father (whom he has never seen) was also a criminal. This was most recently reported in a study by Hutchings and Mednick (1977) who investigated the outcomes of 1,145 adoptions of male children in Denmark. It seems clear that a genetic factor does exist either for some types of criminality or for some percentage of criminals.

I would draw only one conclusion from this fact. Individual biological factors must be in part responsible for some types of crime or for some percentage of criminals.

Fact Number Three: Autonomic Nervous System Deviance in Criminals

In a compelling study, Wadsworth (1976) traced all the males registered for delinquency from a sample of 13,687 births which occurred in England, Wales, and Scotland between March 3 and March 9, 1946 (Douglas and Blomfield, 1958). In 1957 these males had their pulse taken just before a school medical examination (a mildly threatening event). This preexamination pulse rate predicted significantly whether or not a boy would achieve a record of serious delinquency by the age of twenty-one. In a sixteen-year longitudinal study Loeb and Mednick (1977) demonstrated that autonomic nervous system variables predict which of a population of boys would exhibit antisocial behavior. Since Lykken's demonstration in 1957, autonomic nervous system variables have been reliable in differentiating the antisocial individual (see Siddle, 1977).

Fact Number Four: The Chronic Recidivist

The oft-quoted finding of Wolfgang, et al. (1972) that a very small percentage of the males of Philadelphia are responsible for a major proportion of the serious crimes in that city suggests to me that the antisocial behavior of this very small proportion of the male population may be partly explained by individual factors.

Fact Number Five: Biosocial Interactions Relating to Criminal Behavior

Karl Otto Christiansen's twin study (1977a, b) suggests the possibility of a genetic effect in criminality. His work however goes beyond this in demonstrating that this genetic effect interacts in a lawful way with social variables. He showed that in a social context where group resistance to crime is greatest, the genetic effect manifests itself most clearly. Also where the group resistance to crime seems to be relatively smaller, the genetic effect is less manifest. In our own research on physiological factors relating to crime, we have seen an analogous relationship. Where family and group pressures which induce criminal behavior are strongest, the physiological variables are least differentiating. In family situations which seem to protect the individual from crime, physiological variables seem to be more differentiating (Mednick et al., 1977). So, we see not only that the individual biological variables relate to criminality but also that they interact in a lawful way with sociocultural factors.

Implications for Primary Prevention

We have suggested that since individual characteristics as well as sociocultural factors seem to be involved in the etiology of criminal behavior the primary prevention of this behavior might be aided by taking these individual characteristics into account. Perhaps it would be in order to suggest a possible initial research approach to the problem of primary prevention of crime. In view of the fact that individual characteristics seem to be able to predict later criminal behavior (Loeb and Mednick, 1977; Wadsworth, 1976) it seems clear that the early detection of some future offenders may be possible. Once such individuals have been detected in the general population methods of preventing their criminal behavior could be explored. A research design which suggests itself is the intensive assessment of a large population selected at some point before the onset of serious criminal behavior. These individuals should then be followed until this serious criminal behavior has manifested itself. Then it will be possible to identify those who have been seriously criminal and see if there are any combination of items in the original assessment which might be useful in early detection. If such a discriminating assessment battery could be validated and its reliability demonstrated, then it could be applied to a new population and methods of primary prevention could be tested.

A Biosocial Theory of the Origins of Criminal Behavior: An Illustration

There may be some heuristic value in illustrating how biological and social factors could interact to teach or fail to teach a child how to behave in a civilized manner. In this section I will examine the learned bases of obedience to society's sanctions. It assumes that law-abiding behavior must be learned and that this learning requires certain environmental conditions and individual abilities. Lack of *any* of these conditions or abilities would hinder socialization learning and might, conceivably, be partly responsible for some forms of antisocial activities.

How do people learn to be law-abiding? This section describes socialization learning in terms of the interaction of early family training and individual physiological characteristics. If there are lacks in either of these spheres learning to be law-abiding will be incomplete, retarded, or unsuccessful.

Most offenders are convicted of having perpetrated only one, two, or three relatively minor offenses. These offenders are doubtless instigated by socio-economic and situational forces. There is, however, a small group of offenders which may be characterized as extremely recidivistic. In a Copenhagen birth cohort of over 30,000 men (described in Witkin et al., 1977) we found that this minute fraction of the male population accounts for more than half of the offenses committed by the entire cohort. Similar results have been reported for the city of Philadelphia by Wolfgang et al. (1972). It is especially this small active group of recidivists that are hypothesized to have had their socialization learning influenced by deviant social and physiological characteristics. In em-phasizing biosocial interactions the approach also seeks to help in the explanation of those cases of antisocial behavior which seem to have no apparent social cause as well as those cases in which an individual seems extraordinarily resistant or invulnerable to powerful criminogenic social forces (criminal family, extreme poverty, broken home background).

Before going further with this exposition, perhaps I should make clear that I define a criminal as an individual who is registered as having been convicted of a violation of the penal code. In no case will this mean that our studies have utilized a prison population. All the individuals studied were functioning in society. We are concerned about the possibility that hidden crime may be governed by a different set of laws of nature from registered crime. We are, however, encouraged to continue working with registered crime by relatively strong evidence that the hidden criminal is the less serious, less recidivistic criminal (Christie et al., 1965).

Law-abidance Learning in Children

Children almost certainly do not come into the world with a set of inborn behaviors which unfold into civilized behavior. An objective consideration might in fact suggest that the behavior of young children is dominated by rather uncivilized immediate needs and passions. Becoming civilized consists in part of learning to inhibit or rechannel some of these passions.

Hare (1970), Trasler (1972), and others have discussed the possibility that the psychopath and criminal have some defect in avoidance learning that in-terferes with their ability to learn to inhibit asocial responses. Much of this has been inspired by the 1957 study by Lykken indicating the difficulties psycho-paths have in learning to avoid an electric shock. These results have found some empirical support. Hare has suggested that the empirically observed and re-observed autonomic hyporeactivity of the psychopath and criminal may be, partially, the basis of this poor avoidance learning. To better understand this, let us consider the avoidance learning situation. In particular, let us follow Trasler (1972), and consider how the law-abiding citizen might learn his ad-mirable self-control. When one considers the modern urban center in terms of the temptations and, in fact, incitements it offers to a variety of forms of asocial behavior, one is impressed with the restraint and forebearance of the 80-90 percent of the population, who apparently manage to avoid committing repetitive or heinous crimes. Novels such as *The Lord of the Flies* and observations of intersibling familial warfare suggest that there actually *are* some strong instincts and passions that society must channel and inhibit to maintain even the poor semblance of civilization we see around us. The type of learning involved in this civilizing process has been termed passive avoidance; the individual avoids punishment or fear by *not* doing something for which he has been punished before.

Let us consider the way children learn to inhibit aggressive impulses. Frequently, when child A is aggressive to child B, child A is punished by his mother. After a sufficient quantity or quality of punishment, just the thought of the aggression should be enough to produce a bit of anticipatory fear in child A. If this fear response is large enough, the raised arm will drop, and the aggressive response will be successfully inhibited.

What happens in this child after he has successfully inhibited such an asocial response is critical for his learning of civilized behavior. Let us consider the situation again in detail.

1. Child A contemplates aggressive action.
2. Because of previous punishment he suffers fear.
3. He inhibits the aggressive response.
4. His fear begins to dissipate, to be reduced.

We know that fear reduction is the most powerful, naturally occurring reinforcement psychologists have discovered. Thus the reduction of fear (which immediately follows the inhibition of the aggression) can act as a reinforcement for this inhibition and will result in the learning of the inhibition of aggression. The fear-reduction-reinforcement pattern increases the probability that the inhibition of the aggression will occur in the future. After many such experiences, the normal child will learn to inhibit aggressive impulses. Each time such an impulse arises and is inhibited, the inhibition will be strengthened by reinforcement. What does a child need in order to learn effectively to be civilized (in the context of this approach)?

1. A censuring agent (typically the family or peers).
2. An adequate fear response.
3. The ability to learn the fear response in anticipation of an asocial act.
4. Fast dissipation of fear to quickly reinforce the inhibitory response.

The speed and size of reinforcement determines the effectiveness of the fourth point. An effective reinforcement is one that is delivered immediately after the relevant response. In terms of this discussion, the faster the reduction of fear, the faster the delivery of the reinforcement. The fear response is, to a large extent, controlled by the autonomic nervous system (ANS). We can estimate the activity of the ANS by means of peripheral indicants such as heart rate, blood pressure, and skin conductance. The measure of most relevance will peripherally reflect the rate or speed at which the ANS recovers from periods of imbalance.

If child A has an ANS that characteristically recovers very quickly from fear, then he will receive a quick and large reinforcement and learn inhibition quickly. If he has an ANS that recovers very slowly, he will receive a slow, small reinforcement and learn to inhibit the aggression very slowly, if at all. This orientation would predict that (holding constant critical extraindividual variables such as social status, crime training, and poverty level) those who commit asocial acts would be characterized by slow autonomic recovery. The slower the recovery, the more serious and repetitive the asocial behavior predicted. Note that although we have concentrated on electrodermal recovery (EDRec), the theory also requires another ANS characteristic, hyporeactiveness, as a predisposition for delinquency. The combination of hyporesponsiveness and slow EDRec should give the maximum ANS predisposition to delinquency.

Tests of the Theory

In our longitudinal study of some thirteen years duration (Mednick and Schulsinger, 1968), we have been following 311 individuals whom we intensively examined in 1962. This examination included psychophysiology. Since 1962, 36 have had serious disagreements with the law (convictions for violation of the penal code). We checked and noted that, indeed, their EDRec was considerably slower than that of controls. Those 9 who have been clinically diagnosed as psychopaths have even slower recovery.

Siddle et al. (1973) examined the electrodermal responsiveness of 67 inmates of an English borstal. On the basis of ten criteria, these inmates were divided into high, medium, and low asociality. Peter Venables suggested to Siddle et al. that they also measure EDRec in their sample. Speed and rate of EDRec varied inversely as a function of asociality. EDRec on a single trial was surprisingly effective in differentiating the three groups (see Siddle et al., 1977).

Bader-Bartfai and Schalling (1974) reanalyzed skin conductance data from a previous investigation of criminals, finding that criminals who tended to be more "delinquent" on a personality measure tended to have slower EDRec.

In view of the relationships that have been reported between psychophysiological variables and asocial behavior, and in view of our interest in better understanding the apparent genetic predisposition to asocial behavior, we next turned to a study of the heritability of psychophysiological behavior. We (Bell, Mednick, Gottesman, and Sergeant) invited pairs of male twelve-year-old twins into our laboratory. Interestingly enough, EDRec to orienting stimuli proved to have significant heritability (consistently higher for left hand than for right; see Bell et al., 1977). This finding would suggest that part of the heritability of asocial behavior might be attributed to the heritability of EDRec. Thus a slow EDRec might be a characteristic a criminal father could pass to a biological son, which (given the proper environmental circumstances) could increase the probability of the child failing to learn adequately to inhibit asocial responses. Thus we would predict that criminal fathers would have children with slow EDRec. Table 4-1 presents data on the electrodermal behavior of children with criminal and noncriminal fathers. As can be seen, the prediction regarding EDRec is not disconfirmed. It is interesting that the pattern of responsiveness of these children closely resembles that which we might anticipate seeing in their criminal fathers (Hare, 1970). Results of other studies in our laboratory have replicated these findings.

Hare (1975) has recently tested this ANS recovery theory on a sample of maximum-security prisoners. More psychopathic prisoners show significantly slower EDRec than serious, but less psychopathic, maximum-security prisoners. In one figure Hare plots the EDRec of the prisoners along with that of male college students. The prisoner and student curves are worlds apart! In a ten-year

Table 4-1
Skin Conductance Behavior during Orienting Response Testing in Children with Criminal and Noncriminal Fathers

Skin Conductance Function (Right Hand)	Mean Score		F	df	p
	Noncriminal Father	Criminal Father			
Basal level skin conductance	2.51	2.33	0.09	1,193	n.s.
Amplitude (in micromhos)	0.031	0.016	0.03	1,193	n.s.
Number of responses	2.79	1.55	8.51	1,187	0.01
Response onset latency (in seconds)	2.11	2.18	0.07	1,97	n.s.
Latency to response peak (in seconds)	2.05	2.38	5.32	1,95	0.05
Average half recovery time (in seconds)	3.75	5.43	4.26	1,90	0.05
Minimum half recovery time	2.26	4.33	8.80	1,90	0.01

Source: B. Bell, S.A. Mednick, I.I. Gottlesman, and J. Sargeant, "Electrodermal Parameters in Young, Normal Male Twins," in S.A. Mednick and K.O. Christiansen (eds.), *Biosocial Bases of Criminal Behavior* (New York: Gardner Press), 1977. Reprinted with permission.

Note: During Orienting Response testing, the child was presented 14 times with a tone of 1,000 cycles per second.

follow-up study of maximum-security prisoners, Hare reports that EDRec was the only variable in a test battery which predicted recidivism (Hare, personal communication, 1978). Hinton (personal communication, 1975) also finds the EDRec of more asocial prisoners (in an English maximum-security prison) to be slower. In an ongoing study we are finding that criminals reared in a noncriminal milieu have slow EDRec. Children reared in a criminogenic milieu who resist criminality evidence fast EDRec (see Mednick et al., 1977).

In conclusion:

1. There is a theory of social learning of law-abiding behavior that has a unique and key element, the specification of specific autonomic nervous system factors as useful aptitudes for effectively learning to inhibit asocial behavior.
2. Some empirical tests were described that could have disconfirmed this hypothesis. No grounds were found for rejection of the hypothesis in experiments conducted in Denmark, Sweden, England, and Canada under a large variety of situational conditions and criterion group definitions.

Please note that my emphasis of these physiological factors in this chapter should only be understood as an attempt to call attention to this type of approach. The percent of text devoted to the physiological variables does not relate to their perceived importance in the total field of criminology.

5 Sociological Criminology and Models of Juvenile Delinquency and Maladjustment

Denis Szabo

The title of this chapter, sober and scientific, would lead one to expect a detailed account of the contribution made by sociology to an explanation of juvenile maladjustment. I had hoped to be able to report remarkable progress in theory and methodology and thus provide a multifactorial explanation of juvenile delinquency.

I must admit I was mistaken, however. I soon found that the sociological literature is considerably dated. Existing works deal with the efforts, and sometimes only the attempts, of researchers to answer a need contingent on living conditions and social change. They echo intellectual fashions which disappear as rapidly as they appear on the scene. Who can fail to remember the heroic efforts of the late Gluecks, in the twilight of their lives, to leave a legacy of so many works proclaiming their faith in the results of four decades of research, which in large part were devoted to juvenile delinquency? Rarely has so much talent and perseverance been placed at the service of science. Yet few references to these works can be found in the scientific literature of the past few years.

Why this break with tradition? To what is this change of interest due? Is it a profound reorientation in research, or rather a passing orientation due to intellectual curiosity? The fact is that it is the concept of "delinquency" itself that has changed. The very basis of research has been questioned once again.

How, then, are we to proceed with our account? I shall first remind you of the crisis that has taken place in sociological thinking and research over the past ten years. I shall then deal more at length with the consequences of this crisis on research and the explanatory models this discipline offers today concerning our subject—juvenile delinquency.

The Crisis in Contemporary Sociology

This crisis in contemporary sociology, like others that have occurred in varying degrees in all the social sciences, includes three elements: (1) criticism of epistemology; (2) criticism of methodology; and (3) criticism of policy.

Criticism of Epistemology

It must be remembered that the social sciences were born at the end of the nineteenth century, amid the birthpangs of epistemology. They have vacillated since then between two paternities—the natural sciences and the sciences of the mind, traditionally called in France the moral sciences, or ethics. It was a case of epistemological models that were diametrically opposed. The conflict has persisted throughout the entire history of the social sciences. In Europe, the model inspired by the natural sciences has shown a marked preeminence since the end of World War II, mainly under the influence of the American social sciences. These, with their pragmatic and positivist approach, were clearly in line with the epistemology based on the analogy between the sciences of nature and those of culture. The structural-functional approach, which had its origin in the thinking of Emile Durkheim, Vilfredo Pareto, and Max Weber, dominated the theoretical scene in Western Europe as well as North America. Social phenomena were considered "things." Phenomena sui generis, irreducible to biological, psychological, or extrasocial political realities, the social facts had to be dealt with by methods derived from the natural sciences. The analogy between the biological human organism and society, its structure, its organization, and its culture inspired the epistemology of the social sciences, more or less faithfully following the various schools of thought.

The theoretical principle was integration: the sociocultural functions had to be linked in a general interdependence. That which was not linked would fall into disorganization. The mechanisms of conformism were considered an integrating process; the mechanisms of nonconformism were classed in the category of "pathology." The concept of organization is analogous to that of disorganization. The concept of normality has its counterpart in abnormality. The idea of social "health" presupposes that of "pathology" or social malady. The concept of sociocultural "change" would describe the changes inherent in the actual functioning of systems.

Since the mid-sixties, this hegemony of sociology, modeled on the natural sciences, basing itself on positivist traditions, a large share going toward the empiric approach, was called to account. Its epistemology was declared naive as was its theoretical position. The analogy between "nature" and "culture" was harshly criticized. The consensual model of social relationships was compared with the conflictual model. The latter looked upon the social aggregate as entities which maintained a conflictual relationship in terms of their conflicting interests. In the consensual model, the solidarity of the components was due to a principle of equal organization and suggested a sort of homeostasis of the system. All elements were related by subtle interactions causing equal retroactions modifying the whole and contributing to its cohesion. In the conflictual model, opposing interests create conflicts between individuals and social groups. These conflicts are not resolved by adjustment, adaptation, research and the establishment of a new equilibrium that overcomes the conflict, as is the case in the consensual model. It is a matter of conflicts that are not only unsolvable, but that emanate from the very nature of the social organization which it is their mission to radically change. All social relationships should be judged in terms of their contribution to, and their significance in, these conflicts. They are the natural instruments to bring about a more just, less alienated society, reconciling man to himself.

These two models are also two basic paradigms on which contemporary sociological interpretations are based. My use of the term *paradigm* refers not only to the idea of the model but also to an intellectual tradition deeply rooted in the history of philosophy. When a sociologist puts forward one or another paradigm he will refer to an intellectual tradition, to a certain manner of analyzing and interpreting social reality. In fact, the consensual model relates to a paradigm that considers the reality a fact which must be discovered; the conflictual model sees in it a reality that must be constructed. The same opposing interpretations of tradition show up in the actual exercise of power, the crowning concept that caps the entire structure of society. Social organization and its powers constitute the explanatory key and primary object of analysis in the consensual model. Social class, defined by the relation of individuals to the ownership of the means of production, is the opposing paradigm. In the final analysis *all* social phenomena are explained in terms of class conflict in the paradigm which gave birth to the conflictual model; whereas *all* social phenomena are explained in terms of interaction, of domination, between numerous organizations of a national, religious, ethnic, and professional nature, according to the paradigm associated with the consensual model.

As Westhuess (1976) aptly notes, the mind of the sociologist impregnated with one or the other of these paradigms, in looking at the same reality, perceives radically different phenomena, somewhat like geometric figures drawn on a background in multicolored lines. The one will see, analyze and interpret the geometric figures, the other will see only the colors.

This renewed interest in epistemology revived the discussions that raged at the turn of the twentieth century. Today to open a book like that of Sorokin (1926) on the history of sociological thinking, is like leafing through a recently published book! All these controversies, buried under the output of an empiric sociology of three-quarters of a century, sound surprisingly current to our ears. We note, by the way, that it is not by chance that elderly survivors of this heroic era of *Méthodestreite* experienced renewed vigor when this occurred: the septuagenarian Marcus is a very good example.

This epistemological debate brought sociology back to basics. Its contemporary representatives, however, often lacked even an elementary course in the philosophy of science during their university training, and their lack of formal training added even more to the confusion, alas quite usual in these discussions.

Very briefly, it can be said that two concepts of man in his relations with his milieu have been presented side by side: one whose most eminent representative was Rousseau, at the beginning of the modern era, and another which is close to the thinking of Tocqueville.

The first concept postulates an extreme plasticity in human nature. The good savage is degenerated, alienated, and perverted (according to the vocabulary of one or the other school of thought) by the influence of his environment, which included physical nature and above all sociocultural and spiritual nature. By manipulating the environment, understood in terms of holistic theory, one could pave the way for the advent of the *Homo Novus*—essentially a *Homo Socius*. Opposed to this optimistic conception of man is that of man tainted by original sin, which because of his heritage from the animal kingdom, casts its shadow over all actions, all behavior. These are registered within the strict limits marked by the biological and psychological organism, which is part of the web of human evolution—of divine origin for some, a breaking away from the higher primates for others.

This school of thought, which could be called either pessimistic or realistic, is skeptical about the possibility of changing man. It sees his flexibility strictly limited in the face of environmental influences. Man's instinctual equipment, the innovative and conservative elements of his mind, is not receptive to every influence exercised by external forces. The human condition in the hypothesis of the good savage means the condition that can change the human being. This same expression uttered by adherents of the hypothesis that upholds the principle of a nature, points out the limits to his changeability.

Then, too, we must point out the importance of the postulate on the equality or inequality of man, implicit in the two models.

The consensual model assumes that man faces life endowed with a highly complex biogenetic and sociocultural legacy. Placed in certain historical conditions, in a given socioeconomic structure, man develops in different ways according to his learning processes. This differentiation, based on his specific sociological and genetic heritage, gives him a status in society that will be higher or lower than that of others who have a different heritage. This inequality is a fundamental fact of the human condition; it should be corrected to some extent by the sense of justice existing in each era but cannot and should not be entirely eliminated.

The conflictual model assumes the ontological equality of man. Everything that leads to inequality in a given past society must therefore be corrected. This does not happen through natural adjustment. It is achieved through conflicts, confrontations, and revolutions. Thus conflict is at once a principle of explanation and a principle of justification. Consensus, the ability and the need to adhere to a certain common good, has the same significance for the consensual model.

These two conceptions of man are expressed, of course, with a great many variations. The history of scientific ideas presents an exhaustive supply of them.

It is not surprising to see that they naturally oriented sociological thinking and theory in opposite directions. The structural-functional school, which was very strong between 1930 and 1960, taking its support mainly from the works of Durkheim, Pareto, and Weber, could make do with a conception of man which did not postulate a total plasticity in the face of the socializing forces of the environment. The conflictual school, both in its Marxist and interactional variation, was more naturally based on the concept of man in which his characteristics were either the result of a socioeconomic evolution subject to certain laws, or a system of definitions and stigmatizations created by the elite in power.

Criticism of Methodology

The methodological consequences of the recrudescence of epistemological discussion are considerable. The scientific methods of investigation derived from the natural sciences and adapted to the specific problems of the human sciences dominated sociological methodology before 1960. Everything had to be expressed in quantifiable indicators, from the rate of urbanization to the perception of norms. These quantifiable variables had to be submitted to statistical treatment, amplified later by computer analysis. The hypotheses had to be expressed in propositions which could be verified empirically and logically, tested by appropriate techniques, and replicated by other researchers. The cumulative nature of the results obtained by the use of observation and experimentation was the true criterion of the scientific quality of the research. The sociology of both Durkheim and Pareto was based on the use of objective, positive methods like the ideal technique of investigation. All the specific sociological studies, those of the family, religion, education, the city, labor relations, produced research whose main characteristics were to test theories or hypotheses of medium scope, in the words of Robert Merton, whose thinking dominated the methodology of this sociology as did Talcott Parsons in the conceptual and theoretical area.

The consensual model was well suited to the positivist methodology, having a preference for quantitative methods. An analysis of the interdependence of factors, in, for instance, the effects of social mobility on the integration of the family or in the mother's role in the adoption of specific behavior in the relationships between adolescents and adults, could alone contribute sufficient knowledge of an acceptable scientific exactness. It was the only acceptable way of contributing to a theory of society. The social facts were taken as they were, assuming the objectivity and neutrality of the researcher in the gathering of the facts and the interpretation of the results. The relative detachment of the researcher from the conflicting interests being debated was an article of faith that was proclaimed in the very first chapter of methodological treatises. "To know more and more about increasingly restricted subjects," the adage of the exact sciences that largely characterized the positivist methodology, applied as well to the social sciences. The rest was qualified as literature—somewhat pejoratively (Coser, 1975).

The conflictual model gave preference to qualitative methodology. Assigning itself the task of redefining the basic facts of the social reality, the translation of this reality into simplified indicators did not suit the objective of this sociological theory. Is the rate of divorce an indication of family disintegration or does it reflect a new form of relationships between the sexes? Does the increase in suburban population mean the failure of urbanization or is it a new type of rural life? There are many such examples. What must be remembered above all is the questioning of the positivist functions of the interdependence of the variables that constitute the social structure. The significance of the data takes precedence over precision (in the quantitative sense), change over stability, and the accessory takes on the aspect of the possible essential. The first question in methodology will not be assurance to the world of the objectivity and neutrality of the researcher's approach. On the contrary, he will be asked to show his colors. What side is he on? Who is he working for?

To redefine, to reconstitute the sociocultural reality, this is the message, particularly of the trend in phenomenology inspired by Alfred Schutz. A whole new sociology will be created around the hopes and aspirations of certain social groups—the masses as they are called by some—based on values that are forming which are opposed to those that constitute the cornerstone of today's society. The methodology of the social sciences must channel this potential for change, these aspirations for authenticity of men, whose true nature has been usually alienated, caught in a stranglehold by the existing social institutions.

A methodology very close to theory, extensively using participant observation, producing works of a literary nature—this is the image presented by most of the works closely or remotely connected with the conflictual model. With the resources of this methodology, sociology poses rather than solves problems. If social engineering, close to economics, was the model for many of the positivist sociologists, it is social criticism which attracts the adherents of most qualitative methodologies. Incidentally, Marxism comes closer to one or the other model depending on whether or not power is in the hands of Marxist-Leninist parties. As Raymond Aron (1971) rightly said, the social scientist of the first school sees himself as the counselor of the prince, the other as the confidante of providence.

Criticism of Policy

The social sciences have never been detached from the political context. Progress in the exact sciences went hand in hand with the unhampered examination of the secrets of nature. This freedom of inquiry was opposed, sometimes violently, by the often religiously inspired philosophies that tended to limit total freedom of exploration. The newly developing social sciences met the same type of opposition from the established order in the path of their progress. The mere disclosure of the social reality as it truly is, contrary to the assertions of the dominant ideologies, constituted a questioning of the social organization, and sometimes of the holders of power of the moment. Sciences like the social sciences were leftist in the beginning, to the extent that the right represented tradition and the left the challenging of this tradition. Very quickly, however, within the two scientific traditions, the natural sciences and the cultural sciences, as Dilthey liked to call them, the many possible applications of research results created a great many schools of thought in terms of their political significance.

Scholars who were engaged in the fundamental sciences were more easily able to maintain a certain distance with regard to the political, industrial, economic, and commercial powers which benefited from the exploration of the results of scientific research. For some, the results of scientific research were not in themselves either good or bad, it was the *use* made of them that posed a moral problem. Others, in increasing number, were interested in the social function of science, and wanted to know from the very beginning of the research project the possible use of the results obtained.

In our two models, significant differences can be found. In the *consensual model*, concern about the political implications of research is mediated by the methodological principle of relative neutrality on the part of the researcher. It does not follow that research itself and the application of the results of research for political purposes will, in this perspective, constitute two entirely different things.

This does not mean to say that many researchers working in the positivist tradition do not consider themselves engaged politically. But the majority will deny any direct connection between research, its conception, development, and realization, and definite political intervention. This would not be the opinion of most supporters of the conflictual model. In their view, to define a subject is already to take sides in a conflict in which those who are on the "good" or "bad" side of those in power are opposed. The most brilliant work on this thesis, albeit a bit diagrammatic, is that of Benoit Verhaegen in his *Histoire immédiate* (1974).

It should be noted that the epistemological, methodological and political stands taken are largely interdependent. The body of contemporary sociological thinking has many cross-currents, combining and creating subtle differences in rich and complex intellectual traditions. It was not my intention to give an account of these, merely to recall their existence. In the English language, Gouldner's book, which appeared in 1970, and that of Coser published in 1967, mark the outburst of this triple crisis in sociology. The events in the spring of

1968 and the writing of Edgar Morin, in my view, constitute the same line of demarcation in sociology in the French language.

Because sociology experienced this identity crisis in the sixties, it is only natural that its contribution toward explaining juvenile delinquency must reflect it. We can also throw some light on sociological explanations of juvenile malad-justment through our two models, consensual and conflictual. It is a question of ideal and simplified types. All the sociological explanations furnished since the beginning of the century can be grouped under the guiding principles of these two models.

Thus identified with the consensual model are ecological theories relating to structure, organization, and social control. Among the contributions of the conflctual model are the Marxist contributions (in the eastern European coun-tries), interactionist and ethnomethodological.

I well realize the danger of such a simplification, whatever the didactical justification. The thinking of most authors has many more nuances than are shown here. However, to encourage thought and to provide an overview of the subject in reasonable length, I decided to risk these perfectly justifiable criticisms.

It must be pointed out once more that the two models, based on two fundamental sociological paradigms, cannot produce hypotheses whose verifica-tion can have any effect on the truth sought within the framework of the opposite paradigm. These paradigms are too deeply rooted in the history and aspirations of man. Empirical verifications only feed one or another trend and the debates within these trends. However, each paradigm has its "highs" and "lows" in the eyes of the public, anxious to see some beneficial effects on the quality of its own life. The testable propositions derived from each paradigm and developed within each model provide or do not provide the anticipated results. To the uninformed, the general public, it is a question of observable experiments. This is the strictly scientific role of the researcher, and therein lies his contribution, whatever his adherence to opposed patterns of tradition.

To sum up, the crisis in sociology is closely linked with the social, political and moral crises of the second half of the twentieth century. The liberal and pluralistic democracies cannot conjure up demons that will only partially dis-integrate them, and only during great events or when collective danger con-fronts them. The industrial and scientific revolution of the nineteenth century, the tragedies of the two world wars, are such uniting factors. But the birth or rebirth of doctrines, of theories justifying the negation of a pluralist, liberal democracy, based on freedom and individual responsibility, and inviting its destruction, are a cyclical phenomenon.

The arguments are similar, only the vocabulary changes. Experience is never transmitted, only dogmatism is, as Aragon said. This we shall find in the microcosm of the criminological literature on juvenile delinquency.

Models of Sociological Criminology and Juvenile Maladjustment

The Consensual Model's Explanation of Juvenile Delinquency

In the light of the reservations already mentioned, we have gathered here works which, in the final analysis, accept the premise of the adaptation of the social organism to the exigencies of change inherent in the functioning of the social system. The idea of adaptation is opposed to that of the fragmentation that occurs when adaptation has not run its normal course. It is presumed that adaptation, the adjustment to changing conditions, is the rule in the functioning of society. Should fragmentation occur, it is the result of a failure of the process of adaptation.

The first sociological works on juvenile delinquency were done in Chicago between 1925 and 1945 (for a summary, see Szabo, 1960). Let us remember that it was the ecological study of society that dominated the theoretical background of the first important American school of sociology, borrowing from biology the concept of the "community" where a society is organized in complex interaction with the physical resources of the environment and later on with the sociocultural milieu. The concepts used were those of "occupation," "implantation," "organization," with a view to the exploitation of resources, "cooperation," "conflicts," "disorganization," "invasion," and "desertion," or "extermination". Here we have the transposition of the conceptual device of the sociology of plants and animals onto the human population. Those who, like Shaw and McKay, Trasher, Whyte, were interested in the dark side of social organization, considered delinquency a pathological phenomenon of rejection. It was the result of blockages, of faulty functioning in the sociocultural mechanisms which were supposed to assure the well-being of society. Examining the "cells," or the sociocultural "molecules" composing the organism, these sociologists observed a variation in the rate of delinquency between the diverse ecological areas of large cities. As a very general explanatory principle, they put forward the decreasing influence of norms on the behavior of increasing numbers of individuals. It was assumed, then, that there were norms, generally shared, which reflected values whose contravention immediately labeled the individual as delinquent.

The influence of the environment and the interaction between the environment and social groups constitute the first formulation of the consensual model. Inasmuch as the transmission of community values was taking place, thanks to the constraint exerted by the imposition of norms of conduct, it was enough for the sociologist to identify, describe, and analyze the factors which prevented, distorted, or changed the natural tendency of young people to conform to the expectations and restraints of their milieu: family, neighborhood, school, peers, work. This accounts for the concentrated and persistent interest of this sociology in identifying the problems occurring in all these milieus and which accounted for the delinquent behavior. Broken homes or families in conflict, neighborhoods deprived of sociocultural resources, peers dominated by gangs with antisocial leaders, schools ravaged by vandals and producing illiterates, a labor market exploiting or dismissing young people ill prepared to face competition—these are the findings of thousands of pages of investigations, of statistical tables and essays of interpretation, that were produced by sociologists of the Chicago school.

Soon, and in this same perspective, certain authors concentrated on some explanatory factors which they believed were strategically more decisive than others. Thus Cloward and Ohlin (1960), after Durkheim and Merton, showed the effects of the socioeconomic organization on the chances of young people to adjust, particularly those who came from underprivileged social milieus. They concluded that the fiction of equal opportunity, an article of faith in a liberal democracy, was meaningless for those who started life with handicaps accumulated for generations. The legitimate paths to success being barred, the behavior and destiny of many juvenile delinquents was explained by resource to forbidden means to reach the goal desired by everyone—to be well off and to feel respected. This they could achieve only by illegal means.

The conclusion drawn from these studies tended, for the most part, to follow the direction of the consensual model. There must be a move, through appropriate social policies, to assure the handicapped a truly equal chance in the competition of urban living. The great society of the sixties largely conforms to this ideal. The consensual model was the driving force, the helping hand in a reformist social policy. Social democracy, the complement of political democracy, was the result of this action.

Those who set out to study the idea of the subculture more thoroughly, such as Wolfgang and Ferracuti (1967), Downes (1966), and Terrence Morris (1957), for example, were intrigued by a sort of inverse integration of young people in mini-societies which were established marginal to, or at odds with, the community. For these authors, the very term *subculture* indicates a kind of writing off of a part of the society, of the great whole whose mission it is to actively harmonize all parties, categories, classes, and groups which make up a global society. Nonetheless, the numerous monographs written on delinquent subcultures showed their members strongly integrated around values opposed to those of the society as a whole. By means of punishment and reward, the conduct of their members was determined by rigid norms. Yinger (1960) developed the idea of the "counter-culture," which is probably the most extreme formulation in the consensual model.

Within this same broad perspective, but drawing upon different sources, are those who subscribe to social regulation. The difference between this and the ecological tradition lies mainly in the fact that the mobility of the population within the urban area had increased. This fact assured greater prominence to theories which stressed the psychosociological elements of integration rather than the physical milieu. The black ghetto in large American cities is still an appalling reality; its inclination to change, however, appears minimal.

Starting with Durkheim and his concept of mechanical solidarity, which derives from states of conscience common to all members of a society, assuring cohesion based on essential similarities between the members of that society, these researchers, like Empey et al. (1971), Hirschi (1969), and Jessor et al. (1968), include in their perspective the contribution of Tarde (1924), Mead (1934), Dollard et al. (1950) and Skinner (1972). This tradition of social psychology stresses the importance of socialization, of acquiring norms of motivation and behavior through experience or imitation. Sutherland and Cressey (1974), who were less interested in the problems of juvenile delinquency, are of this same tradition, as is Walter Reckless (1973). The former, with their concept of differential experience within differential associations, the latter, with his theory of containment, that is, of a balance between endogenous and exogenous forces, centrifugal or centripetal, concentrated their explanations within the general framework of the regulation of conduct.

The team of the Research Group on Juvenile Maladjustment, of the University of Montreal, supported this trend, and I shall now borrow the arguments of Maurice Cusson (1976), to present this point of view. His theory is based on sociological theories which consider the processes of exchange as the basis of social interaction. The "exchanger" is always concerned about the consequences of his behavior. His actions are based on the principle of reciprocity and mutual and complementary interests. Man is considered a rational being who calculates the advantages or disadvantages that his actions will elicit. Neither subconscious impulses nor environmental forces can alone explain the motivation behind human behavior.

In a community, in a group, the norms will be respected to the extent that those who are in agreement with them resort to rewards and penalties to impose them. In a group where nonconformists are too numerous and conformists too spineless, there cannot be respect for the established norms. A youth will be deviant, then, to the degree that he finds little gratifying exchange with the members of the group, that he spends his time with other deviants who protect him against the possible pressure of conformists, and who approve sufficiently of his behavior, the result of the contravention of norms for which respect is no longer enforced.

When an individual is strongly integrated in a conformist society, he has little motivation and few sociocultural grounds to create a milieu where antisocial conduct can crystallize. Certain individuals in certain milieus are thus deeply set in their conformist pattern of behavior. When this integration is weakened, when social regulation is exercised only partially and by fits and starts, defiance, deviance, and confirmed delinquency occur.

Adherence to a deviant norm, at a given moment, gives a profile of the makeup of the delinquent personality as it was analyzed, by analogy with the

phenomenon of conversion, by De Greeff (1946) and developed and standardized by Pinatel (1975).

If integration in delinquent subcultures reinforces the making of a delinquent personality, the accompanying exclusion from the conformist society
does likewise; as Cusson observes, theft is the antithesis of exchange. In the ideal
model of exchange, each partner gains from the transaction. In theft, one partner profits at the expense of the other. The basis of exchange is agreement; that
of theft is force or trickery, a negation of agreement. Exchange prospers where
there is understanding and mutual trust. Theft and aggression break the relationship, setting individuals against each other.

Thus delinquency can be analyzed from two points of view, stemming from
the principle of reciprocity which this approach proposes. It concerns (1) delinquency as a negation of reciprocity in social relations based on the exchange
of services and manufactured goods, and (2) the violation of a norm which is
considered a rule of the game accepted by common accord, and which assures
justice and fairness to all parties concerned in the exchange.

The model is constructed by combining the variables, including and stan-
dardizing the transactions of the young person with his milieu. They are:

1. What the subject receives from the milieu. Material and spiritual needs are
    mainly assured by the parents, and indirectly by the society, to the extent
    that the latter supplements parental efforts and makes up for their de-
    ficiencies.
2. What the subject contributes to the milieu. All the responses he makes to
    the expectations of the group: affection and obedience to his parents,
    success in school, participation in and contributions to youth groups at
    the community level. This includes his acceptance of the general rules of
    the game conveyed and administered by society as a whole.
3. The aspirations of the subject concerning his physical welfare and spiritual
    well-being. This includes rewards, affection, approval for success in school.
    These are true rewards for efforts to conform.
4. The demands of the milieu with regard to the young person, the counter-
    part of his own aspirations. He will be rewarded to the degree that he
    responds positively to the expectations and demands of the community.

The combination of these four variables will depend on the effects of social
regulation in a given community. Reciprocity of expectations should correspond
with a reciprocity of services furnished. The explanation of delinquency will
therefore be based on the following reasons:

1. Insufficient gratification of the subject by his milieu.
2. A lack of reciprocity between the contribution of society and that of the
    subject.

3. Too great demands on the part of the milieu.
4. Little gratification of the young person, creating a feeling of injustice.
5. A general decrease in the exchanges between the young person and his milieu (alienation).
6. A general decline in the quality of the exchanges with the milieu amounting to a near rupture.
7. A greater number of gratifying relations with nonconforming subjects or groups or those which are marginal to the community.

If all these variables follow the same direction, the result is the exclusion of the subject and his chosen milieu from the community. This exclusion is based on the lack of established authority in the pursuit of exchange relations based on confidence and reciprocity. At the same time, the individual is freed from all the controls inherent in exchange relationships. He is therefore labeled, based on the bad reputation resulting from the seven variables enumerated above. Once labeled, the subject's ability to engage in gratifying exchange relationships is practically nil.

Maurice Cusson rightly concludes that the model of social regulation, based on the concept of exchange, easily fits in with the other sociological models explaining juvenile maladjustment. These are:

The educational model. Parents and educators teach their children a respect for the law, resorting to disciplinary measures, inducements to behave well, offering help and encouragement, evaluating their behavior, supervising them, and so forth. The effectiveness of these methods is strongly affected by the quality of the relationship between the subject and the person exercising the authority.

The work model. The young person who likes school, does well in his studies, who feels esteemed for his success in school, is more inclined to enter the labor market, and as a result, is more easily integrated in the community.

The cultural model. Importance is given to the influence exercised by norms which are more or less in harmony with those of society as a whole, the political society and its laws. The norms of the group mediate the influence of society as a whole, and reinforce, neutralize, weaken, or reject it. We see a more or less strong tendency toward delinquency depending on the influence exercised by the group.

The model based on stigmatization. Delinquency is considered the result of a major breakdown in the process of education. By the act of exclusion, stigmatization weakens the regulating influence of the conventional groups which compose society as a whole, and at the same time increase the influence of delinquent subcultures. The institutionalization of young people provokes further deviation.

The criminal personality model. This is essentially biogenetic and psychogenetic. The hypothesis on which it is based seems perfectly compatible with the social regulation model. The inability to enter into exchange relationships, based on the principle of reciprocity, is affected by breakdowns in the socialization process, both in the fields of education and work. Labeling reinforces the stigma of the rejected, the scapegoat, the deviant, and confirms the antisocial inclinations of the subject.

Impact on Social Policy and Practice

This then, very briefly, is the consensual model's explanation of juvenile maladjustment. We have noted, throughout this chapter, the epistemological, methodological, and political postulates which accompany and inspire this archetypical model. Recalling them, we now note the impact and significance of this model with regard to social policy:

1. Man is evil but, under certain conditions, capable of giving his best; left to his own devices, however, the indomitable forces of evil will prevail. The basic problem is that of evil; it must be seen as a fact of the human condition. This evil is embodied in the hostility of nature (suffering, sickness, death), in the hostility of the interior world of man, his own wickedness, and his inability to live up to his own aspirations (Baechler, 1975). All great civilizations have tried to interpret the evil, the existence of which is a universal fact. The source of the evil is in man himself, not outside him. From Pascal to Jung we find this tradition, which is still voiced among contemporary thinkers with as different approaches as those of Baechler (1976) or Kolakowski (1969).

2. Good and evil being inextricably mixed in man, there is no hope for the advent of an ideal society. By persistently hunting down what is considered evil, we risk setting up regimes or tyrannical practices that in order to suppress the sources of evil, suppress freedom at the same time. This dualism makes it necessary at all times to consider the consequences of remedies proposed to cure an evil. History has proved that the remedy is often worse than the disease.

The slightest element of what we call progress has exacted a price, and we cannot establish comparisons between the loss and the gain, observes Kolakowski. "It is our duty to fight all the sources of affliction, but we do so without the hope of ever being sure that the tree of progress will bear fruit" (1969, p. 134; free translation).

This skepticism about means, which does not exclude the passion for justice, is a very special characteristic, and aptly illustrates our point.

3. If we cannot increase the good without increasing the evil, we can only hope for modest and partial results from any social policy. According to Baechler (1975) the massive increase in resources has created a great deal more envy. The waning of religious fanaticism has been compensated by a greater secular fanaticism. Free education has made it possible for the leisure classes to have the state—and thus everyone—pay some of the cost of their children's

education. The only way these conditions can be equalized is by increasing the role of the state, which means increasing the inequalities in terms of power. Generalized participation in decisions would only mean a tremendous loss of time in idle talk, would result in utter boredom, and would inevitably be changed into a stratification of the autonomous individual. The rational conclusion, therefore, is a reformism accompanied by great prudence, and a refusal to replace the present solutions by others which have not proved themselves. One might say that the latest works of Daniel Bell (1973), Irving Kristol and Daniel Moynihan in sociology, and J.Q. Wilson (1975) in criminology, subscribe to this point of view, and their influence today is far from negligible.

The Conflictual Model in the Explanation of Juvenile Maladjustment

The consensual model dominated criminological theory and research almost exclusively up to the mid-sixties. Rehabilitation and resocialization: these were the key words of the criminal policy of the era. During the crisis in sociology described above another theory appeared and another interpretative model developed, the conflictual model. As in the consensual model, it is an archetype, combining a whole series of approaches, traditions, explanations, and methodologies, which, incidentially, may seem in certain respects to oppose one another. As in the previous model, in a way this model belongs less to a school than to a community of thought.

The concept of power and its exercise seems to be central to this model. It is presumed, straight off, that those who exercise power make it an instrument of oppression, reserved for their exclusive profit. The very nature of power is oppressive, its exercise arbitrary. The unequal treatment of the citizens that results always benefits those in authority, to the detriment of the poor. This discrimination, which stems from the very nature of the existing social organization and which establishes inequality as a principle of organization in this society, is a scandal in the eyes of criminologists of the conflictual model.

The research which gave birth to this interpretive model increased toward the end of the fifties. Finding that the majority of delinquents, both adult and juvenile, came from the poor and underprivileged classes, the sociologist's first step was to question the validity of the measuring instrument that established this image. This was the reason for the studies on hidden delinquency, started by Nye and Short (1957). Although it was not clear at the beginning, the desire to redefine the data on delinquency in terms other than the established ones became manifest. The result of these works was the perception of a delinquency distributed much more generally throughout the various social classes. It was found that breaking the law was not limited to representatives of the poorer classes that filled the institutions, but that many norms protected by the law and its agencies were violated by the middle classes. The latter furnished not only the law makers but also the administration charged with enforcing the law (police officers, magistrates, social workers, educators). Very quickly the question was asked: Could delinquency be the expression of an attitude, a defiance, of one social class toward the other (Miller and Conger, 1966)?

Since the majority of these studies were done in the United States, the fact that the dangerous classes were black and belonged to the urban subproletariat played a considerable role in the sensitivity which oriented these studies and these interpretations. George Vold (1958) was among the first non-Marxist criminologists who stressed the unyielding conflict of interest which set people against each other as members of social strata or classes, and to consider delinquency a consequence of these conflicts and confrontations.

The substitution of the term *deviant* for *delinquent* marks the schism between the consensual model and the conflictual model. Albert Cohen was the first to make the change in his famous essay in 1966. According to him, deviance was a concept that encompassed delinquency which was itself a result of a purely juridic and sociologically accidental technicality. Deviance is defined as the opposite of conformism: all those who did not submit to the canons of morality, good behavior, in short, all who were opposed to the truths transmitted by tradition and supported by the established authorities, were considered deviants. In the end, all innovators in the arts, literature, sexual morality, and politics aroused reactions of defiance, rejection, and persecution on the part of the conformist majority. Soon delinquency became part of a whole series of behaviors which had in common the refusal to accept the rules of the game established to assure the uninterrupted functioning of society for the benefit of the rich.

For those who upheld the conflictual model, this society was not characterized by a spirit of solidarity, as Durkheim believed, or by an interdependence based on the play of complex interests, in instant balance, as Pareto saw it. No, this society was based on social classes in conflict with each other, having opposing interests, some reconcilable, some not. Some researchers focused on the legislation responsible for juvenile justice. The works of Platt (1969), Chambliss and Seidman (1971) and Quinney (1974) pointed out the extent to which these laws had no other purpose than to dispose of a class enemy in the fight to maintain the power of the bourgeoisie. To have the workers subdued, disciplined, accepting the salaries offered them, this was the reason for penal legislation that had to dispose of the headstrong who seek to defend the interests of the oppressed. To oppose the law, is this not delinquency?

An analysis of the important agencies of criminal justice by Cicourel (1968) and his collaborators, who advanced the theory of Harold Garfinkel, pointed out the use of criminal law and criminal justice as a tool. The role of this tool was to maintain order and conformity with this order for the benefit of the ruling class.

The values and norms imposed by the law and its agencies on the people should therefore be a priority subject for a critique by the sociologist. To accept the definition of the situation as it results from the present functioning of the system is impossible. The critical function of science must prevail. One cannot look for solutions to problems posed in terms of postulates and premises that are declared unacceptable, that are challenged on philosophical and moral grounds. It is in this perspective that the question of Howard Becker (1964) becomes meaningful: On what side is the sociologist? He must take the side of the victim of a rule, instituted by those in power to maintain that power intact, and intended for the exploitation of the people of postindustrial society.

The sociologist as critic reminded us that to define the problem is to become involved. We will therefore pose the problem by asking the delinquent the significance of his act, the aspirations that led him beyond the pale of a society that does not accept him, but which he too rejects. In the interpretation of all the criminogenic factors previously enumerated, we see the introduction of a radical criticism of contemporary postindustrial society. Among the latter's victims are the delinquents.

The concept of man and society put forward by this model is very different from the preceding model. Here man is as conceived by Rousseau, and all evil is external; as Sartre said, hell is other people. Other people, groups, societies, all the sociocultural and economic environment must be changed in order to save humanity. The Dionysian concept of man postulates the expansion of the ego to the limit. It promises to break the narrow corporal prison in which we are all captive by affording a glimpse of the exaltation of communion with the infinite. The end of alienation, of fragmentation resulting from the contradictions of involvement in the complex and sometimes contradictory networks of interpersonal relationships, will be proclaimed, once these contradictions are removed. The elimination of these contradictions leads to a new-found human society, where at last the tug of war between the forces of good and evil will no longer exist, since their main function will have been eliminated during the destruction of the socioeconomic base of capitalist exploitation.

The hope of a community without conflict, above good and evil, is an integral part of the philosophy underlying the new criminology. "It is forbidden to forbid" was the anonymous graffiti appearing on the walls of the Sorbonne in May 1968. "We want a society where the power to 'criminalize' will no longer exist because it will have no object," proclaim the authors of the *New Criminology* (Taylor et al., 1973).

Let us enumerate the characteristics of this model as defined by one of its most gifted representatives, Michael Phillipson (1971).

1. Instead of looking for the cause of delinquency, we seek the *significance*. We try to understand, in the Weberian sense of the term, the process by which the actors arrive at their specific conduct. By means of empathy, we take the actor's point of view in order to clearly understand the meaning he gives for his

action; on the contrary, the consensual approach looks for indicators by which it can infer behavior and which presuppose a certain determinism underlying the act. The conflictual approach prefers to use the subjective method of participant observation. Due to the relationship of trust which the sociologist establishes with the subject of his study, he is able to obtain reliable data which enables him to understand and analyze the delinquent. The study of universals, which is the basic approach in the consensual model, gives way to the requirements of the ethnographer for specificity and irreducibility in his findings during his observations.

2. Based on the perceptions of the actor, we shall try to describe the emergence, transmission, perpetuation, and modification of the sociocultural significance of the delinquent act. From this point of view, the social structure could be considered a vast network of symbolic clues that are diversely shared between various individuals and groups in the society. The role of the sociologist is to take the part of the subject he is studying, in this case the delinquent, and to understand from his perception of these clues the scope and meaning of his act. The sociologist does not have to take the place of judges, parents, or educators. He has only to explain the delinquent. We note, incidentally, in this approach, the major importance of the role of language as a symbolic vehicle whose analysis becomes an excellent tool in the interpenetration between the mind of the researcher and that of the delinquent.

3. The persons thus analyzed belong to groups, to social classes, however, whose existence and conscience are determined by a common dependency on those who exercise power through the control of the economic system. The discovery of the "sociologically typical", therefore, will at the same time be the discovery of relationships of dependency, exploitation, the manipulation of the weak by the strong, of labor by management.

4. The subject's decision to act is not due to objective calculation, to a rational choice of available alternatives. For the sociologist working in this perspective, the alternatives seen by the actor cannot be reduced to objective and rational data. His actions can never be construed, and consequently, cannot be evaluated in the light of the sociologist's view of the facts or his definition of the situation. Spontaneity, freedom, subjectivity are the key concepts in searching for the motivation of a deviant act. A determinism which accepts the rules of the game, the use of which makes discrimination or prediction possible, is repudiated.

5. Delinquency belongs in the vast category of deviant behavior, some of which is innovative, while some reflects the refusal on moral grounds to accept odious values. The conflictual explanatory model puts the definition of the rules of the game where it belongs, among the social actors, thus removing this weapon from the hands of the ruling classes who use it via legislation and law enforcement agencies for their exclusive benefit. The sociologist is thus freed

from the service of the establishment. He is entrenched in his mission of observer, analyst, and above all, critic.

6. By detypifying the concept of delinquency, the sociologist points out the existence in society of forces of dynamic change, which constantly redefine the objectives, methods, and orientation of society, its groups and classes. Delinquency cannot be understood as simply a break in a contractual relationship subject to the conditions of those who exercise the power. Delinquents, like the mentally ill, the political terrorists, or those who indulge in deviant sexual practices or use drugs, may constitute the manifestation of new social forms corresponding with the emergence of alternative value systems to those in force. The sociologist's place is not in the service of the old regime. On the contrary, he should contribute to the establishment of new rules. Delinquent behavior is essentially *problematical*; it cannot be considered an objective fact.

7. Statistics as indicators of delinquency are rejected. However, they can be accepted as indicators of the functioning of the judicial and social control systems, in other words, as a way of measuring alienation, oppression, and dispossession. These statistics tell us nothing of the significance of the act of the human being, the delinquent. On the contrary, they deprive it of meaning.

8. We tend to consider delinquency an expression of social conflict (Lofland, 1969). The Marxist adherents of the conflictual model look upon the penal law as an instrument of oppression and manipulation in the hands of the bourgeoisie. The idea of power is of the essence in the conflictual perspective: it is a confrontation between value systems, between views of the world, between hope of a new society and stubborn defense of the status quo. In this new society, completely egalitarian, where, according to Lenin, power can be assumed by every person since all the constraints of exploitation and alienation will have been removed and since control will be forbidden, criminals are the result of a truly universal consensus. In all other societies, state Taylor et al. (1973), deviance and delinquency are acts of resistance against the oppressive and illegitimate authorities.

9. In the light of these considerations, it seems clear that nothing in the deviant act itself qualifies it as such; it is in the *eyes of others* that the deviant act becomes delinquent. These others, who have the power to discredit such an act in favor of other acts which they support as legitimate, are actually the possessors of a historically determined power. Sociologists of the conflictual model attach great importance to the historical genesis of the laws and believe them to be an expression of the desire of certain groups to dominate others. As early as the seventeenth century, young people swelling the ranks of the unemployed were interned in forced labor camps. Young persons who invaded the cities, where, for lack of employment and training, they constituted a threat to the safety of property and those who owned property, were placed in reform schools. The laws protecting the workers were annulled because of strikes and of

sometimes bloody conflicts. The laws protecting the consumer, the public, the social heritage, were slow in coming. The hidden powers fought to maintain their privileges and their impunity in the face of acts of plunder and fraud. Fair taxation, the fight against organized crime and white-collar crimes, industrial security, these are the demands of a sociology which is bent on establishing an alternative view of vice and virtue in contemporary society.

10. With regard to methodology, this model is characterized by a total distrust of the value of official statistics, of the gathering of opinions stereotyped and conditioned by the mass media, by the Gallup poll method of survey. It is by participant observation, empathy, that the researcher penetrates his subject's world. Here he tends to see either the victim of an unjust society or the rebel who is seeking new frontiers through personal and collective experimentation— experimentation that might lead to the discovery of a society finally free of the constraints, compromises, alienations, hypocrisies, and the organized violence that we encounter daily.

Impact on Social Policy and Practice

The impact of the conflictual model on social policy is not easy to assess. Its protagonists have more critiques of social action than concrete proposals. Apart from sporadic experiments in communes or the very special case of the kibbutzim in Israel and the communist countries, there has been no integrated social model designed that would evolve from the breakdown of the present society.

It must be pointed out, however, that efforts, to decriminalize victimless acts can be attributed to adherents of the conflictual model. Certain homosexual and heterosexual practices and the use of certain drugs are being removed from the control of the criminal law, which sanctioned them by a loss of civil rights. Other behavior, particularly white-collar crimes, should be more severely criminalized in the conflictual view. However, the subscribers to this model certainly do not have a monopoly in fighting for these reforms.

Generally speaking, efforts to limit the role of criminal law to areas which seriously endanger the physical and spiritual integrity of individuals were supported by research. The study of more or less radical alternatives to the present system of criminal justice was encouraged as well.

Conclusions

What effects have these two models on criminal policy and on the activities of those working in the field of juvenile delinquency? It is certain that the consensual model, an offshoot of the existing system, accepts the rules of the game. What it proposes is to rectify the rules where there is cheating and redefine those where a reasonable consensus can be obtained. Researchers should show the reality as it exists, as it is experienced by others, and as it is exemplified not only by the subjectivity of the actors but also by the institutions with their constraints, traditions, and influence. The consensual model supports the possibility that contradictory interests can be resolved, but within the context of the natural and necessary hierarchy of the needs of the conformist majority and the deviant minority. Practitioners and clinicians should try to guide those in their charge in order to better prepare them to make a place for themselves in the social system. Justice in the labor market, in the school, and in the family: these are the criteria which will give these workers the moral integrity they require vis-à-vis those to whom and for whom they are responsible.

Obviously then, social criticism is not lacking in the consensual model; it is an integral part of it. It can become a basic principle if conditions so require. Its adherents' conception of man and society makes them particularly heedful of the fact that to replace one tyranny by another means, as history has shown, a general loss of freedom and an inferior way of life. The most unjust "protectors" of society know that it is they who would lose the most by the change.

But the subscribers to the consensual model foresaw the correctness of the thinking of the philosopher Kolakowski. Our corruptibility is not contingent. According to Kolakowski, we know that the very process of living is a source of anxiety, conflict, aggression, uncertainty, and care. No coherent system of values is possible, and any attempt to apply it to individual cases will fail. The moral victory of evil is always possible.

If the above model is well suited to an Apollonian civilization, the conflictual model is directly in keeping with the principles of a Dionysian civilization. In this perspective, researchers try to find in the world of nonconformists, of deviancies and delinquencies, premonitory signs of a liberation from the constraints arbitrarily imposed by an unjust society, the cause of all the alienation, perversion and misfortunes of humanity today. The first task of the researcher is to compare nonconformist values with conformist values. As soon as it is felt that neutrality is impossible for the scientific investigator, it seems to be an inevitable deontological rule to use research as a weapon of accusation in the class struggle. It is the researcher's moral obligation to denounce the production of other researchers as so many means of defense in the service of the ruling classes and their regime of privilege.

With regard to practitioners in the juvenile justice system, their situation seems to be untenable in this perspective. Either they must admit their role as mercenaries in the service of the unjust and illegitimate authorities or continue to delude themselves. Inasmuch as they admit to neither one of these conclusions, their duty, within the limits allowed them by the law and by society, is to denounce the iniquities of the present system. What side are we on? There is no doubt about the answer, and many magistrates and educators have joined with researchers to show, each with the means at his disposal, their refusal to automatically shoulder the responsibility for the injustices of the system.

Truth takes precedence over efficiency. The promise of a total well-being, the hope of a benevolent apocalypse which will give man back his innocence, is the supreme source of hope and the direct motivation for action.

In summary, I have grouped a whole series of ideas, often very different from one another, into two somewhat arbitrary paradigmatic models. They are paradigmatic because they are actually two fundamental approaches, unyielding to one another and each commanding an epistemology, a theory, a methodology, and a deontology which, without being exclusive, are specific. In fact, they constitute communities of thought.

Throughout this chapter, I have tried to keep in mind the influence of epistemology on theory, of theory on methodology and strategy in social policy. We must also remember that the cultural revolution which eroded sociology toward the end of the sixties left its mark on sociological criminology just as the wave of antipsychiatric feeling did on clinical criminology.

Intellectuals, men of science, advisers of the prince in the matter of criminal policy, lawyers assigned by law to the delinquent, and the criminologists of today must bear the weight of these contradictions that the constant changes in scientific methods and approaches impose. Our moral and intellectual discomfort, however, must not be greater than that of preceding generations. Each time there is a breach in the spiritual and material structure of the world, the contradiction becomes more destructive. These periods are much more frequent than those in which intellectual well-being prevails, assured by the security that is derived from well established truths.

The views of the world that have been described and the contemporary interpretations of juvenile maladjustment that have been presented are based on a tradition that has existed in the Western world for centuries. Upon their dialogue and the results of their confrontation depends the quality of today's society and that of the future.

I have tried to present objectively the two models of sociological explanation of juvenile delinquency. I have tried to outline their proposals for contemporary criminal policy. I have now only to say a word about my own thinking on these matters.

I have cited the philosopher Kolakowski (1976) a number of times because, essentially, my personal position coincides with his. I believe, as he does, that the unity of man is not possible. If it were, we would do everything possible to bring it about. Even the most oppressive governments needed no other reason than this. Their protagonists had no other motivations. The greater our hopes for humanity, the more we are tempted to offer it all sorts of sacrifices. The words of Anatole France are frighteningly true today: never have so many been killed in the name of a doctrine which proclaims the innate goodness of man. And we could add that never have we been so hard on man as when we impose sacrifices in the name of humanity.

The evil in us can only be held in check, at least partially, by doubt, which should be cultivated and firmly exercised in the judgments we make, not only in science but also in politics. The greatest ruse of the devil is to have us believe he does not exist, said Baudelaire. It is by thinking of him and his power as the fallen angel that the intellectual, the man of science and the criminologist must confront and evaluate the adverse dangers implied in each act and each decision he makes when trying to deal with the difficult problem of delinquency.

6 The Myth of the Respectable Traffic Offender: Twenty Years Later

Preben Wolf

In Denmark only infringements of the penal code (indictable offenses) have normally been regarded as criminal acts. The principles as to what constitutes an infringement of the penal code have, however, not always been consistent. Nor have the statistics of crime followed a definite policy through the years. Thus it may be said that the inconsistency of the legislation and the diffidence of the authorities in classifying criminality under special laws and under the penal code proper have blurred the boundaries between these two categories of offenses.

Violations of the penal code comprise the traditional crimes against the state, against persons or property, and sex crimes. The punishable violations of special laws are mainly traffic and driving offenses and offenses against price regulations, rationing laws, economic laws, tariff laws, police regulations, and so forth. These offenses are mainly what Vilhelm Aubert (1964, p. 86) has called "modern offenses" originating from conflicting interests in society—offenses which are often met with more restitutive sanctions than those otherwise applied within the criminal justice system.

Special law offenses are looked upon with much more ambivalence and toleration than are the traditional criminal offenses dealt with in the penal code. As a consequence there has been and there still is a tendency in societies where this distinction is valid not to consider offenders against the various provisions of the special laws, for example, traffic laws, as real criminals. They are rather seen as ordinary, respectable citizens, who may have been incompetent and perhaps wanton drivers, but they are neither the intentful nor the immoral wrongdoers that real criminals are generally supposed to be. Other special law offenders have been looked at in similar ways. During recent years there has, however, been an increasing awareness in Denmark and elsewhere of the importance of offenses against the special laws. This increasing awareness is probably correlated with the fact that the cost of special law violations appear greatly to exceed the costs brought about by penal code offenses. One consequence of this has been serious discussions among experts and politicians in Denmark of redefining, for example, tax evasion as a real crime by making the offense part of the penal code and not just an act punishable according to special law. Another consequence has been the inclusion since 1974 of special law offense figures in the tables of the official publications of crime statistics (Kriminalstatistik, 1976, 1977).

Estimating the Incidence of Crime in Denmark

Statistics of crime and criminals have been officially published in Denmark since 1828. For obvious reasons this does not mean that longitudinal comparisons can be made for the whole 150-year period. The main obstacles have been the changes that have taken place in law, the administration of justice, and in the compilation of criminal statistics.

Most of the statistical computations have been made yearly, and in some cases every five or every ten years. In any case they are presented in simple tables showing registered crime figures over a certain period of time, and as such they may be utilized in computing the annual volume of crime or the incidence of crime, for example, the number of penal code offenses or offenders registered within a year per 100,000 or per 10,000 of the total Danish population. Thus in 1954 the incidence of crime in Denmark as measured by number of penal code offenses known to the police was just over 2,500 offenses per 100,000 of the total population. Twenty years later the volume of offenses had increased 2.5 times to about 6,500 per 100,000 population (Wolf, 1976).

Computation of the incidence of crime is the most usual way of presenting crime statistics for longitudinal comparison internationally or nationally. This measure is very suitable if one wishes to follow the development of the registered crime figure during a period of time.

Such computations do not, however, say anything directly about the number of registered offenders or offenses that are represented in a population at a certain point in time (prevalence of crime) (Hurwitz and Christiansen, 1968). It is difficult and often costly to make descriptions of the prevalence of crime or criminals in a population. So normally we must be content with more or less systematic estimations based on the official criminal statistics.

In the early 1950s Kallestrup (1954) estimated that the penal code offenders in Denmark made up about 8 percent of the male population in the country at the time. Karl Otto Christiansen (Christiansen and Nielsen, 1959) estimated the frequency of crime (penal code offenders only) on the basis of the official statistics of crime and population around the early and mid-fifties. He found about 8 percent registered criminals in the total Danish population of males aged fifteen and over. In a random sample of 3,032 men and 606 women, who in 1953-1954 were twenty-one years of age or more, Wolf et al. (1958) found 569 men (18.8 percent) and 14 women (2.3 percent) registered in the Central Police Registry (Rigsregistraturen) of Denmark. The number of women was too small to warrant further investigation on a statistical basis. The males, however, comprised 292 (9.6 percent) offenders against the penal code and 277 (9.2 percent) violators of special laws outside the penal code. The fact that we found more penal code offenders in our material than was estimated for the population at the same time by Kallestrup or computed by Christiansen and Nielsen, was mainly caused by differences of procedure. In contrast to the others we had included offenders against the penal code who had experienced waiver of prosecution, warnings, and/or fines only. Having adjusted our material according to the definitions of Kallestrup and Christiansen and Nielsen, we too found a criminal frequency of 8 percent for all adult males in Denmark at the time (Wolf, 1962, 1965).

Changes in the Prevalence of Offenders (1956-1975)

The random sample of the male population of Denmark on which our 1958 study was based had been drawn in 1953-1954 by Svalastoga for his study of social stratification and social mobility in Denmark at mid-century (1959). In 1956-1957 the sample was checked for registered crime by Kaarsen and Wolf in various criminal registers, mainly the Central Police Registry for the whole country.

Another random sample of the male population born not later than 1960 was drawn by Erik Høgh in 1975 (Høgh and Wolf, 1977). This sample has been checked for registered crime and delinquency in the same way as Svalastoga's sample had been checked twenty years before. In the fifties we found 569 registered offenders, or almost 19 percent of the sample comprising 3,032 adult males (twenty-one years and over). Twenty years later we found 333 (24 percent) in a similar sample of 1,380 adult males living in Denmark in 1975-1976.

The increase in the prevalence of registered offenders from the mid-fifties to the mid-seventies is mainly due to an increase in the frequency of penal code offenders, from less than 10 percent in the fifties to about 14 percent in the seventies. One should remember that, as the increase in prevalence of offenders over the twenty-year period appears to be less dramatic than the increase in the incidence of offenses previously mentioned, the units of measurement are not the same. A comparatively small group of very active offenders are responsible for a relatively large number of offenses registered (Wolf, 1965). Furthermore, offenses may have been committed by females and by persons under the age of twenty-one, or by offenders who have never been registered officially. The prevalence of those registered for special law offenses only increased from just over 9 percent to about 10 percent.

Unlike the sample from 1953-1954 the later sample comprises males fifteen and older. So it is possible to compare the various distributions for the age categories of fifteen to twenty with those of the age categories of twenty-one and over in 1975-1976, but it is the latter categories only which can be compared with the material available from the fifties. The total frequency of registered offenders is practically the same in 1975-1976 for the age category fifteen to twenty (25 percent) as for the category of twenty-one and over (24 percent). On the other hand, young offenders under twenty-one are differently distributed over offense categories from the offenders above that age. The distributions over penal code offenses, traffic offenses, and other special law offenses are shown for the two age categories in 1975 and for the offenders in the old sample from 1953-1954 in table 6-1. It is worth noting that of male offenders registered in 1975-1976, the younger group (in Denmark there is no liability for punishment before the age of fifteen) had predominantly violated traffic laws. In fact even the eight boys who had been listed as penal code offenders had all been registered for traffic offenses as well. Among the adults in 1975-1976, this distribution is significantly different, with the penal code offenders as the dominant category.

The proportion of penal code offenders among those registered in the 1950s does not differ much from the corresponding proportion in the 1970s, but the composition of the groups of special law have changed completely over the twenty years. Of the special law offenders living in Denmark in the mid-fifties, less than half were traffic offenders. This proportion has increased to more than 80 percent in 1975. This shift is not surprising if we take the enormous increase in motor vehicles and traffic during the last twenty years into

Table 6-1
Distribution over Offense Categories

	Offense Categories			
Age and Year of Sample	Males Registered for Penal Code Offenses	Males Registered for Traffic Offenses	Males Registered for Special Law Offenses Only	Number Registered in the Central Policy Registry of Denmark
15-20 1975-1976	8 (21.6%)	27 (73.0%)	2 (5.4%)	37 (100%)
21 and Over 1975-1976	188 (57.3%)	116 (35.4%)	24 (7.3%)	328 (100%)
Total 1975-1976	196 (53.7%)	143 (39.2%)	26 (7.1%)	365 (100%)
21 and Over 1953-1957	292 (51.3%)	115 (20.2%)	162 (28.5%)	569 (100%)

Source: Wolf (1977).

Note: In 1975-1976 8 registered males, for whom no specific offense could be ascertained, have been excluded.

account. Furthermore, the special law offenders of the registered offenders in the early fifties were still dominated by violations of price and rationing regulations from World War II and the immediate postwar years.

The Respectability of the Traffic Offender Called into Question

It has been mentioned above that during the last twenty years the image of the special law offender may have changed somewhat in the direction of less respectability because of the greater cost to society of these offenses, including traffic offenses. Still, traffic offenses are so common that it is not easy to think of them as seriously deviant, antisocial, or criminal acts.

During the fifties and early sixties European studies of the traffic offenders' records of traditional criminality began in Germany (Kaiser, 1976), England (Willett, 1964), and Denmark (Wolf, 1964). These and later studies elsewhere (Council of Europe, 1966; Baldassini-Faini, 1969; Separovic, 1971) found that traffic offenders frequently had a record of previous appearances in court in connection with other types of offense. Earlier studies in the United States and Canada had reached similar conclusions (Tillman and Hobbes, 1949; McFarland and Moseley, 1954). Willett's study of the *Criminal on the Road* (1964) is probably the best known of all these various studies, but as was pointed out by Steer and Carr-Hill (1967), his results differed somewhat from the results of other studies, such as the contemporary Danish one (Wolf, 1964).

The immediate postwar years were characterized by few motor vehicles in Denmark. It was not until 1949 that the rate of highway vehicles reached the prewar level of 1939 with just under 4,000 vehicles per 100,000 population. Between 1954 and 1957, while the material for the Danish prevalence study mentioned above was collected, the relative number of motor vehicles passed 8,000 per 100,000 of the population in Denmark. Now, twenty years later, this figure is fourfold (Banks, 1971; Statistical Yearbook, 1977). As was shown by Svalastoga (1970), there is a positive relationship between a country's number of cars per capita and the annual number of road deaths per capita, and this seems to hold for car densities below a certain level not reached by Denmark yet.

So it was toward the end of the first decade after World War II, when the number of cars per capita in Denmark had doubled, that forensic doctors and heads of casualty wards first began to suspect that there might be a connection between traffic accidents and criminality among drivers. Their suspicions were published in the daily press (Jensen, 1956) and it was decided to include a study of this problem as part of our researches of crime in Denmark at mid-century (Wolf et al., 1958; Wolf, 1964; Wolf and Høgh, 1975).

Two alternative hypotheses were put to test in our study of criminality and traffic in the mid-fifties:

1. Traffic offenses aside, registered traffic offenders are just as law-abiding as other adult citizens who have not been registered by the police for violation of traffic regulations.
2. There is a significantly higher frequency of other registered offenses (for example, penal code offenses) among registered traffic and motoring offenders than there is among people who are not registered as traffic offenders.

If it is correct that traffic and motoring offenders are just as law-abiding as anybody else, and if we take a representative random sample of the adult male population and study it, then we should expect to find approximately the same percentage (frequency) of registered penal code offenders in the group of registered traffic offenders as found in the remaining sample of males who had not been registered as traffic offenders. The same would hold for the percentage of other special law offenders, when the two categories are compared. This was tested in the random sample of all adult males (twenty-one years and over) in Denmark which, as mentioned above, had been drawn by Svalastoga (1959) in 1953-1954 and studied with regard to criminality between 1954 and 1957 (Wolf, 1964, 1965).

From table 6-2 it can be seen that hypothesis 1 was not borne out twenty years ago. It appears that there are between three and four times as many registered penal code violators among the traffic offenders as in the remaining

Table 6-2
Distribution of Penal Code Offenders and Special Law Offenders

Type of Law Violation	Registered Male Violators of Traffic Laws (%)	Males Not Registered as Violators of Traffic Laws (%)	Total Males 21 Years and Over, 1953-1954 (%)
No violations registered	55.4	86.0	84.2
At least one violation of Penal Code	30.7	8.4	9.8
At least one special law offense but no Penal Code offenses	13.9	5.5	5.9
Number (%)	166 (100.0)	2,866 (99.9)	3,032 (99.9)

Source: Wolf (1977).

male population and more than twice as many pure special law offenders. These differences are clearly significant. So hypothesis 1 is not borne out, and hypothesis 2 seems to hold so far.

On the other hand, the product-moment correlation (*r*) between violations of traffic laws and violations of the penal code is not very strong (*r* = 0.1715), and the correlation between pure special law offenses and traffic offenses is even less so (*r* = 0.0941). Still, the conclusion of our studies in the mid-fifties must be that registered traffic law offenders were more frequently real criminals (penal code offenders) than were the male population as a whole. It worked the other way as well: "A special point of interest is that traffic and motoring offenses are registered three or four times as often for real criminals (violators of the penal code) as for unconvicted persons" (Wolf, 1965, p. 224).

The question now is whether such a conclusion would still hold if the research were repeated in the same way in the mid-seventies. In view of the fourfold increase in motorcars, the corresponding increase in traffic accidents, and the fact that mopeds have since become abundant on the Danish roads, it is conceivable that it has also become more common, more normal, for ordinary noncriminal people accidentally to commit a punishable traffic offense. According to Svalastoga (1970) it should hold for Denmark, that for constant population the number of road deaths will increase from 3 to 4 percent whenever the number of cars increases 10 percent. This may very well be the case since the noncriminal, male traffic offenders have increased from just under 4 percent in 1953-1957 to a little more than 8 percent of the male population twenty-one years and over in 1975-1976. Thus, the relative number of traffic offenders who have not violated the penal code has increased 100 percent during the last twenty years or so. If we then take a look at the percentage of those who have violated both the traffic laws and the penal code, we shall see that among adult males it has increased from almost 2 percent in 1953-1957 to almost 6 percent in 1975-1976. This means that it has more than trebled during that period, while the percentage of penal code offenders who have not only committed traffic offenses has changed very little from the mid-fifties to the mid-seventies.

From table 6-3 it can be seen to what extent the conclusions based on the distributions shown in table 6-2 still hold. It is immediately observed by comparison of the distributions in table 6-3 with those of table 6-2 that our conclusions from the fifties must still be considered valid in the seventies.

The connection between registration for violation of traffic laws and registration for violation of the penal code has become even more profound than before. It is more highly significant, and the correlation has become stronger (*r* = 0.3149). In contrast to this there is today hardly any correlation at all between traffic offenses and other pure special law registered offenses. If we then consider young males between fifteen and twenty years of age included in table 6-1, we find that the previous conclusion holds for them as well. The

Table 6-3
Distribution of Penal Code Offenders and Special Law Offenders

Type of Law Violation	Registered Male Violators of Traffic Laws (%)	Males Not Registered as Violators of Traffic Laws (%)	Total Males 21 Years and Over, 1975-1976 (%)
No violations registered of Penal Code nor of special laws	58.8	88.7	84.5
At least one violation of Penal Code	40.2	9.3	13.6
At least one special law offense but no Penal Code offenses	1.0	2.0	1.9
Number (%)	194 (100.0)	1,180 (100.0)	1,380 (100.0)

Source: Wolf (1977).

Note: In 1975-1976 5 males, 21 years and over, for whom no specific offense could be ascertained, have been excluded.

proportion of penal code offenders among the traffic offenders in this group is over 18 percent, while it is less than 2 percent among those not registered for traffic offenses. This difference is clearly significant in spite of the smallness of the categories. The correlation coefficient is also very close to that of the twenty-one years and older members of the sample ($r = 0.3083$), but still very moderate.

Conclusion

Expanding the above-mentioned formulation we conclude that male registered traffic offenders are more often real criminals (penal code offenders) than are other Danish males beyond the age of liability to punishment (fifteen).

The results of the two Danish studies described here seem to establish that the view of the traffic offender as an otherwise law-abiding and respectable citizen is to a large extent, but not completely, a myth. As has already been mentioned, similar results have been reached in other countries, at least for certain of more serious kinds of traffic offenders. Suggestions have been put forward in the press and elsewhere by Danish physicians (for example, Palle Hjort, the county medical officer for the County of Copenhagen) to the effect that half the drunken drivers are mentally deviant in one way or another. It is considered an established fact in Scandinavia that a large proportion of the drunken drivers have serious and rather permanent alcoholic problems (Nielsen, 1974; Nordisk Råd, 1977). Furthermore, the conclusions with regard to the criminality of registered traffic offenders mentioned above have been corroborated specifically for drunken drivers in several Danish studies during the sixties. Thus Karl Otto Christiansen found 45 percent registered penal code offenders in a sample of 302 male drunken drivers in Copenhagen; Frode Henriksen analyzed 150 persons serving sentences of mitigated imprisonment (*haefte*) in Danish prisons for driving or attempting to drive while under the influence of alcohol. He found that 50 of those persons (33 percent) had also been registered for penal code offenses. In a similar study of 69 persons serving the same type of sentence for the same type of offense, Reventlow and Jørgensen found as many as 44 or 64 percent registered for other offenses (Straffelovrådet, 1970). Berglund and Johansson (1974) have summarized a number of similar studies from Sweden. Sveri (1970) found 40 percent registered penal code offenders (indictable offenses) among 242 drivers under the influence of alcohol. In a later study by Willett of 188 English traffic offenders he found 40 percent registered with criminal offenses. In his earlier study from 1964 he had found 23 percent with sentences for indictable and nonindictable offenses other than traffic offenses. In Holland, Buikhuisen and Van Weringh found as many as 52 percent of 1,873 traffic offenders who had sentences for nontraffic offenses as well (see Berglund and Johansson, 1974).

The variations in the frequencies of other registered offenses among registered traffic offenders from one study to another undoubtedly partly result from differences in the definitions applied, in the characteristics and representativeness of the samples studied, and the methodological procedures and criteria of what constitutes crime. Most of these sources of variation were ruled out when the Danish study from the mid-fifties was replicated in exactly the same way twenty years later. This is not the time or place, however, for a more elaborate comparative study of all these various results and the reasons for their variations. Suffice it to say that the conclusions from our Danish study during the fifties have been upheld by the replicated study twenty years later. Furthermore, the results of both studies are corroborated by a number of more specific studies carried through by a number of different researchers in Denmark and elsewhere at various points in time between 1957 and 1977.

It may still be a matter for discussion whether traffic offenders are really more criminal than other people, as Willett contends, or whether they are registered more often by the police for other offenses because they have been registered already, and thus are better known to and more easily detected by the police, as has been suggested by other criminologists (Chapman, 1968). There is probably some truth in both points of view.

I favor Willett's contention. The burden of proof must lie with those who claim that the connection between traffic offenses and real criminal offenses is an artifact caused by some of the purely technical conditions of normal police investigations.

From the point of view of the practitioner and the average person, this discussion is probably less interesting than the possible consequences of the fact that registered penal code offenders appear to constitute an appreciable safety risk, not only as criminals but also as motorists. Penal law offenders appear six times more often as registered traffic offenders than do other Danish males beyond the age of fourteen. In the metropolitan area of Copenhagen (Høgh and Wolf, 1977) alone, the relative number of drunken drivers among penal law offenders is about three times larger than the corresponding figure for the remaining sample of noncriminal males born in that area.

A very recent study of victims of traffic accidents and of crimes in a small community north of Copenhagen (Wolf, 1977) suggests that victims of traffic accidents are twice as likely to be victims of crimes as nonvictims of traffic accidents in the same area.

The two main Danish investigations described in this chapter both differ from most other criminological studies by basing their conclusions on nationally representative samples of the whole Danish population of adult males at two points of time separated by approximately twenty years. It has been possible for the mid-fifties and again for the mid-seventies to ascertain the frequency of registered law-breaking activity for the two samples of males in Denmark. The results show an increase in the number of registered penal code offenders from about 10 to about 14 percent of all Danish males aged twenty-one and over. The corresponding increase for pure special law offenders was from 9 to 10 percent, but with the traffic offenses in the seventies taking the place of other special law offenses, which had become obsolete since the fifties with the disappearance of rationing and price restrictions from the war and immediate postwar years.

The further conclusions (partly corroborated in the meantime by other more specific studies in Denmark and elsewhere) that traffic offenders tend to be real criminals to a much larger extent than do nontraffic offenders, and that conversely penal code offenders present themselves as real road safety risks, were more than confirmed by the replication of the study in the seventies. The myth of the otherwise law-abiding and respectable traffic offender was unmasked by the studies in the mid-fifties and later. It is suggested that the myth has been weakened but that it is still alive.

The present study has documented that the rapid development of motoring and highway traffic has not made the traffic offender more law-abiding with regard to the penal code. Now, twenty years later, his respectability still seems to be largely a myth.

7

A Copenhagen Youth Gang: A Descriptive Analysis

Karen Berntsen

The basic material for this research was collected in 1963 at the Youth Clinic in Copenhagen, which was established in 1960 in order to carry through criminological research of juvenile delinquency. The work of the Youth Clinic at that time consisted of collecting social and psychological information about a certain number of juvenile male delinquents aged fifteen to twenty years who were on probation. The purpose of the research was to try to prevent recidivism.

In January and February of 1963 the Youth Clinic began conducting a practical treatment experiment. At this time we began with four boys (later more) who knew each other well, who lived in the same area of Copenhagen, and who more or less had committed their delinquent acts, which had brought them to the Youth Clinic, together. One of our means of treatment was group counselling, or discussions. We tried this with these boys but we soon realized that they were only a small part of a much larger gang. This gang met every evening at a certain cafeteria, a square, or in a park, and in many ways they were a nuisance for the police and for the neighborhood. At the Youth Clinic we soon felt it insufficient to work with only the small part of the group who were our "probationers." The influence we could have by these group discussions once a week had to be considered of minimal importance in comparison with the influence of their peers with whom they met the other nights.

We therefore decided to open up the Youth Clinic once a week for the rest of the group, and we suggested that the boys should invite their friends. There were two main reasons for this experiment. The first one has already been mentioned; the other was that we felt uncomfortable knowing about this rather big group of youngsters who continued committing more or less serious crimes and behaving in a provoking, disturbing manner, without any one attempting some positive measures.

The weekly meetings for our "probationers" started in February 1963, and in May the same year the meetings were opened up for "guests" as an "open house." The youths came at about 7 P.M. and stayed until 10-11 P.M.

The Youth Clinic was financed by the Ford Foundation. In charge of this research were professor, dr. jur. Karl Otto Christiansen, superintendent, dr. med. Georg K. Stürup, and professor, dr. jur. Knud Waaben.

Table 7-1

Number of Persons Attending Meetings at the Youth Clinic from February 1963 to April 1964

Number of meetings	1-5	6-10	11-15	16-21	22-26	27-31	32-36	37-41	42-46	47-51	52-55
Number of persons	19	24	38	82	151	204	38	49	45	42	15
Average number of persons	4	5	8	14	30	41	8	10	9	8	4

During the first five meetings (1-5) nineteen persons came, averaging four persons at each meeting. After the meetings were opened up for the friends of our probationers more and more youngsters of both sexes came, and during meetings 16-21 there were a total of eighty-two persons, with an average of four-teen per meeting. As there was no room for such big groups at the Youth Clinic, we had to find other facilities, and in July 1963 (meeting 22) we got hold of a vacant youth club in the neighborhood, and until September 1963 the weekly meetings were held there. As seen from the table more and more youngsters attended. But for various reasons we had to close down. We suggested that they join the ordinary youth club. Some did so but some did not, and they asked us to continue. In October 1963 we therefore opened up again at the Youth Clinic (meeting 32) and continued until April 1964.

Why did they come? They knew that we wanted them to stop their criminal activities, and that we wanted to influence them in this direction. One attraction for them, of course, was free coffee, cakes, and a limited number of cigarettes. Their own answers to the question were, for example: "We have no place to be together." "It is nice sitting and talking." "It is better to be here than at home." "As long as we are here, we don't commit crimes."

During these evenings we discussed general phenomena such as parent-child problems, school and work conditions, sex, alcohol (drugs such as marijuana, LSD, morphine, and heroin were not a problem in Denmark at that time). But primarily the discussions were concentrated on crime in general as well as specific types of crimes, especially car theft, wanton destruction of property, and homosexual promiscuity. As time went on, it became clear that many of the group members continued their criminal activities. As one boy said, when asked why he continued to come to the meetings even though he continued with crime: "You hope that it will help to come and talk about it. Perhaps then little by little you understand that you must stop." The Youth Clinic started negotiations with the authorities regarding establishing a special youth club for the group, but did not succeed.

In the fall of 1963 we decided to get more concrete and formalized knowledge about the history, structure, and activity of the group or gang as well as the registered crimes of the individual members. At that time quite a few of the members had been arrested and sent to youth prison or institutions, and we had to be quick to get the relevant information. We then constructed a questionnaire with seventy-four questions concerning the history, organization, and leadership, of the gang, in addition to a form for a social interview. We payed $1.50 for answering the questionnaire and the same for the social interview. In total we succeeded in getting this information from fifty persons, thirty-seven boys and thirteen girls. Of these, eleven boys and one girl were interviewed in prison or institutions, the rest at the Youth Clinic. We also got information from the Child Welfare Organization and the Central Crime Register concerning 90 persons whom we then considered as more than sporadic members of the gang. Later the number was limited to seventy-eight persons, fifty-seven boys and twenty-one girls, because the last twelve persons were found to be irrelevant concerning any relationship with the gang. For the seventy-eight persons studied in 1964, a follow-up study with regard to registered crime was made in July 1967 and in January 1977.

One of the reasons for trying to analyze some of this material is that Karl Otto Christiansen was deeply involved in the research and was especially interested in this subresearch, in which he actively participated. He discussed and improved the questionnaire which was used, and he interviewed some of the group members. In the research design he put much emphasis on getting information on the size, development, and kind of juvenile gangs in Copenhagen; he especially wanted to know if it was possible to find more structured criminal gangs as described in the American criminological literature.

The Structure of the Group

By working on the answers to the questionnaire and the information at the weekly meetings we have tried to get a picture of the development of this special group. The history of the group can be divided into three periods:

1. From 1960 to June 1962 there existed in this particular area of Copenhagen different small groups of youngsters. Some of them were simple street corner groups, others were a little more structured, for instance, they had special names. One was called the Sunbeams, another MTU (these three letters in Danish stood for "motor crazy youth" or "total extermination of virginity"), a third one, and perhaps the most important, called themselves the Pils (Danish beer). In the beginning only six boys met in a cellar where they started drinking beer and talking; they continued by stealing the beer and then stealing cars. They got tired of their cellar and moved to the square where there were two cafeterias. At the time, about June 1962, some of the other groups moved in the same direction.

2. The period June 1962 to August 1963 was the time when the group's activities, especially delinquent and criminal activities, culminated. There was an inner circle consisting of about fifteen to twenty persons, and around them were some forty to fifty boys and girls. They made so much trouble that they were expelled from the cafeterias. The movie theater at the square, where midnight shows were played on Saturday nights, took special precautions. They would only sell two tickets to each youngster so that they could be spread apart; they left every second row empty to have space for an official to calm down the youngsters. The activities of the group included crimes, noisy and disturbing behavior, and teasing and provoking adults in general and police officers in particular. Their territory was the square and the park.

3. In August 1963 there was a change because a large part of the inner circle was arrested; eight boys were sent to youth prison, and two boys and one girl were sent to institutions for youth. In the fall we collected the material for the research by getting the social interviews and the questionnaires. When we sensed that two boys from the periphery were trying, through criminal activities, to rebuild the group, we at the same time tried to split it up by moving away our "probationers." By the spring of 1964 the group no longer existed. It was not easy to find out who belonged to the group and how the group was structured. Our material consisted of the observations we made during the fifty-five meetings at the Youth Clinic and the analysis of the fifty questionnaires.

At first we had more or less complete names of about one hundred boys and fifty girls. This number was slowly reduced because some could not be identified, and others were omitted because of a very loose attachment. Therefore, we ended up with seventy-eight persons, fifty-seven boys and twenty-one girls. But this in itself shows that it was a rather loosely organized, unstructured group. Nearly all the members lived within half a kilometer from the square where they met, and they knew each other from school, the neighborhood, or work.

The question of how to become a member was answered by the majority of the youngsters with: "It was not a real membership. When you came to the square, you belonged to the group." Only a few from the inner circle would reveal that some special performance was necessary, as for example, a fight or a criminal activity such as stealing a car.

Although it was not a strictly structured group, the analysis and observations showed that there were some youngsters who had a more prominent position than others. By analyzing the fifty questionnaires and counting the number of times each person is mentioned as belonging to the group, we derived the following division of the group into three parts:

1. The core consisted of five boys and one girl. They were mentioned in thirty-one to forty-three questionnaires.

2. The inner circle consisted of ten boys and eight girls, mentioned in eleven to thirty questionnaires.
3. The marginal circle consisted of forty-two boys and twelve girls, mentioned one to ten times.

For reasons of discretion and in order to facilitate the statistical work, we assigned each group member a number instead of using their names. The boys were given numbers below 100, the girls above 100. Of interest is the fact that eighteen of the seventy-eight persons were related to each other. In four cases there were two brothers; further there were a couple of twin brothers and their cousin, there was one sister and her brother, two sisters, and three sisters.

Of three of the boys who belonged to the core group, boy number 5, who participated in only a few meetings at the Youth Clinic, played a great role. Before he came to the clinic he was often referred to with pride and shudder because of his daringness, his devil-may-care attitude, and his activities. When he arrived at the clinic, he certainly lived up to the expectations and dominated the evenings by telling stories about himself and his criminal behavior. Number 9 was also an important person. He was a nice looking, charming boy who the girls especially admired and fell in love with. He was bright, well behaved, and polite when outside the group, but often aggressive and impudent within the group. Number 32 tried to impress the group with his physical strength and his oratorial talent. He was the clown of the group and tried to spoil every attempt at serious discussions by laughing and telling jokes.

The girls tried to dominate the meetings and tried to make favorable impressions on the boys. They behaved as if they had a high status in the group, but analysis of the questionnaire showed that neither the boys nor the girls considered the girls of great importance.

Concerning the leadership of the group five questions in the questionnaire have been chosen to show the structure:

Question 9. Who is to decide that you belong to the group?

Question 24. Has anyone more to say than any of the others?

Question 28. Does anybody in the group have especially good ideas?

Question 55. Who do you think would be best suited to be a leader?

Question 56. If you were the leader, who would you choose as your right hand man?

Boy number 5 got the most votes (seventy-six) and was chosen as number one for all questions except question 56. Here boy number 9 came first. The answers show that different abilities are mentioned as important for the second in command than for the leader. The second in command must be a "good friend," "one you can trust, clever, realistic, just." Eleven youngsters chose number 9, and only five chose number 5 as second in command.

Concerning question 55, who they would choose as a leader, number 5 received thirteen and number 9 twelve votes. Either number 5 was chosen without remarks, or after at first being chosen, he is later rejected as not possessing the suitable capacities of a leader. As one boy put it: "Number 5 is too wild and fantastic to be the leader". Nevertheless, the responses show that, at any rate, number 5 came to their minds when speaking of a leader.

The persons who chose number 9 often compared him with number 5, as: "He is more realistic than number 5, he is more just, he has got the brains, and we all respect him."

As mentioned above, number 5 received seventy-six votes on the five questions; number 9, sixty-six votes; and number 3, forty-two votes. In total, eight boys were mentioned by the members as having some of the capacities of leadership, but with fewer votes, ranging from twenty-four down to nine votes.

Therefore, it can be concluded that although it was not an organized gang as such there was, nevertheless, a certain kind of structure with a small core of boys who were accepted by the other members as decision makers, as the leading persons, whose initiatives were followed by the majority of the members.

Of the eight boys mentioned, during the fall of 1963 four of them (among them number 5 and number 9) were sentenced to youth prison, and number 3 was placed in an institution for youth. This was perhaps one of the reasons why the group went to pieces.

Besides the question concerning capacities of leadership of the group we were also interested in knowing something about the positive and negative feelings among the members, because we assumed that a certain amount of friendship ought to be a presupposition for sticking to the group. Yablowski, in *The Violent Gang* (1970), mentions, however, that delinquent gangs are often characterized by little feeling of friendship and solidarity. Among the group leaders there are also persons with whom the ordinary members do not sympathize or whom they even dislike.

The questions in the questionnaire concerning positive feelings are the following:

Question 32. Who in the group do you like best?

Question 53. Name the six persons in the group who you like.

Question 47. If you were unable to meet at the usual places, whom would you like still to be together with?

The analysis of the answers shows that not all persons answered these questions. One answered that there was nobody he liked because he did not trust them, and number 5 answered that he had no feelings for the members, and he had no feelings for anybody outside the group either. Number 9 received the most votes (thirty-eight), number 1 received thirty-two votes, whereas number 5 received only fifteen votes. There were few mutual choices; only four persons, with number 9 in the center, seem to form a structured group.

Concerning the negative feelings only one question was analyzed:

Question 49: Is there anybody in the group you do not like?

Supplementary question: Who and why?

Twenty-three persons answered the question with no or yes; the remaining twenty-seven persons mentioned certain individuals. Most of these were only mentioned once, but number 5 was mentioned by eight persons, number 3 by four, and number 9 only by one person. Number 5 was characterized by the boys as "bragging and screaming", and having a "big mouth"; and by the girls as "never clean," and as having "a bad influence on the others."

In conclusion it can be mentioned that the two most important members of the group were number 5 and number 9. Number 5 was accepted as a leader type, but as an instrumental leader with whom most of the group members did not sympathize; they disliked him and did not want to be friendly with him. He, on the other hand, did not like anybody at all. Number 9 was both chosen as a leader type, as the second in command, and as a friend who was respected, and to whom one would listen. He was the emotional leader of the group.

The Criminal Activities of the Group

As mentioned earlier the Youth Clinic came into contact with some of the group members because of their criminal activities in the early sixties. In all, twenty of the fifty-seven boys (35 percent) were on probation at the Youth Clinic during 1962 and 1963. This did not mean, however, that these twenty were the only ones with registered crimes, but other measures such as warnings, fines, or imprisonment were taken.

Concerning the age of the group members, table 7-2 shows their years of birth. When referring to the age of the group members, we have used July 1, 1962, when the active group period started (see below), as the basis. At that time the boys were from 12 to 20 years old, with an average age of 16.7. The girls were younger, from 12 to 16, with an average age of 14.3.

One of the purposes of this research was to try to get an impression of the development of the criminal careers of a group of youngsters who in a period of their lives were attached to a group or a gang, the main activities of which were delinquent and criminal acts. We wanted to know if such a group mainly

Table 7-2
Year of Birth

Year	1942	1943	1944	1945	1946	1947	1948	1949	Total
Number of males	2	5	10	15	18	5	–	2	57
Number of females	–	–	–	–	5	2	10	4	21

attracts youngsters who, before the group was formed, had been registered as criminal, how much criminal activity was committed during the active group period and by whom, and how many of the group members continued their criminal activity after the group broke up.

In order to answer these questions it is necessary to work with some fixed time periods. In this case we are working with three periods.

1. The time before the active group period, i.e. before July 1, 1962—in reality it is a period of eight years, from May 1954 when the first criminal activity, a bicycle theft, was registered, to June 30, 1962. Before this time the gang was in no real contact with each other and were only together in small groups of two or three persons. The criminal activity during this period is labeled "previous crime."

2. The active gang or group period from July 1, 1962, to December 31, 1963. During this year and a half, the seventy-eight group members in shorter or longer periods met each other at the same meeting places and participated in the same activities. In reality it is, of course, not true to say that the group started and ended at two fixed dates, but in an analysis it is necessary to do so. The period was determined on the basis of a general impression and on the answers to the questionnaire. Half of those we interviewed had started coming to the meeting places before the end of 1962, and the rest began meeting in September 1963. Concerning the end of the group period, the majority reported that they stopped coming to the meeting places before the end of November 1963. Twelve persons were unable to continue because of imprisonment, thirty said that they stopped voluntarily, and the rest did not give real answers. The crime committed during these eighteen months is called "actual crime."

3. The first follow-up study was made in June 1967, after three and a half years, the last one in January 1977. In 1967 the criminal records were examined; in 1977 the information came from the official crime register and thus contained less exact information about single criminal acts. The crime committed during this thirteen-year period is called "later crime."

Previous Crime

As mentioned earlier, the period before the gang was established covers eight years, from May 1954 to July 1962. During this period twenty-seven of the fifty-seven boys (47 percent) had been registered for criminal activities. None of the twenty-one girls had been registered. Therefore, the following will only refer to the male group members.

There is an age difference between the thirty previous nondelinquent persons and the twenty-seven previous delinquent. The first group had only 10 percent in the age group seventeen to eighteen, while the remaining 90 percent were younger. The previous delinquent group had 41 percent in the age group seventeen to twenty, with 49 percent younger. The twenty-seven boys had committed seventy-eight crimes during this period. Two-thirds of these had to do with thefts of bicycles, motorbikes, and cars, and the rest consisted of a few thefts by breaking and entering, other thefts, two robbery attempts, and two cases of indecency.

We analyzed whether the criminal acts were committed alone or together with other persons. In most previous research it was found that the younger the delinquents are, the greater the possibility that two or more persons are involved in the crimes committed. In our study we found that of the seventy-eight previous delinquent acts, twenty-three (30 percent) had been committed alone, mostly bicycle thefts and the like.

We also analyzed the involvement of more than one group member in the crimes. This was only found in twelve of the seventy-eight delinquent acts. Furthermore, it was found that four of these twelve were committed by two brothers, three by twin brothers, one by another couple of brothers, and one by two cousins. These eight boys all became members of the gang. Only in three cases were the criminal acts committed in common by boys who became members of the gang but who were not related by family ties. The majority of the previous crimes was committed together with boys outside the gang.

Concerning the outcome of the criminal activity done by the twenty-seven boys, half of them (thirteen persons) received only a warning or a fine, thirteen persons were put on probation, and only one boy was sent to an institution for children and youth.

The conclusion from the analysis of the crimes committed up to July 1962, before the active gang period, must be that the gang had attracted both nondelinquent and delinquent boys, but in general it must be said that there were only a few of the delinquent boys who had committed serious crimes, the majority, seventeen boys, had only committed one to three acts, and only one boy had been removed from home.

Actual Crime

The gang period covers eighteen months, from July 1, 1962, to December 31, 1963. During this period forty-seven of the fifty-seven boys (82 percent) were registered for delinquent and criminal activities. The same goes for six of the twenty-one girls (29 percent).

None of the six girls committed their delinquent acts alone; in five cases one or two boys from the gang were involved, and in the last case the girl shop-lifted with a girl outside the gang. The girls were generally passive partners in the crimes, for instance, as passengers in stolen cars, or receiving stolen goods. In one case the girl's boy friend (also a gang member) had stolen 10,000 D.kr. (about $1600) by breaking and entering, and they both went to Majorca where they spent the money. When asked through the questionnaire if there was somebody in the group who had specially bright ideas, many of those inter-viewed mentioned this boy and referred to this event. The outcome of the delinquency committed by the six girls was of little importance; three received warnings, three fines.

The criminal activity committed by the forty-seven boys during the eighteen months was of quite another nature. Two hundred eighty-eight criminal acts were registered in which one or more boys from the gang were involved. In 168 of these (58 percent) two or more group members participated, in 69 (24 per-cent) the boys were alone, and in 51 (18 percent) one of the group members was with persons from outside the group.

The criminal activity culminated during the months January to June 1963, when 53 percent of the crimes were committed. In January 1963, forty-five crimes were committed, that is, one and a half each day. There is another peak in June 1963 with thirty-two crimes, but after this month the criminal activity rather abruptly ended. We will try to find some explanation for the pattern of development of the criminal activity of the gang.

The types of crimes which were committed during this period are shown in table 7-4.   We know from the discussions with the group and from the ques-tionnaire that most of the crimes were not planned in advance. They would meet at the square, not know what to do, somebody would make a suggestion about taking a drive, and they would then find a car on the street. Often they

Table 7-3
Crime Committed during the Active Group Period July 1, 1962 to December 31, 1963

July - Dec. 1962	Jan. - June 1963	July - Dec. 1963	Total
86	153	49	288
30%	53%	17%	100%

Table 7-4
Types of Crimes during the Active Group Period

	Theft of Cars or from Cars	Theft of Bicycles or Bicycles with Motor	Theft by Breaking and Entering	Shoplifting or Theft from Slot Machines	Robbery Violence	Other Crimes	Total
Number	136	33	46	28	17	28	288
%	74.2	11.2	16.0	9.7	5.9	9.7	100.0

would put the car back in the same place if there was enough petrol in it. Or they just strolled along the streets, found an unlocked car and took it. Before they abandoned the cars, they often took a radio or other things. As will be seen later, a few of the boys were more active in proposing and fulfilling crimes than others.

As can be seen from table 7-4, car theft was the most common type of crime. The most serious crimes committed were the seventeen cases of robbery and violence. These were nearly all committed in the park between May and June 1963. The victims were homosexuals who strolled along in the park to make acquaintances. The gang members disliked the homosexuals and had a very intolerant attitude toward them. As one of them put it at a discussion: "The police have a right to try to hunt us because we are juvenile delinquents but in the same way we have a moral right to hunt and rob the homosexuals because they are a nuisance." Concerning the twenty-eight cases of other types of crime, these were mostly theft from job, family, fraud, etc., often committed alone.

As mentioned above, in 168 of the 288 crimes more than one group member was involved. In 70 percent of these crimes (car theft and stealing by breaking and entering), however, only two group members were together. Only in a few cases (less than twenty) were more than three members together, for example, in the attempted robberies.

Also as mentioned before, ten of the fifty-seven boys had not committed registered crimes during the active gang period. Five of these had had previous crime, mostly one or two bicycle thefts or theft from slot machines. The other five boys had no previous crime. However, forty-seven boys had been involved in crimes during the active group period. But how much registered crime has the individual group member been involved in?

As can be seen from table 7-5, about half of the forty-seven boys were only involved in a few registered criminal activities (one to four crimes), whereas a small group of five boys were involved in the majority of the cases. As an example we can mention boy number 5 who participated in eighty-four criminal

Table 7-5
**Number of Crimes Committed by the Group Members during the Active
Group Period**

Number of crimes	1-4	5-9	10-21	25-84	Total
Number of boys	23	11	8	5	47

acts (35 percent). He did not commit crimes during the active group period with outsiders, and in seventeen cases he was alone, in sixty-seven with other group members. He presumably preferred to be together with only one other person, and this was either boy number 2 or boy number 78, or all three were together. Neither boy number 2 nor number 78 had committed a crime before the active group period, and neither was registered after the active group period. Boy number 2 had the second highest number of crimes in which he was involved (fifty-three), and number 78 committed twenty-one crimes.

Regarding the types of crime boy number 5 was involved in, half of the car thefts were committed by him and twenty-three of the thirty-nine thefts by breaking and entering. Boy number 9 who, together with number 5 was earlier mentioned as one of the most influential boys in the group, committed twenty-seven crimes. Of these, however, only two were car thefts, and ten were thefts by breaking and entering, or other types of crimes. He was either together with number 5, alone, or in a few cases with his brother, number 64, as well as with number 5.

In conclusion it can be mentioned that although the criminal activities of the male group members during the active period were rather great and most of the boys were involved, the criminal activity, however, was dominated by only a few persons. The three most criminally active boys were involved in 146 crimes. The rest of the criminal cases were committed without these three persons by forty-four other boys who were comparatively inactive.

As mentioned before, the criminality culminated in January 1963. At that time two boys, number 8 and number 64, were arrested and charged mostly for car thefts. They were both put on probation by the Youth Clinic, and they stopped their criminal activities. Number 5 continued until he was arrested in June 1963. In June and August 1963 the last criminal peak showed up, especially involving robbery against homosexuals. As a result, some other group members were arrested and imprisoned, and that was nearly the end of the group crimes.

It is difficult to determine how much was accomplished by the work and efforts of the Youth Clinic, which started in February 1963, by individual work and the weekly open house meetings.

We were also interested in knowing the legal outcome of the criminal acts committed by these forty-seven boys during the period July 1, 1962, to

Table 7-6
Legal Outcome of the Crimes during the Active Group Period

Legal outcome	youth prison	placement in institution for children and youth	conditioned sentence with probation	fines or discharge of case	Total
Number of boys	8	5	25	9	47

December 31, 1963. We found that more than half of the boys got a conditioned sentence with probation, but thirteen were either imprisoned or sent to an institution. The difference here was due to the age of the individuals. The eight boys who went to youth prison were older (over 18 years) than the other five boys.

Later Crime

The information about registered criminal activities committed after the active group period was obtained from the official crime register. The first follow-up study was made in June 1967, the last in January 1977. As the active group period was decided to have stopped on December 31, 1963, the observation period covers thirteen years.

Concerning the age of the group members at the time of the last follow-up study, the male members are now between 27 and 34 years old, with an average age of 30.8. The female members are between 27 and 30 years, with an average age of 28.4.

Of the twenty-one female members, only two of them have registered crimes during the observation period. Both of them were involved in criminal activity during the active group period. One of them was involved in two car thefts with some of the boys in 1963, and in 1965 she shoplifted with a girl-friend (outside the group). For this she got a fine. The other girl committed shoplifting in 1963, and at the same time she left home several times. She was then fifteen years old and was sent to an institution for girls. She often ran away from the institution and was sent back, but after two years she was allowed to return home. At the age of nineteen she was married and had two children. Later she lived alone with the children, had only sporadic work, and lived on social relief. In 1973 she was charged with fraud. While on a train she had found a checkbook and succeeded in getting about 2,000 D.kr. by using the checks and signing them with false names. She was given a conditioned sentence.

With regard to the criminal activities of the female members, it can be concluded that in general it has played a very small role in their lives during the thirteen-year observation period since they were members of this gang. Perhaps more of the girls were actually involved in criminal activities during the active group period than the six girls who were registered. From the discussions and the questionnaire one gets the impression that the boys found it gentlemanlike not to give the girls' names to the police when the girls participated in the crimes. Another interesting point was that the girls occasionally made the boys commit the crime, for example, by telling them that they wanted a special thing, a handbag from a shop window or the like. As we, however, are only interested here in registered crime, the females' activities are not significant to us.

The later crimes during the last thirteen years committed by the male members present quite another picture, as can be seen in table 7-7. The number of male members without and with previous crime (the period up till July 1962) and without and with actual crime (the period from July 1962 to the end of 1963) is related to the number of persons who were registered for crimes committed from January 1964 to January 1977 (later crime).

In total, twenty-six persons (46 percent) were recidivists during these thirteen years. The subgroup which committed crime both before and during the active group period has the highest percentage of recidivism (64 percent) while the ten persons who did not commit actual crime have the smallest percentage of recidivism (10 percent).

Of the later crimes, theft by breaking and entering and ordinary theft make up nearly half of the registered criminal acts. Forgery and fraud, which were of no importance during the previous and active period, are the next highest criminal types during the later crime period, whereas car theft seems to have lost its importance.

It has not been possible in all cases to see exactly how many single criminal acts and what types of crime were involved. There seems to have been about

Table 7-7
Previous, Actual, and Later Crime

	Later Crime		
Without previous crime Without actual crime	5	0	0%
With previous crime Without actual crime	5	1	20%
Without previous crime With actual crime	25	11	44%
With previous crime With actual crime	22	14	64%
Total	57	26	46%

two hundred different crimes committed during the thirteen years, and one person, number 79, has alone committed more than sixty of these, while ten of the twenty-six males have committed only one to two acts each.

Concerning number of sentences, ten males had only one sentence each during the thirteen years; nine males, two sentences, five persons, three to four; and two persons, seven sentences (numbers 79 and 46). The most serious sentences for the twenty-six persons were the following:

1. Warning, fine or case concluded by
   continued probation by child welfare   5
2. Twenty to eighty days imprisonment   3
3. Conditioned sentence   11
4. Youth prison or six to twelve months prison   7

As seen from this, only seven persons were imprisoned for a long time. The conditioned sentence with or without probation was still used for most persons.

From my point of view, one of the most interesting aspects of this follow-up study must be to analyze the length of time since the active group period in which the members have been crime-free. We now know that five of the boys were never registered for criminal activities, and that four persons were not registered after July 1962, and twenty-two were not registered after January 1964.   The twenty-six persons with criminal activities after January 1964 committed their latest crime as follows:

1964	3
1965	7
1967	1
1968	2
1969	1
1971	4
1973	2
1974	1
1975	3
1976	2
Total	26

As seen here, ten of the twenty-six persons stopped their criminal activities in 1964-1965. One could think that the crimes committed during these two years had something to do with membership in the group. The fact is that six of these ten boys did commit the crimes with other members of the group. In no criminal cases committed after 1965 were other group members involved. Eight persons stopped their criminal activities between 1967 and 1971, and since 1973 only eight persons have committed crime. This means that forty-one persons of the fifty-seven male group members (72 percent), have been crime-free since 1965, and forty-nine persons (86 percent), have been crime-free since 1971. Only eight persons (14 percent) have been registered for crime from 1973 to 1976.

For two of these eight persons one can talk about a more constant criminal activity during these years; for the rest there were one to three sentences, mostly conditioned sentences with longer crime-free periods in between.

Concerning the last two persons, one of them, number 46, has been sent to youth prison four times since 1963, after which he received three months imprisonment, one year three months, and in April 1976, one year imprisonment. He has in all been incarcerated for nearly five years during the observation period.

The next, number 79, was also sentenced to youth prison in 1963, was in there twice before November 1967, was later sentenced to eight month- and six month- prison terms and two conditioned sentences, and in 1976 he was charged with violence toward an official, a case which has not yet been concluded.

As mentioned earlier, there were five boys who made up the core of the group. Were these the ones who continued with criminal activities during the observation period? No, two of them had no later registered crime, one stopped in 1964, and the last two in 1971.

What happened to boy number 5, who had committed the largest number of delinquent and criminal acts during the active group period, and who belonged to the core of the group? The Youth Clinic had the first contact with him in April 1963, when one of the psychologists went to his home because the day before he had been given a conditioned sentence with probation from the Youth Clinic. He was then eighteen years old, had been unemployed for the previous six months, and lived with his mother and her two younger children. The father, who was an alcoholic, had left home some years before. Number 5 wanted to join the military as soon as possible, and he succeeded on May 1, 1963. A month later he visited the Youth Clinic, and reported that he was happy, liked military life, and had had only minor disciplinary difficulties. But shortly after he was moved to another regiment, was unable to adjust there, deserted and went home. He was then brought back by the military police and deserted again. In June 1963 he committed a new crime and was arrested and sentenced to youth prison in July 1963. With two other prisoners he escaped in December 1963, stole a car, was brought back and finally released on parole in March 1965. However, he committed robbery in May the same year and was put back in youth prison a week after. In July 1967 he was released on parole.

In January 1964 professor Karl Otto Christiansen had a talk with boy number 5 in the youth prison. He was there without hope, seemed to be deeply rooted in his criminal attitude, and did not think he could benefit from the youth prison. He planned to escape a few times (which he did), was quite uninterested and negative toward the future, and thought that in all probability he would end up in the detention center for psychopaths—"Everybody says so."

In August 1967, after having been released for one month from the youth prison, he committed a theft from a honosexual and later got drunk and started a barroom fight. He was arrested and received a conditioned sentence with probation. He lived at that time with a girl and worked for the girl's father. In January 1968 he married the girl, who had a child, and they had another child together. The probation officer reported that he was cooperative and positive and that there was only a minor alcohol problem, which was related to marital conflicts. In 1970 he and his wife committed a jewelry theft from a woman they visited. He was sentenced to eighty days in prison. His wife left him, and they were later divorced.

In 1971, 1973, and 1974 he violated the Road Traffic Act; the last time he was drunk. He received two fines and for the last case, fourteen days imprisonment. At that time, in 1974, he moved away from Copenhagen, remarried and had one child. His wife, who had had polio, was pregnant again. The couple bought a house in a small village where he was employed. The police officer in the little village recommended his petition for delay of serving the fourteen days in prison in order to help promote the positive development of his life situation. In reality this meant that as of January 1977, he had been crime-free since 1971.

He really was one of the group members whose criminal career we expected would last longer. We also had thought that he would end up in the detention center for psychopaths. Perhaps his new wife and the move away from Copenhagen changed the course of his development.

Concerning violation of the Road Traffic Act, these violations are not considered to be delinquent or criminal acts and, therefore, are not included in the survey of crime. It should, however, be mentioned that twenty-one of the fifty-seven boys (37 percent) have broken the Road Traffic Act once, twice, or three times. This has rather often been caused by driving while drinking, and some of the boys have had their driver's licences taken away for one or two years; four of them have been told to start treatment for alcohol abuse.

Concerning the drug abuse problem, which in Denmark started among the younger generation in 1967, this seems to have been of little importance for this group. Perhaps they were too old at the time and preferred beer and alcohol. Only one person has been sentenced for violation of the narcotic law, in 1968, and he was asked to seek treatment for drug abuse. There is no further information, and as far as we know, he has not been sentenced.

Another person had a drug problem, and in 1973, at the age of twenty-six, he committed suicide by an overdose. He left a farewell letter in which he said that the reason why he wanted to die was that his girlfriend had committed suicide a month earlier.

Another boy died in June 1965 in a traffic accident. He was twenty-one years old and had been released from youth prison six months before, after which he obtained his driver's licence and a motorbike. He drove too fast, collided with a car, and was killed.

Thus, two of the fifty-seven boys are dead, and a third one disappeared in 1972, just after he was released on probation. Since 1963, when he was sentenced to youth prison and until he disappeared, he had been imprisoned for more than five years.

Some Final Remarks

We have concentrated on the registered criminal activities of the male group members through a rather long number of years, from childhood to adulthood; the average age at the end of the follow-up study was 30.8 years. Our starting point was the year and a half in 1962-1963 when fifty-seven boys and twenty-one girls were more or less involved with each other as so-called members of a gang. The main activities of this group were delinquent or criminal acts, where two to three boys worked together, and the main type of crime was car theft.

A rather large proportion of the boys (47 percent) had been registered for delinquency before they joined the group, and the same goes for the observation period, in which 46 percent were registered. But at the time of the follow-up study it was shown that most of the male members (86 percent) had been crime-free during the previous six years, and 74 percent for the previous eleven years.

When we started this survey in 1963—and by "we" I also include Karl Otto Christiansen—we were mainly interested in analyzing the structure and organization of the group and its criminal activities. As time passed without the research being published, the interest turned to another aspect. I became interested in finding out if it was possible to prove whether membership in a group like this would have any influence on future lives.

The observation period, which covers thirteen years, ought to be long enough to come up with some conclusion. But the results of the follow-up study leave me uncertain as to whether I am able to prove anything at all.

The first follow-up study was made in 1967, with an observation period of three and a half years. At that time only ten of the fifty-seven boys had committed new crimes, and only two to three persons were not yet released from prison. My hypothesis then was that the criminal activity during this observation period still had something to do with the group as such. From my point of view it was an aftereffect from the active group period. I expected that the number of crimes and criminals would have diminished during the following years. My conclusion could then have been that membership in a peer group, even if it is dominated by criminal activities, at the age of fifteen to seventeen, does not increase the risk of criminality later in life.

The results, however, of the last follow-up study in January 1977 do not prove this hypothesis because too many of the male members continued with crime or were more sporadically involved in crimes, and besides that were also involved in traffic violations. Of course it has been shown that the group with both previous and actual crime has the highest percentage of recidivism, but the group with crimes only during the actual group period has 40 percent recidivism.

Here, as in much other research, it is dangerous to talk about causes and consequences. It is safer to only give the facts without trying to explain them. The facts are that the majority of the boys were only involved in few and not very serious criminal activities during the active group period, but a few of them were rather heavily involved in crime at that time. The same picture emerges during the observation period: the majority have only few and not serious crimes, and only a few have continued with criminal activities. And of the five most active criminal boys during the group period, only two were registered after 1964, and even number 5 seems to have stopped in 1971, whereas some of the boys who were not very criminal during the active group period have continued.

As a conclusion, nevertheless, I will dare to point out that during the last thirteen years this group of youngsters has been more involved in criminal and other illegal activities than at least I would have expected. One explanation could be that because most of them, during their group membership, were already registered in the files for delinquent and criminal activities, they had a greater risk of being detected and found by the police later.

Another explanation might be related directly to their belonging to a group or gang, in which delinquent or criminal behavior was accepted to a certain degree. Could that in general mean that in their later lives they had less social control, less resistance toward illegal activities, were more easily tempted to break the law, or took more chances than people in general? Or is there no relationship at all between their group membership and their later criminal activities?

In this chapter it has only been possible to analyze some of the information and data procured through the questionnaire, the discussions and the official sources. The description of the district in Copenhagen in which they were brought up, the background and the social history of the individual group members, and the nonregistered crimes, have not been mentioned here.

The follow-up study ought perhaps not to have been concentrated on criminal activity alone but also on the social and psychological situation later on. For instance, it would be interesting to find out if they were still living in the same neighborhood, if they were still in contact with each other, who they married, and what kind of jobs they have.

It is always easier to obtain information about those who remain in touch with different authorities through crime, hospitalization, and so forth, than it is to get information about those who become the so-called well-adjusted members of society.

8

Masks of Psychopaths: Relations between Personality and Environment as Elements in Criminal Policy

Georg K. Stürup

A modern penal code was introduced in Denmark in 1930. The principles had been discussed for decades between lawyers and politicians. This law gave better possibilities for an active criminal policy based on the humanitarian principle that it is an ethical necessity to treat individual prisoners in ways which would be least harmful to the sentenced and to society. The law provided that courts should select abnormal prisoners in need of special treatment and place them under psychiatric care. After the first ten years of the implementation of this law, two problems emerged: No research program had attempted to analyze the rate of success for this selection program, and no special treatment had been established.

The psychiatric superintendent of the special institution for psychopaths at Herstedvester (near Copenhagen) was at the same time prison doctor at the nearby state prison and psychiatric consultant to the Department of Prisons, Ministry of Justice. This superintendent, Dr. Poul Reiter, had planned a cross-sectional survey of the inmates at the state prison. At that time the prison had about 3,400 prisoners; most of these were recidivists who, for the second time or more, were serving a sentence in a state prison. There was also a group of first offenders over twenty-five years of age.

The research project was started as a criminographic, sociological, and psychiatric survey of the population in this maximum security prison. Karl Otto Christiansen, later to have a distinguished scientific criminologic career, started his career as practical assistant to this research project. In 1942, shortly after this was started, I succeeded Dr. Reiter and thus automatically also became the director of this program. A lifelong fruitful collaboration with Karl Otto Christiansen began.

Karl Otto Christiansen had a broad theoretical knowledge in philosophy, sociology, and psychology and was experienced in interviewing offenders before they were sentenced. My own previous experience was based on psychophysiological research and the handling of social-psychiatric problems of adults with physical handicaps and of so-called difficult children. I had no previous experience or interest in forensic psychiatry.

From 1940 to 1943 the life stories of 335 prisoners were collected. All material in the police and court files was studied. These many reports from the prisoners' childhood up to their last sentence were summarized. Then followed rather long interviews concentrating on the social and economic background of the offenses (Christiansen), and a complete medical and psychiatric investigation (Stürup). All together this was used for a sort of diagnosis. In lengthy discussions we finally tried to agree on a classification in accordance with the new laws' intentions, but we soon lost interest in these sterile questions. Besides collecting suitable material for comparison with the Herstedvester population, we attempted to shed light on the still unresolved theoretical question of the causal importance of the environment and personality.

At Herstedvester it was possible to experiment with treatment programs. The control of the treatment used was placed under the Ministry of Justice in the department already responsible for psychotic and mentally defective criminals placed in many different hospitals. The prison department only had jurisdiction over our security and finances, not our treatment. This arrangement "under two masters" allowed Herstedvester great freedom in introducing new treatment methods.

The definitions arrived at in the research project became useful tools in our daily planning of individualized, integrating growth therapy, a program which was slowly developed over the following years (see Stürup, 1968, 1977).

Description of Sample

Offense Classification

We found a classification related to the criminal career to be the most useful in differentiating different groups in relation to their need for specialized therapeutic assistance and their rate of recidivism. Our sample was divided into three main groups: first offenders, intermittent offenders, and chronic offenders.

First Offenders. In our sample there were seventy-six persons over twenty-five years of age. In the Herstedvester sample there were many rather young first offenders sentenced for very serious crimes, as well as some below eighteen years of age, who could not be sentenced to more than eight years imprisonment. It seemed that psychiatric advice to use an indeterminate sentence resulting in placement in Herstedvester was, in these cases, easier for the prosecution to accept.

Intermittent Offenders. In our sample there were ninety-four recidivists with one or several crime-free periods of three to five or more years duration. This group was determined on a purely descriptive basis, and no specifications were made as to causes or types of offense resulting in sentencing. The persons in this group were further subdivided:

1. *Episodic criminals.* That is, relatively few isolated episodes of sentences in an otherwise sentence-free life.
2. *Periodic criminals.* In these cases the crimes evaluated in the sentences were accumulated in rather clearly distinct periods interrupted by one or several longer crime-free and sentence-free periods.

Chronic offenders. These offenders only have short crime-free intervals. In our sample there were 163. Some had many short sentences and many short crime-free intervals; others had been in prisons for longer durations and therefore fewer times, but they also had short crime-free periods. This last group also dominated the detainees found in Herstedvester.

A brief follow-up from 1948 (Stürup and Berntsen) demonstrated clear differences between the recidivism rates of the three career types. For first offenders the rate of recidivism after seven years was 19.7 percent; for intermittent offenders the rate was 50.5 percent; and for chronic offenders the rate was 77.2 percent. Almost the same figures were found for the distribution of these prisoners according to their rearing conditions. For example, some sort of defective upbringing had been registered for 53 percent of the first offenders, for 75 percent of the intermittent offenders and for 85 percent of the chronic offenders. The number of intermittents was also correlated with the rates of recidivism of the different criminal career types.

The more traditional classification system, based on the type of dominating offense, presented greater difficulties, especially in the Herstedvester group, where rather many had more than four different types of offense, and several presented parallel criminality. Using common sense, the latter were placed in one of the dominating crime groups, and the former were classified as polycriminals. As can be seen from table 8-1, although the rate of recidivism is highest for the polycriminals, the overall differences are relatively small.

Psychiatric Classification

The psychiatric classification proved more difficult than foreseen. An evaluation strictly according to Schneider's principles (1940), with an emphasis on the supposed inheritance as used by Reiter, had to be abandoned after the first cases were analyzed. Instead of estimating the importance of hereditary factors in abnormal personality, we stayed with the clinical observation and called all the deviating persons character-insufficients. We continued to use Schneider's subclassifications.

Physical health and bodily strength seemed to be as relevant as personality

Table 8-1
State Prisoners According to Dominating Type of Offense and Recidivism

	Number	Number Recidivists	% Recidivists
Burglars	102	68	66.7
Ordinary thieves	62	40	64.5
Embezzlers	33	16	48.5
Swindlers	50	19	38.0
Sex offenders	38	14	36.8
Violent criminals	13	6	46.2
Polycriminals	33	24	72.7
Total	331	187	56.5

and intelligence in determining how the subject would handle a given situation. It became clear that individual characteristics and social factors were not the only determinants of criminal behavior. An unfavorable personality could itself result in an inadequate environment, and conversely, unfavorable environmental conditions could result in unfortunate personality development, which then could bring about a significant risk of criminality. In some cases neither environmental nor personality factors were found to be defective. In these cases it was supposed that special criminogenic situations had provoked the criminal act. Thus it was not psychiatrically possible to predict the behavior of the individual, especially in terms of his criminal personality. Personality crime factors are not independent of environmental factors, least of all subjective environmental factors, which are not quantifiable. Even those social factors for which we had data, for example, childhood conditions, occupational and financial status, marital and social information, had to be considered as biased by the special circumstances in which they were collected.

It seemed probable that observations of personality and environmental crime factors could be influenced by our knowledge of the criminal career of the subject. These considerations did not encourage the investigators. The figures remained intriguing, especially the fact that 37 percent of the chronic criminals studied were diagnosed as having character insufficiency, as compared to 5 percent of first offenders and 19 percent of intermittent offenders. Besides the traditional biological concept that some basic personality deviation was the cause of the development of severe criminal behaviors, several other possibilities were considered:

1. The prisoner, being a persistent criminal over a period of years, was unable to adapt himself to life as a law-abiding citizen in a socially acceptable manner. Conscious attempts were made to avoid this tautology.

2. Living the life of an offender creates character insufficiency. This life includes repeated incarceration in an authoritarian institution separated by free periods with new criminal offenses leading to new police investigations. Feelings of being "hunted" by the police and being at odds with society are accompanied by the stress of further court appearances, the censure of the mass media, ending in yet another term of imprisonment. Such experiences may be responsible for character deviations which are indistinguishable to the clinician from classical psychopathic (constitutional) deviations.

3. The criminal career is related statistically to certain environments where criminality is prevalent for other reasons and in which there is a high frequency of psychopaths. In such cases we cannot draw conclusions as to the possible criminogenic effect of the observed personality deviations.

Despite pessimistic considerations it was still hoped that with great caution in the methods used and the judgments made, an analysis would give some tentative results which could lead to some further hypotheses concerning the relationship between personality elements and social elements involved in the making of a criminal. A qualitative evaluation would probably not be satisfactory. Eminent criminologists, like the psychiatrist Healy (Healy and Bronner, 1936) and the psychologist Sir Cyril Burt (1938), had found multiple causation of criminal behavior. In spite of this, both concluded that psychological factors were of dominating importance. A more sociologically oriented criminologist evaluating similar results would easily arrive at the final conclusion that environmental factors were of dominating importance.

Because of this it was felt necessary to evaluate the relationship between environment and personality by quantitative means. To do this our statistical collaborator, Georg Rasch, used a discriminating analysis. Three indices resulted from the analysis: an environmental index, a personality index, and a combined environmental-personality index. Of these, the environmental index differentiated strongly between our three career categories. The combined environmental-personality index gave only a slightly stronger differentiation. This index decreased with the increasing age of the chronic offenders, both the age at the time of the first conviction and the age at the time of the most recent one.

The chronic offenders began their criminal careers at an early age, and the total load of crime factors appeared to be greatest in the early years and to decrease with increasing age. This fits well with the clinical observation that criminality decreases with increasing age.

A classification based on environmental factors proved to be a better prognostic indicator than one based solely on personality factors. However, the main result was that these two sets of suspected crime factors, when studied and compared in this way, did not produce a useful basis for further scientific research. We started to doubt the value of such general labels as psychopathy, but continued to accept the fact that some people have greater difficulties than others in managing day to day problems. Some of these persons cause great inconveniences to themselves and to those around them. The syndromes presented by these behavior disorders are varied and probably of different origin. (For a fuller description of the simplified diagnostic labels we used, see Stürup, 1968).

From a psychiatric point of view, it seemed necessary in future work to aim at a deeper study of interpersonal relationships, including the interaction of the person who became identified as the perpetrator of the crime and the others involved in the crime.

We doubted the deterministic belief in the stability of the personality, with its tendency to blame the parents or the social situation in early childhood. At Herstedvester, interest was more and more concentrated on the circumstances underlying criminality, and I soon became convinced that these had as much importance as childhood history.

The main difficulty was, and still remains, that we have no accurate means of giving a verbal evaluation of a person's receptivity to the environment in a given situation. An attempt might be made in this direction by collecting and describing the details of criminal careers without prejudice. At Herstedvester we had an opportunity to study our inmates as experimental subjects who we could observe under varied circumstances in the institution and then on their own. This allowed us to observe the importance of chance factors.

We found that it did not help to enter into complicated discussions centered on possible etiology, which was the main thrust of the psychiatric literature as well as of the psychiatric reports presented to the courts. It was found more satisfactory for treatment purposes to concentrate on the actual situations in which our charges became involved. I commonly expressed this in a polemical way, saying that we did not try to cure psychopaths, but merely to help offenders with "character insufficiency" to be "nicer" psychopaths so that they would not differ too much from "normal" psychopaths found throughout society.

Until 1973 most of the severe criminals officially diagnosed as psychopaths and then placed in Herstedvester were serving indeterminate sentences. All had caused much suffering as a result of their criminal acts and their way of living. The experienced psychiatrists in the Medico-legal Council considered it relatively certain that their psychopathic pattern would continue.

They fitted the Schneiderian definition of psychopathic personalities, and they also agreed with Cleckley's (1964) vivid and eloquent description of the intelligent psychopath—a person without guilt feelings, who had charm and no paranoid ideas, no disturbance of thinking, and no nervous symptoms. But do our cases really fit these descriptions?

The Concept of Psychopathy

Cleckley (1964) gives many illustrative case histories but, like other authors, does not abstract from these how well developed the characteristic elements should be, or how many are necessary to give a satisfactory diagnosis. In spite of this, the core group of Cleckley's psychopaths fit, to an acceptable degree, those of Schneider, and are easily recognized.

Many borderline cases cannot be labeled as psychopaths, even after prolonged contact. Cleckley sees the disorder as a persistent entity, a serious and subtle disorder at deep levels, disturbing the integration and normal appreciation of experience—"such a patient does fail to experience life adequately in its major issues."

My criminal case load had many common characteristics which separated them as a group from those Cleckley had observed in private psychiatric practice and in general hospitals treating nonpsychiatric patients. All cases handled in Herstedvester had been sentenced by the courts for their unusual and dangerous acts. The majority had been acting in a criminal manner for a long time. They were observed by the same members of the staff over long periods of time, both inside the institution and in periods of freedom, out in society, after a spell in Herstedvester. Thus there was an opportunity to observe them when they were at ease, at times when they were still full of hope, as well as at times of severe distress. It was common to see cases who looked as if they were psychopaths, but who later developed a normal pattern of behavior.

With the following cases an attempt is made to clinically illustrate the differences seen in our case load and the variability of the symptomatology.

Case History: Arne

As a member of the Medico-legal Council, I took part in the evaluation of a complicated homicidal man. At the age of thirty-seven Arne had choked to death a seven-year-old girl whom he had met in the street. When found in a trunk near his home, her vagina was severely lacerated.

She had followed him willingly and in her play had mentioned the name of her girlfriend. This happened also to be Arne's wife's name and this had, he explained, provoked him to attack her, choke her, and with what must have been great force, masturbate her. After depositing the body, he had calmly gone away, bought a newspaper and gone to his girlfriend's home. Here he had seen the blood on his hands and clothing. He had washed himself, had hidden the blood-stained clothes in a box and buried it in the garden. At the same time, he stressed that he did not know where the blood had come from, that it had only been as a "measure of precaution" that he had tried to get rid of the soiled clothes. Later, while drinking in a bar, he had heard about the murder and had then had a vague feeling that the police might want to talk to him, as the body had been found on his premises. It was only after a long examination that he admitted to the crime.

Shortly after he was jailed, he was investigated by the local medical officer. Later he was placed in the security section of a psychiatric hospital where specialized psychiatrists analyzed his personality structure over several months. He alleged to have a loss of memory over a short but crucial time period and said he remembered nothing of the murder.

Arne came from a stable family background, but may have had a rather harsh upbringing. As a boy he began pilfering, played truant from school, and when twelve years old, he ran away from home. He was placed in a children's home. On leaving school he had numerous jobs, and many different girlfriends. He married three times and had two children by his second wife. In spite of the fact that he had obtained the right to see the children, in fact he never did. He was sentenced four times for petty offenses, but it was not until the last of these that he actually went to prison. At this time his third wife, a former prostitute, left him and returned to her old way of life. This troubled him greatly, but what it was about this that troubled him never became clear. He insisted that society was responsible for his crime. He maintained that his wife had left him because he had not been granted parole, and it was this that had resulted in the homicide. But there had been many difficulties in the marriage. He had been unable to satisfy his wife's strong libido by traditional sexual activity, so he had regularly masturbated her as he had the child.

In the first as well as the second psychiatric report he was described as having normal intelligence, and being emotionally callous, while at the same time being hot-tempered and easily boiling over into anger and hysterics.

The Medico-legal Council accepted these descriptions, stressed the self-assertive elements and classified him as a socially unstable psychopath. It was found likely that at the time of the criminal act he had been in a tense state of mind, but the council found itself unable to evaluate the importance of the fact that the girl mentioned his wife's name. The short span of time for which he claimed loss of memory could have been due to a temporary repression of his serious criminal act. The deviations in his personality structure were estimated to be considerable, and, it was added, there was a substantial risk that this deviation would develop further in the coming years. In order to try to counteract such a dangerous development, the court was advised that he should be placed in the special detention institution at Herstedvester for an indeterminate time. (The sentences used in the Danish system differed from the British sentence "at Her Majesty's pleasure," especially as the court maintains the authority to change the security measures. No board or other administrative body was involved.)

The court did not follow this advice. Instead, Arne was sentenced to life imprisonment. He appealed against the sentence and finally the supreme court upheld the sentence, but with one of the judges dissenting. This judge, le Maire, had on an earlier occasion called such life sentences "detention without treatment." Based on the psychiatric evidence and all the circumstances of the case, le Maire found the man not fit for a prison sentence and voted for his placement in the special institution.

In prison Arne suffered from several headaches and became more and more nervous. After six months I was called upon to give advice to the prison authorities concerning him. I tried to explain, both to the prisoner and to the prison administration, that his nervous reactions were to be expected from the psychiatric findings before the sentence, and that as the court had decided not to use psychiatric care in his case, it would be best for the patient if he could adapt to the situation as he found it, since he could not escape from it.

As the warden could not accept the remarks in the last part of the advice from the Medico-legal Council, I tried to make the following points in a letter:

1. That in the surroundings of the psychiatric institution we could obtain a deeper insight into the development of the prisoner's dangerous propensities. Acute exacerbation of his condition, which would occur periodically, could, when special rapport had been established, be used with great therapeutic benefit.
2. That it would have been valuable to try to help the prisoner build up a new self-respect. The point was made that a life sentence did not lend itself to such an attempt.

This was a case where the psychopathy was absolutely clear-cut and agreed upon by all the psychiatrists involved, myself included. The prisoner had been unstable in work and in his love affairs and was egocentric and irritable. The unusual and brutal act he had committed had an inadequate motive and he seemed to be unpredictable.

The fact that the court disregarded our advice, in spite of the special warning from the Medico-legal Council, can be attributed to the traditional pessimism concerning the possibility of influencing severe psychopathic behavior. Also the court was influenced by the modern Western negative attitude toward the efficacy of treatment.

From the first fairly intensive interview I made unexpectedly good emotional contact with the prisoner, who clearly appreciated the straightforward way the situation was presented to him. Eight months later, in a kind letter to me, he told me that for some time he had been in a depressed state, which was accompanied by nightmares. Thus, in spite of only minimal direct contact, it was clear that some sort of transference was being established. But a transfer to Herstedvester was at that time, unfortunately, not easy to arrange for a person with a life sentence. In some years not a single life sentence is given.

A few months later he wrote to me again. He was now afraid of losing self-control. He still did not remember his criminal act, but often had terrifying dreams. He dreamed that he was driving a bus at high speed into a group of people. He had little contact with his fellow prisoners and thought that they probably despised him. Staff in the maximum security prison were not supposed to spend too much time talking to individual prisoners about personal matters. Drugs were given to him fairly liberally by the prison doctor, but he did not feel that these were any help to him. He showed interest when it was explained to him that such reactions as he was having to the situation he was in were normal, but his problems continued and it became necessary to transfer him to Herstedvester.

Under our regime he soon felt better. For some time he had had bladder trouble, and a polyp which proved to be malignant had been ablated. He established a good rapport with several staff members, but his fellow inmates did not like him. He again mentioned his lack of memory for the gruesome act he had committed and seemed to doubt his guilt. He stated that it could have been committed by the man who had been his wife's "friend" while he, Arne, was serving his first prison sentence. On another occasion he said that he himself was "probably the worst criminal in Denmark."

After a spell when his emotional condition had for some time been practically normal, he was returned to prison, in spite of his desire to stay at Herstedvester. Some months later he was again in need of help from us. Three and a half years after his sentence, he was again returned to Herstedvester. Now and then he would come into conflict with the other inmates, but with the staff he presented no problems. He was treated with strong radiotherapy for his cancer of the bladder. At one time he expressed a wish to get in touch with his children whom he had not seen for many years, but his former wife did not want them to know of his crime; he accepted this and did not insist further. He was thankful for all that was done for him at Herstedvester and expressed his thanks to the doctors and Ministry officials controlling the institution.

Thus, when Arne met a realistic and friendly attitude his aggressive behavior disappeared. He accepted his sufferings. He wanted the surgeon to operate to try to prolong his life in spite of his situation. The operation was not very successful but he did not complain. He suffered pain and knew that the disease was malignant. He died almost one year after being admitted to Herstedvester for the last time.

Our attempts to help this man were not related to any theoretical concepts as to the cause of psychopathy. Although the life sentence made things more than usually difficult, it was easy to establish good emotional contact with him, partly because of his marginal position in relation to his fellow prisoners. From the first psychiatric interview I had with him, I found his attitude different from that described in the psychiatric report. Special psychotherapeutic techniques were not used. The only therapy was the effect of the total atmosphere of the institution and the supporting attitude of the therapist and other members of the staff. This raises two questions:

1. Is personality a much less stable pattern than is usually supposed?
2. Is the very substantial change observed in this and other cases due simply to a suitable change in his objective environment, and also his subjective environment?

Few psychiatrists who think of psychopathy as an entity have, like Kahn (1931) taken an interest in the different careers of psychopaths and described episodic, periodic, and permanent psychopaths as well as those with psychotic features. These important differentiations have met with little interest in the literature and in clinical practice.

David Henderson (1947) regretted that psychopathic states "were not tackled with sufficient conviction, firmness and modified optimism." To some extent, he was influenced by psychoanalytic attitudes, but he does not attempt to differentiate psychopaths from Alexander's character neurotics. He was "much more interested in judging each actual situation or case on its merits and in the setting of the life history, without at this stage laying down an interpretation which is common to all."

The following case may illustrate the necessity of not regarding psychopathy as an entity with common and stable patterns of reactions.

Case History: Wulff

As part of the preparation of a case for court procedure most of the chronic criminals received in Herstedvester had in relation to former court procedures been submitted to psychiatric observations. This history is derived from these official reports.

Wulff was nineteen years old when first officially classified by an experienced legal psychiatrist reporting to the court. This report, which included a description of his upbringing, his personal and social development, and psychiatric observations on him, concluded by describing him as a spineless, self-assertive, work-shy, and callous psychopath. Furthermore, he was unreliable and seemed completely unable to resist criminal impulses. Since the age of fifteen he had been drinking too much.

He had already served one eighteen-month sentence, and following this report he was sentenced to three years imprisonment. At the age of twenty-one he was paroled, and soon after this he married a sixteen-year-old girl who was pregnant by him. At twenty-four years of age he began a new series of economic offenses. He was then hospitalized for nearly four weeks in Filadelfia, a special Danish hospital for epileptics. The detailed report from this hospital mentioned that at the age of five years he had suffered a severe lesion of the head resulting in a change from right-handedness to left-handedness. At twenty-one years he had a second head injury with loss of consciousness and was in the hospital for ten days. A month later he had his first epileptic fit, and six months after this he was admitted to the university neurological clinic in Copenhagen where he was diagnosed as an epileptic and a psychopath. An EEG recording showed a generalized dysrythmia. Later, this was mostly localized to the left temporal lobe, but later again, in Filadelfia, it was found to be more diffuse and his condition was diagnosed as traumatic epilepsy.

He had been unstable at work and had tried to obtain an invalid pension, which was recommended by physicians at Filadelfia. He began a series of larcenies and when arrested was subjected to further psychiatric observations.

The psychiatric report produced for the use of the court mentioned that during his last sentence he had been considered immoral, with a warped mind, and deficient in his personality structure. During the police investigation he had appeared oversensitive, unbalanced, and pitiable, and he later wept in court. The local medical officer who saw him in the prison did not have the slightest doubt that Wulff was a psychopath. His epileptic fits had not been observed directly in any hospital and, therefore, the possibility of hysterical fits was suggested. It was thought that there should be further investigations in a psychiatric hospital. After two months in the hospital Wulff was recorded as a psychopath of the spineless, reactive, self-assertive, dysphoric type, who had also misused barbiturates over a period of time. He was again accepted as an epileptic, even though again, fits were never observed. Detention was recommended and, as this also had the support of the Medico-legal Council, the fact that he was sentenced to be detained came as no surprise.

We in Herstedvester doubted that he was a true epileptic. He had no fits, even though he was getting no anti-epileptic medication. When the evidence was examined carefully, we found his arguments so consistent (that he had not committed a robbery against a homosexual, for which he had also been sentenced), that we felt it necessary to support a request for further investigation.

His protestations of innocence for this crime proved to be correct, and this was, of course, a great help in establishing a satisfactory therapeutic contact with the therapist and other staff. He became emotionally stable under our regime and a steady worker. Since, after elimination of robbery from the crimes committed, he was only sentenced for larceny, it was possible after a year to transfer him to the open section. Here he continued to be a steady worker, presenting no dysphoric moods or neurotic symptoms. We found him of rather high intelligence.

When, after one and a half years, he was paroled, his wife told him on his first day of freedom, without warning, that she could not resume their marriage. There followed a difficult period, with divorce and a legal battle over the custody of the two daughters. This ended with his wife realizing that she was unable to control the eldest daughter, and this girl was left with her father. In need of special psychiatric help, the girl was placed in a special home for the treatment of neurotic children. Wulff himself became very unbalanced, clearly dysphoric, and subsequently attempted suicide. During this neurotic phase he met and married a somewhat dominating woman who soon after the marriage was unfaithful to him. She had an affair with one man for a short period, and later she had an affair for six months with another man. When he discovered this, he tried to win her back, and they decided to have a two-month trial period together before they gave up their marriage. He felt that he could "not live without her." However, the day after this decision she provoked him severely, told him she was leaving him and pointed a knife at him, cutting him on the hand. It was then that the disaster occurred. He does not remember what happened after that. He only remembers seeing her screaming near the window with a knife in her back. The autopsy revealed several stab wounds as the cause of her death. It was clear to the social assistant who had seen him the night before the stabbing that he had been very anxious and emotionally unbalanced, but the killing was a great surprise to her.

Once again, he was investigated in a psychiatric hospital, and a depressive reaction was noted. His personality was now found to be highly sensitive, self-assertive, and dysphoric. The Medico-legal Council still called him a psychopath, and he was now classified as spineless and emotionally labile, and the council drew attention to the misuse of meprobamate in the period just before the crime. The former diagnosis of epilepsy was not mentioned. At the time of the crime he was said to have been especially unbalanced and in a very emotional state, but the depressive reaction noted at the hospital was thought to be mostly secondary to the criminal act.

He was returned to Herstedvester by a new court order. For the first year he was emotionally unbalanced and at times depressive. During the following five years he became well balanced, with a growing realistic evaluation of his situation. He maintained contact with his daughter during this time, and when she was involved in a severe traffic accident, he reacted in a completely adequate manner. As she grew older, their correspondence was straightforward and warm as between any normal father and daughter. After six years we obtained legal permission for him to have monthly, six-hour leaves, and during this time he visited his daughter and relatives. He spent six months in the open section of the institution, and after about seven years he was again paroled.

This time he was able to maintain his normal mood and steady work. When I met him six years later quite by chance on a ferry, he spoke to me. He was still employed at the same industrial plant. He had met a girl after the first year, and after some time they began to live together. At the beginning of their relationship, they had had some difficulty getting used to one another. Some time during this period he had asked the social assistant if he could help him to obtain a death certificate for his second wife, as "it would be too uncomfortable for him to go to the office himself," and when he got this he explained to the therapist that this was "good to have," but that he did not plan an immediate marriage. After some time, however, they did marry, and it seems to have been satisfactory on both sides. They spent regular holidays with his eldest daughter.

Seen in retrospect, Wulff, paroled at thirty-eight years of age, kept his emotional balance during the three years we followed him closely. Now, at forty-seven years, he has still kept clear of the police, has demonstrated a natural, emotional tie with his daughter, and seems during this time to have established a stable and good relationship with a woman, now his wife. He greeted me, when we met, as an old friend, and wanted me to be happy in knowing that we "may have good results" with some of our patients.

The difficulties in making a satisfactory prediction are obvious. At nineteen years he belonged, without any doubt, to the core of psychopaths judged either by the Schneider or Cleckley classification methods. There was nothing to indicate a character neurosis.

His first marriage, at twenty-one years, may have been an extra burden, but it cannot be reckoned to have had a substantial influence on the long series of crimes of larceny of which he was convicted. The possible epileptic fits were well substantiated by the EEG results, but in spite of this they were found to be mostly of emotional origin. Under favorable institutional circumstances he matured and became more balanced. When exposed to unexpected, serious family problems, he developed a definite neurotic pattern with depressive and suicidal tendencies. This period culminated in an emotional homicide. When given reasonable support he regained his balance and became a stable worker with normal emotional ties.

Now, at forty-seven years of age, he presents a perfect example of a young man in whom many experienced psychiatrists had not been able to recognize that his psychopathic behavior had been only a mask. Although he had passed through a neurotic phase he was now without obvious psychopathology and had no complaints.

Some similarity among our group of chronic criminals has already been mentioned. They have nearly all been in other institutions before finally coming to Herstedvester, and these other institutions show great reluctance to take them back. We, on the other hand, added voluntarily to our group of detainees cases like Arne who had suffered a great deal in prison, as well as a number of prisoners who themselves made life for those around them too difficult, so that staff and other inmates were glad to get rid of them. Psychologically they had a common set of experiences which conditioned their standardized pattern of behavior. They all felt degraded but were reluctant to admit either this or their lack of hope for their own future. Most had been described by the mass media as worthless, and this had commonly been done in an insulting manner.

Their view of themselves had been influenced by their criminal career. After their arrest they had felt keenly the criticism of the authorities and of their relatives and friends. It is my impression, not perhaps a universal opinion, that many prisoners, described as incurable monsters, accept such descriptions of themselves as true. While not openly admitting that they believe this, they act in accordance with such predictions. Cases can be studied, who, at the initial interviews, only remember the darkest elements in their early life and who seem to live in an illusion that their former social life was somewhat of a delusion. They do not realize that it is common in "normal" people, occasionally, to have "dirty" or antisocial thoughts which are usually soon forgotten; this can help to explain their willingness to subscribe to the most pessimistic view of their future prospects.

Cleckley and many other authors mention the psychopath's incapacity for feeling guilt or shame. Their behavior is said to be deceptive and to promote confidence, which is then misused. My experience, on the other hand, seems to indicate that such basic skepticism can have disastrous effects.

Instead of this negative attitude which could lead to the risk of suicide, psychopaths or former chronic criminals need to be helped in their attempts to regain true dignity. It is an urgent ethical problem to acquire a better knowledge of the risks involved and the possibilities we already have for helping these men in their fight against frustrating disbelievers.

One case which illustrates these problems is the story of Paul, described in Stürup (1968, pp. 135-136). It is summarized below.

Case History: Paul

Although Paul grew up in a happy, united family, he became a self-assertive, quarrelsome, psychopathic thief and housebreaker. He felt unjustly treated by society. We learned, rather late in his criminal career, that he had once hoped to be an artist. He was sent to Herstedvester at the age of thirty-eight as a chronic criminal. Behind his aggressive pattern of behavior we succeeded in finding a deep-seated insecurity. What he really most wanted was to become a normal, law-abiding citizen. After parole he systematically strove to regain respect and trust, but after two and a half years he was still not accepted socially, and he lost hope. When he was rejected for a job for which he was well suited because of his previous record, he committed suicide. His sensitivity can be seen clearly in his farewell letter, written after he had taken an overdose of sleeping pills. He appears in this to be a considerate, very unhappy person. To quote only one sentence: "Forgive me for the trouble I am causing you [the social assistant], but I cannot avoid it; I dare not go on."

The "lack of remorse and guilt feelings" dominant in Paul's earlier life had become quite opposite feelings long before his suicide.

Feelings of guilt have a relation to our common moral values, but it is difficult to differentiate between healthy and neurotic guilt feelings. In principle, we are not referring to neurotic guilt when we say that psychopaths are without guilt feelings. Rather, it is the lack of guilt shown by those who perpetrate immoral acts that we have in mind.

When used in criminology, the word *guilt* is in accordance with the daily use of the term. Western penal codes exempt from guilt, in any legal sense, children below a certain age and adults who are mentally ill or intellectually subnormal. The question of what makes the guilty person feel guilty is seldom asked. Seldom are questions asked about the mechanism of normal guilt feelings and the related remorse and shame. We must attempt to answer these questions from the facts presented by our clinical observations before we evaluate the psychopathic "lack of guilt."

Without a complete analysis of these problems, I would postulate that it is not necessarily the actual breaking of the rule in the penal code, that is, doing something morally wrong, that releases guilt feelings in normal people. The last few years have seen the publication of many analyses of self-reported offenses. When interviewed, most young people report being guilty of (meaning, having performed) one or more criminal acts, mostly minor offenses, but a substantial number of those offenses reported anonymously were of such severity that they could have been subject to sentence as felonies if they had been admitted to the authorities. No remorse had resulted on reporting the offenses, but possible remorse could have been repressed. I have seen no reports mentioning that acute or delayed reactions had been observed subsequent to such a possible repression. The aftereffects of guilt feelings are not known.

A part of this hidden criminality will be known to no one but the perpetrator of the act, and a part, sometimes, to the victim. Some part will be known to the police but will not be established. Only about one-quarter of the known offenses are established, and only some of these will be sentenced in court. Fewer still will lead to the serving of a sentence. Some inmates have been sentenced without a direct confession. Of 335 prisoners investigated by us between 1941 and 1949, 12 percent insisted on their innocence. Several of these, when returned to prison later with a new sentence, admitted they had been guilty the first time, but again stressed that this time they were innocent. These cases gave a clear indication that the feeling of "not being guilty" represented a kind of defense mechanism. This "not guilty" group does not attempt to claim any real miscarriage of justice, and they have no special interest in our concern.

Those prisoners in our sample serving sentences of longer than four months regularly regarded themselves as criminals. Other evidence seems to indicate that persons only fined or given suspended sentences certainly do not feel that they must class themselves as criminals. It seems that the basic elements leading to remorse or shame are (1) the fact that the offense is known, especially to someone loved and respected who will disapprove; and (2) that it is no longer hidden. Many offenses would be prevented if the offense itself would result in remorse. Society's moral code would work well if this were the case, but in today's society it is unusual to meet a "not depressed" (psychotic) person confessing to an old offense for the reason that he does not want to be "alone with his secret any longer."

We should not expect the prisoner to suffer severely because of his offense, and it would be unwise to criticize him for a lack of shame. But this should not prevent the therapist from making the prisoner realize in detail the possible consequences of his offenses. Once good emotional contact has been established, an anamnestic analysis may be made of the actual criminal acts.

The discussion of the likelihood of his ever committing the same sort of offense again may lead to a deeper examination of all the circumstances surrounding the criminal act, that is, the total criminal stiuation. It will then be possible to progress beyond a discussion of the value of the goods stolen or of the harm which the victim has suffered. The prisoner will readily be able to understand the importance to everyone of privacy and freedom from fear, and it is important for him to empathize with the victim. It is during such emotion-laden moments that both the prisoner and the therapist may get some understanding of otherwise unmentioned facts which lie behind a particular pattern of behavior. Here again we use the environmental subjective factors which have surrounded the prisoner and which were active at the time of the crime. These will be the deciding factors in any restructuring of his present life in prison and his future life when released.

The medicolegal advice given to the court in the following case used the same labels as those used in former cases but the man's life story was not at all like the others.

Acts of aggression are, in Denmark, usually directly situational, like those of Wulff. Now and then, however, we meet someone usually later labeled as a psychopath who has built up a confidence with his victim in order to be able to choose a suitable moment to attack. This was the case with Hans.

Case History: Hans

Hans came into detention at twenty-two years of age after attempted homicide. He grew up in a very poor family. His father pictured himself as a social reformer, but in his own home he beat his wife. The father's brother killed his own wife, his five children, and himself. When Hans was seven years old, the father left home. At thirteen his mother died. He missed her so much that it was difficult to convince him that she would not come back. Three school reports stated that he was intelligent, industrious, and kind. His elder sisters tried to keep the home together, but when Hans was sixteen, they gave up. He was then placed in a home for juveniles. Several attempts were made to keep him in an apprenticeship, but he would not cooperate.

At eighteen he was on his own and we know little about what happened to him from eighteen to twenty-one years of age. He worked for some time abroad, but he was unstable and once attempted suicide, proving that he was unhappy. At twenty-one he received a suspended sentence for petty fraud. Shortly after this he received a four-month sentence which he served.

After this imprisonment he seems to have been restless and unbalanced. Later a psychiatric investigation revealed that he had considered whether he would jump in the harbor, but he still had enough hope of making a new chance for himself to avoid this second suicide attempt. He hoped to get a job in another part of the country but needed a small sum of money to pay his travel fare. He remembered that someone had told him that an easy way to get money, when you needed some, was to go home with a homosexual and then rob him. Later that night he went home with such a man, where, after a good meal, they went to bed. During the night, while the man slept, Hans went into the kitchen for a knife with which to cut his host's throat. He found this scheme too awkward to carry through, so instead he again went to the kitchen, brought back a full bottle, and hit the man hard on the head. The bottle broke, however, and the man sat up. Hans then tried to choke him, but the contents of the bottle had made the man's throat slippery. After this failure he gave up.

When seen by a psychiatrist in prison he was diagnosed as probably psychopathic, but psychosis was not completely ruled out. He was transferred to a psychiatric department. Here he explained that he himself had phoned the police because he felt that to spend some time in prison would be a good way out of his troubles. He felt disappointed at failing to kill the man. During a prolonged stay in the hospital, it was found that his emotional contacts had deteriorated ever since puberty. He had become emotionally callous, work-shy, pig-headed, and nearly autistic. To kill a person, he maintained, "did not matter much" if it was done quickly and without pain. He would plan his actions and then carry them out without scruple.

The court report concluded that he was "a severe constitutional psychopath, completely lacking in emotion." During observation he had been completely without regard for other people's needs and only interested in material gains for himself. He was work-shy and asocial, as well as antisocial and amoral. He took no interest in his own life and had no goals. A developing psychosis had been suggested as a diagnosis, but this was found to be unlikely. He was considered to be highly dangerous to the life and property of others. The Medico-legal Council accepted this description, but abbreviated it to "emotionally callous and amoral psychopath."

In prison he had exhibited odd behavior. He was sentenced to detention and was sent to Herstedvester. He continued to be only interested in material goods. In a letter to his sister he described all the material advantages he now enjoyed, but his cynical attitude remained toward those around him, and he added that the contents of the letter did not mean that he had any great optimism for the future. The first year at Herstedvester he was still civil but unreliable and very lazy. In the third year he began to work more steadily, and in a letter to his sister he commented on this fact, telling her at the same time that his unusual honesty would guarantee him several years longer detention than "was reasonable." In this letter he described the doctors as "like bulls in a china shop." On the ward the staff praised him and said that he was very pleasant.

In the fourth year at Herstedvester, the systematic treatment of persuasion seemed to have helped establish a transference with his therapist. He was now granted eight-hour leave permits. During these periods away from the institution, being with the same staff members during these hours, he was able to establish positive contact with "normal" people. He was rather shy. His emotional contact with his sisters in their homes seems to have been completely normal.

At the age of twenty-six, he began to take the initiative and discuss his former antisocial attitude. After a long time spent in self-analysis, evaluating his former patterns of behavior, he reached the conclusion that his attitude to the community had been wrong. He realized that we could not accept this new insight at its face value, but he insisted all the same that he himself was convinced that the risk of his committing another crime, which he admitted he would once have done, was eliminated. He accepted the fact that we must keep him under observation for a long time and not simply accept what he said about himself, although this was also important. He also explained his new outlook very seriously to his sister, but he did not give up using cynical verbal expressions like "if one is a psychopath then it is good to keep emotionally cool, it saves pitying yourself and others." Boasting remarks like this may reflect a deep and basic need for personal independence, and a very well-developed need for freedom from any attempt at intrusion in his personal life. The officer who accompanied him on his eight-hour leaves supported this theory. He reported that Hans often blushed like a schoolgirl.

Together with Hans his therapist once more studied his whole life history. The result of this repeated anamnestic analysis was satisfactory. His explanation of his former bitterness against society as he now saw it was that it was related to his teen-age experiences, that he had been left on his own and that no one cared. In this way, he maintained that society had made him a criminal. He said he had thought that all people were malicious like him and enjoyed hurting others. He admitted that the five years at Herstedvester had taught him that this was not true, and he had therefore been wrong. He did not complain about the treatment he had received from the staff.

He was then placed in the open section of the institution in order to put this new social attitude to the test. He maintained a good relationship with the officers in this section, and when questioned about the likelihood of his escape he said that he saw no risk of it since he felt that the confidence the officers had shown in him was so valuable to him that he did not feel it possible to misuse it. He remained in this open section for six months when, on our advice, he was paroled. He accepted as quite understandable the fact that the public prosecutor was not happy that the court followed our advice, and understood that the supreme court must first approve the parole.

Some weeks after his parole he wrote a letter about his feelings. He wrote that, like "everyone," he "likes to be a free man." Furthermore, he wrote,

"My new outlook has made me trust my fellow-citizens and made me understand much of what I before despised, but the best is that I like my work and can avoid dissatisfaction when I meet difficulties."

Eight months later he had an economic crisis. He met this in "the most miserable way" he could think of, "but the only way left"—by working harder. He had now overcome the crisis successfully. After two years of parole he had a girlfriend and said that he very much hoped to be a good father to her child. He managed to establish a nice home, and after living with the girl for a year, they married. After some years he complained that she did not look after the home properly and they began quarrelling. He moved away for a few months and they got a divorce, but later, in spite of this, they came back together again. At times he was unemployed, but he rationalized this in his traditional philosophical way. After five years of parole he got a license as a taxi driver and he kept this job for seven years. During this period his wife had another boyfriend and Hans moved out again and went to live with a sister. A month later he disappeared and wrote a farewell letter to his wife. He returned to the sister's house without having made any suicide attempts, but his wife did not change her mind. It seems evident that he had established a very strong emotional attachment to her.

Shortly after this it was found unnecessary to continue supervision and he was finally discharged. Some information has come through to us about his later life from different sources. We did not discover why he gave up his job as a taxi driver, a job that he had enjoyed for many years.

Fourteen years after being paroled from Herstedvester he was involved as a receiver in some property offenses. He served a rather short sentence. One member of the group was a chronic criminal who was returned to Herstedvester. When Hans was freed he wrote to me asking if he could come and visit this man, his friend, a peculiar personality like himself.

Hans is now over fifty years of age, and the risk of his committing any new offenses is, as he himself wrote in a letter to me, "quite negligible."

Conclusion

In our earlier survey of inmates in a Danish maximum-security prison, the first criminological research carried out by Karl Otto Christiansen and me, we found the environmental crime factors of the chronic criminals were much more severe than in the group of first offenders over twenty-five years of age. The environmental factors also seemed more important for the prognosis than the personality factors observed in the psychiatric interview, based on the offender's life career. We often regretted that the results of this research were not published in time to influence the criminal policy of the day. But in other ways our research was of great importance. In May 1945 the Danish prison system was confronted with the enormous task of handling more than 12,000 "political" prisoners, when the population was already increased from 3,000 to 6,000 due to the war situation. Based on our practical experience and the results of our investigation into the still-existing prison system structure, we proposed a scientific analysis of the group of political offenders. These persons were traitors to the country and had collaborated with the German forces.

In addition, the conclusions reached from the first project, reported above, have been important in our understanding of the part played by the often crucial situations which we found regularly when we studied the life careers of the detainees in Herstedvester. In some cases it would appear that the situation was simply accidental, as when the young girl used the name of Arne's wife. The use of her name seemed to act as a trigger mechanism. Other cases like this have also been found.

Sometimes one unpredictable situation seemed to have released tragic events which, in hindsight, we know could have been predicted if all the facts had been known. In the lives of both Wulff and Paul we have examples of such events. Wulff's first unsuccessful parole was not something which we could have prevented with a better knowledge of Wulff's personality. Rather, we would have needed to know more about his wife. Probably her actions were based on the popular idea that it is a spouse's ethical duty to lie to a penal institution in order to effect the release of the prisoner. His wife had to pretend to be a good wife as she knew that this would promote her husband's parole. Had more facts been known, a safer parole situation might have been prepared than the one Wulff met, which was clearly more stressful than he could possibly manage. It is easy to see how the new situation created by the interrelation of Wulff and his second wife resulted in her death. We had too little knowledge of the family to foresee this.

Paul's suicidal situation was an illustration of such situationally conditioned suicides. This was really a call for help which society was not ready to give. Neither the traditional environmental crime factors nor the personality factors (the diagnostic label) provided sufficient knowledge on which to plan either an approach to useful therapy or a satisfactory prognosis. Our efforts had to be concentrated on careful recording of observations which we hoped would help us understand the crucial points in the criminal careers we saw developing. The interpersonal relationships between our inmates and staff, including prison officers, nurses, therapists, teachers, social workers, and sometimes relatives, became much more interesting than a diagnostic classification of the prisoner, or a special technique of psychotherapy. At times, of course, we made use of all the therapeutic techniques which at any one time we were able to put into practice. One only wishes to warn against the dangers of an overprofessionalized view that limits the possibilities for helping the patient. Our understanding of the criminal, his behavior, and the results of this behavior on himself and others is essential—even more so because we must try to get the criminal

himself to grasp the importance of his own understanding of these complicated matters.

It is not only genetic structure and early childhood history but also the
whole life pattern which must be considered. In addition, we must realize that
this "biological" personality is continually reacting to stimuli from others,
stimuli continually changing as the person senses the intentions and reactions
likely from the behavior of others. We must keep our ideas flexible and rely on
direct clinical observations. We must avoid the temptation to make these fit
into a theory.

In many reported cases we have illustrated the variability of the so-called
psychopath's previous histories. This we have been able to observe because of
our methods of treatment and the fact that we have seen our patients under
extremely different environmental circumstances. This makes it possible to
avoid the danger of seeing these abnormal personalities as all one group. The
biological basis consists of many different abnormalities, and the actual pattern
of abnormal behavior is determined by the earlier, as well as present, experiences.

In one case after another treated at Herstedvester, we saw the pattern of
behavior change, sometimes in a very dramatic way, as in the case of Wulff.
We would not deny that his biological makeup contains elements of great
importance to his personality structure and the way he reacts to environmental
stimuli. Such elements could be openness and need to communicate or a much
more closed type of behavior, emotional stability or instability, lethargy or
energy.

Henrik Sjöbring (1954) made some attempt to produce a psychological
analysis of the basic structures of human personality along these lines. We tried
to use these, but like Sjöbring himself, we did not find any combination of such
structures to be therapeutically useful.

Situationally acquired behavior patterns seemed to us to be of the greatest
importance. The actual relationship of elementary specific personality factors to
adequate and, to such structures, useful environmental factors, is still not understood in a clinically useful way. Schneider's book *Psychopathic Personalities*
was first published in 1923. In it he supposed an inherited predisposition, but he
accepted that environmental influences could be of importance for the further
development of the abnormal personality. Another important contribution was
made by Alexander and Staub (1956); they describe a person whose "whole
life pattern shows typical deviations from the normal." They go on to say that
"his life is very dramatic," and that "he lives out his instinctual drives . . . even
those drives which are unacceptable to the ego, even the antisocial trends"
(p. 116).

Alexander and Staub especially differentiated between these and the "true
criminals" whose personality was "definitely and homogeneously antisocial,"
while that of the neurotic character is not homogeneous. In the neurotic, a part

of the personality condemns the impulsive obedience to his drives. The pathology of the neurotic character is seen as an unconscious battle between the two heterogeneous parts of the same person. His personality seems "split in two, one part acting impulsively while the other reacts to this impulsive behavior in a very moral or even overmoral fashion."

Cleckley (1964) also sees psychopathy as a persistent entity, and with Alexander and Staub stresses that psychopaths differ from the typical criminal. Cleckley writes, "seldom does a psychopath take much advantage of what he gains and almost never works consistently in crime or in anything else to achieve a permanent position of power, wealth or security" (p. 276). Cleckley also observed that only a small proportion of psychopaths will be found in prisons. They are not likely to commit serious crimes. Although they will often be arrested they will soon regain their freedom and then return to their former pattern of behavior. This gives support to my own optimistic observations. Psychopaths have inadequate reactions to their own criminal acts and seem to have an inability to learn from fellow prisoners. Since the psychopath is not influenced by the prison culture, his life can continue without a sense of degradation; this helps him avoid adopting the behavioral patterns of the chronic criminal.

In the special penal institution at Grendon in England, Gray (1973) found that most "chronic habitual criminals" can be described as a group as being "inadequate, aggressive, antisocial, preoccupied with immediate needs, and unable to form any lasting relationships." He sees this as a result of their common experience as "criminals" and this he also sees as responsible for the antitherapeutic culture in prisons. This corresponds closely with my own findings. Most chronic criminals have what I call *masks of psychopaths*.

If the concept of sociopathy, commonly synonymous with psychopathy, is to have any clinical value, it must be reserved for what we could most reasonably call secondary reactions to degrading social experiences which have a better prognosis than is generally made for the classical psychopathies. Blackburn (1975) has used the term *secondary psychopaths* for neurotic, but not extroverted, cases. This has no relation to my own use of the term *secondary reactions*.

I believe that the majority of my cases were such sociopaths, but it must be admitted that only seldom could I have made an early distinction between these two groups. The case of Hans exemplifies this. It is for this reason that I prefer to call them, as a group, *character insufficients*, and to use this vague term to stimulate an individualized treatment.

Fini Schulsinger (1972) has identified a group of people as psychopaths, excluding character neurotics, that is, those with a consistent pattern of neurotic restriction of activity and gratification. His psychopaths present "a consistent pattern of impulse-ridden or acting out behavior" lasting for "a reasonable period after adolescence." As part of another research project he has elegantly used the opportunity to investigate psychopaths in a large sample of adoptees and their relatives. The attempts made in this research to separate genetic and environmental factors are carefully carried out. In spite of the purely descriptive definition used, he finds that genetic factors play an important role in the etiology of psychopathy.

Many of the cases handled at Herstedvester fit Schulsinger's broad definition. In another group the character neurotic elements are dominant. In some cases with a history of psychopathic behavior going back to childhood, a prolonged follow-up of treated cases has shown that the pattern of behavior can change. Schulsinger does not exclude the influence of environmental factors, but he excludes from his study the group of character neurotics. This would have been of value as a second control group. Perhaps in all cases with severe, long-lasting, impulse-ridden, or acting-out behavior patterns observed in relation to specific severe and prolonged degrading experiences, it would be possible to demonstrate an interaction between different specific genetic factors and specific environmental factors. This could mean that a segregation of special groups of maladapted offenders could possibly be the beginning of a safer prognostication from a real identity of the life careers of all the individuals in each group. That would give better opportunities for scientific investigation of the therapeutic process.

Many of our cases have developed their character insufficiencies while living the life of an offender. Some have probably developed a criminal career as a result of a basic constitutional defect. But we must ask in which group each case belongs.

If it should prove possible to also identify and analyze primary psychopaths, it would be of interest to attempt to separate out those of our antisocial, heterogeneous group described above, whose patterns of behavior are mostly secondary to their degrading experiences. Such cases will still occur, and biological explanations will be of as much value as sociological ones. They must be regarded as complementary.

Our legal system intends first and foremost to be egalitarian in its reaction to offenders, but often it tends to be more formal and superficial. Some offenders are more in need of help than others. When we remember Arne's pathological egocentricity, his inadequately motivated killing, and his general poverty in major affective reactions, we (psychiatrists, lawyers, jurors) tend to believe that he must be segregated and incarcerated for life. But if all we do is rob such a man of what identity remains to him and standardize his life in a maximum-security institution (in many countries it will be a huge institution with no possibilities for close contact with a single staff member who he feels he can trust), then we do not offer him a fair chance of changing his pattern of behavior. For less sensitive offenders such help will not be needed.

People who are driven by impulse to antisocial conduct must be given the possibility to regain human dignity. We must help them to obtain emotional contact if we want to achieve egalitarian treatment.

We must always remember our insufficient abilities to differentiate correctly between a psychopathic personality of the hopeless type and those chronic criminals who have adopted the mask of a psychopath—a mask that it is our duty to help him eliminate.

9

Labeling and Beyond: Social Stigma Revisited

S. Giora Shoham

By labeling Wittgenstein as a foreigner of odd personal habits, with an extraordinary, phenomenal, possibly unique, talent for philosophical invention, the English thus defused the impact of his personality and moral passion as completely as they had earlier neutralised Shaw's social and political teachings. —A. Janik and S. Toulmin, *Wittgenstein's Vienna*

Those who fly high catch the eyes of the hunters. —Stuart Bell, *The Elevator*

I have recently reread some of the criticisms against labeling as a frame of reference. I especially reconsidered the critical remarks of Jack Gibbs (1966), the chapter on social reaction, deviant commitment, and career in Ian Taylor et al. (1973), and Walter Gove's (1970) criticism of the labeling premises as applied to mental illness. My first reaction was to review my personal experiences and observations related to the labeling premises since the publication of *The Mark of Cain* (Shoham, 1970) and then to try to react to the contentions of the critics. Indeed, the smeared halo effect of stigma generalizing from some patterns of behavior of an individual or even from a single characteristic to his whole personality passed the acid test of many of my observations and personal experiences. I have seen many people ruined by professional muckrakers. I have witnessed many people whose mere detention for initial investigation by the police made the public view their whole person through the twisted lenses of their stigma. In one instance a successful lawyer, a friend of mine, lost most of his practice after his investigation by the police, although he was not formally detained or arrested and no charge was ever filed against him. Some even went as far as to confide that they knew all along that "deep down he was corrupt through and through," echoing Garfinkel's (1956) statement that "the work of the denunciation effects the recasting of the objective character of the perceived other. The former identity, at best, receives the accent of mere appearance. The former identity stands as accidental; the new identity is the 'basic reality'." In academia "explaining away" a colleague's achievement by means of stigma is a favorite vocation. Smith developed a new field of research; so comes the campus gossip and assures his eager listeners that Smith did an academic market research and ascertained that nobody wanted to deal with that specific area so he decided that that was his opportunity to become a lone shining star. If Taylor publishes too much, the labeler's verdict is that he must be shallow. If he publishes too little he is surely sterile. Jones received an international award so enter the university politicos and spread the word that the awards' committee heard about the death of Jones' wife and the nervous breakdown of his daughter so that their decision to award him the prize was made out of pity. The epitome of vileness and cruelty through stigma was experienced by another friend of mine, whose two sons were killed in the Yom Kippur War. He tried his hand at politics, and his political opponents confided to everybody that he was totally unreliable and should not be elected to public office: "You know, of course, the terrible blow he suffered" they would whisper with a tragic intonation "and this pushed him off the track. It is a great shame but one cannot vote for him because his erratic shiftiness and lack of mental balance are sure to endanger the party."

In totalitarian regimes political stigma creates monsters, nonentities, and madmen, but in democratic pluralistic societies past political affiliations may also curb and sometimes stifle a person's present activities. Such was the case of the McCarthy era in the United States. Also, many people would have nothing to do with the music of Karajan and the philosophy of Heidegger because of their Nazi affiliations. A teacher of philosophy at the University of Jerusalem used to protest against the blanket effect of stigma as follows: "Many of my friends ask me how come an unethical bastard like myself teaches the philosophy of ethics? My answer to this impertinence is, in the Jewish tradition, by another question: Professor F. teaches geometry so does he have to be a triangle?" The stigmatizers apparently do not take seriously our philosopher's logic nor do they heed Voltaire's advice "not to pay attention to the old fool's [meaning himself] ugly face and his all too human frailties, but to listen to what he has to say." They ever expand some of his deeds or characteristics to engulf his whole person. I remember with dismay how my first negative impression of a person formed by stigma and gossip lasted for a fairly long time until I realized that I had been led astray by the derogatory labels. I realized that I was eager to accept the stigmatic image of the person. Labeling and pigeonholing the person put my mind at ease. I did not look for contrary impressions and other views portraying the person as honest and of the utmost integrity, as he turned out to be, but was content to accept the person's stigmatized image without question. My sad experience, time and again, is that human beings are eager, voracious, and sometimes carnivorous consumers of stigma, yet ever ready to rationalize this gluttony by projection, displacement, and a battery of other defense mechanisms.

Revisiting the stigma premises after my interest had wandered for many years to other areas made me think that labeling is not really a theory but a frame of reference, like culture-conflict in criminology. E.W. Hobson's definition of a frame of reference is incorporated in the following passage by H. Becker (1932): "Scientific sociology regards human beings as pieces on the giant chess-board of life; with each succeeding move (social occurrence) they draw closer together, separate or converge in certain respects and diverge in others.... Such approach and avoidance constitute the basis of the socio-logical frame of reference" (p. 39). In other words, a frame of reference is a common boundary of phenomena that has an empirical common denominator. This common denominator may not necessarily characterize the whole phenomenon under consideration; it would be sufficient that a part of its factual manifestation would fit into the common boundary of the frame of reference. By exclusion we may note that the labeling premise is not a theoretical system in the engulfing Parsonian sense; nor is it of similar scope to the conflict theory of society, according to which society (as per the expounders of Simmel's thought) is held together in dynamic equilibrium by diverging normative discord. We hold, moreover, that labeling is also not a "middle range theory" by which Merton denoted the relatively limited theories applied to rather narrow and well-defined areas of study. Labeling conflict is both wider and deeper and at the same time less systematic than a middle range theory. The latter operates on one level of analysis, whereas culture conflict may include in its premises phenomena that occur on different planes of a space which need not have clear-cut delineations.

I still do not think that such physiological characteristics as color or anomalies like blindness which have been included by Goffman (1963) and Schur (1971) within their discussions of labeling, can indeed be fruitfully in-cluded within the stigma frame of reference. These physical attributes and pathologies are so conspicuous by themselves and elicit such a powerful societal reaction that any comparison with social labels attached to the nonphysiological roles and statuses of a person are untenable. Anyone who has seen the excellent film *The Sailor's Return* about an English seaman who marries a black African princess and brings her back home to Dorset, where both are destroyed by British social prejudice, is bound to see the difference between societal reaction to color and social stigma. The latter may be as elaborate as a *danse macabre*, whereas the former is as blunt as a blow on the head.

One of the assets of the labeling premise is that it serves as a methodological contouring technique for studying the normative by its contrast with and exclu-sion from the non-normative. I have stressed this function of stigma in two of my recent books which deal with the phenomenology and ontology of deviance and conformity (Shoham, 1976, 1978a). This, of course, is not new. Freud demonstrated the value of studying mental abnormality in order to understand the normal dynamics of the psyche.

If we turn now to the more specific points of criticism against the labeling frame of reference we have Jack Gibbs's (1966) general complaint that it makes social deviance "relativistic in the extreme." This, however, helps us understand the dynamics of deviance as they are. In the Prohibition era drinking alcohol was a crime, whereas possessing gold was laudatory. Today Americans are on an ever-augmenting alcoholic binge, and possessing gold over a certain amount is a crime. Eskimos used to commit normative patricide. The ancient Egyptian royal families committed mandatory incest, and some of the prostitution in ancient Canaan was sacred. Our hunch is that most, if not all, of the proscriptions in any criminal code book were either normative or indifferent in other times and other places. The objective stability, or universality, of social norms and hence deviance is a myth so that the relativistic approach to deviance inherent in the labeling frame of reference is, as Edwin Schur (1971) rightly says, not a weakness but a major strength.

The Configuration

Some of the criticism against some of the writings of the labeling theorists seems to be justified. Gibbs (1972) quotes the following excerpts from the works of Becker, Erikson, and Kitsuse:

> *Becker*: From this point of view, deviance is not a quality of the act the person commits, but rather a consequence of the application by others of rules and sanctions to an "offender." The deviant is one to whom that label has successfully been applied; deviant behaviour is behaviour that people so label.

> *Erikson*: From a sociological standpoint, deviance can be defined as conduct which is generally thought to require the attention of social control agencies, that is, conduct about which "something should be done." Deviance is not a property inherent in certain forms of behaviour; it is a property conferred upon these forms by the audiences which directly or indirectly witness them. Sociologically, then, the critical variable in the study of deviance is the social audience rather than the individual person, since it is the audience which eventually decides whether or not any given action or actions will become a visible case of deviation.

> *Kitsuse*: Forms of behaviour per se do not differentiate deviants from nondeviants; it is the responses of the conventional and conforming members of the society who identify and interpret behaviour as deviant which sociologically transform persons into deviants (p. 40).

Gibbs then argues that according to these three scholars the societal reaction, that is, the social stigma, in itself and by itself creates social deviance. The infringement of social norms of a given group in a given time and place seems to be irrelevant or expressly excluded by these labeling theorists from the etiology of social deviance. We may add that any model which does not take into account the infringement of a social norm for the probability of being labeled as a deviant is untenable. In other words, any exposition of deviance which implies that the fact that a person has committed an armed robbery in most, if not all, contemporary human societies does not raise the probability of his being labeled as criminal or deviant is patently absurd. Quinney (1970) also abuses the labeling frame of reference by defining crime as "a legal definition of human conduct created by agents of the dominant class in capitalistic society . . . Definitions of crime are composed of behaviors that conflict with the class interests of the dominant economic class . . . Definitions of crime are applied by the class that has the power to shape the enforcement and administration of criminal law . . . An ideology of crime is constructed and diffused in the course of establishing the hegemony of the ruling class." If class conflict and the power of the ruling class is the sole criterion for labeling human behavior as crime, then murderers and rapists from the lower classes should feel that they are doing the right thing when they commit their crimes. Well, Quinney should know, if he has been doing some field work in criminology besides voicing ideological slogans, that most murderers and rapists from all social classes do not claim that murder and rape should be permitted. Most of them commit their crimes although they cognitively legitimize the laws proscribing murder and rape. By regarding class-based labeling as the sole dynamic of creating criminals, Quinney inflates to the dimensions of caricature the role of stigma in the etiology of social deviance.

The fallacy in these extreme expositions of labeling lies first of all in the etiological exclusiveness they claim for stigma. Second, their claim that the labeling frame of reference is mutually exclusive with the non-normative behavior approach to deviance is also untenable. There is no reason why societal reaction, that is, stigma, should not be incorporated within a wider model in which rule infraction is also a probabilistic component. Indeed, the wholistic-synthetic configuration presented in *The Mark of Cain*, envisages non-normative behavior as well as value deviation as raising the probability that a certain individual or group will be branded with the constitutive social label of deviance. A later attempt to integrate between the labeling premises and non-normative behavior was carried out by Pollner (1974). His model I "treats the deviance of an act as existing independently of a community's response. It implicitly posits that certain acts are (or ought to be) responded to in particular ways because they are 'deviant,' that is, their 'deviance' is defined by criteria other than the fact that you or I happen to regard or experience the act as deviant" (p. 27). Model II which is the extreme labeling approach, for example, Howard Becker's, "treats deviance as a property which is created and sustained by a community's response to an act as deviant." Pollner then shows how these two models can be integrated. Black and Reiss, in their paper published the same year as *The Mark of Cain* (1970), also advocate the configuration approach to social deviance. "Deviance itself" they say "should be treated theoretically as a configuration of properties rather than as an unidimensional behavioural event. A critical aspect of the sociology of deviance and control consists in the discovery of these configurations. More broadly, the aim is to discover the social organization of deviance and control." The configuration approach to social deviance as presented in *The Mark of Cain* is that the probability of being branded as deviant increases with deviant behavior, that is, norm infringement, but deviance becomes a social fact only after the given behavior, person, or group has been tagged as such by agencies of social control. The configurational model is, therefore, as follows:

$$\text{deviant behavior} + \text{stigma} \longrightarrow \text{social deviance}$$

where deviant behavior is the predisposing factor expressed in probabilistic terms and the tagging process is the identifying dynamic which crystalizes and ultimately fixates the social visibility of deviance and determines its social consequences. Consequently, Jack Gibbs's criticism against the labeling theorists, that they totally ignore the non-normative act, cannot apply to us because we do recognize its contribution to the configuration of social deviance. On the contrary, non-normative behavior which was not labeled as such by agencies of social control cannot be identified from the phenomenological point of view as social deviance because the interaction, the interrelationship, between non-normative behavior and tagging produces deviance. One might as well ask whether hydrogen or oxygen is more important for the production of the water molecule. Also the configurational approach is not vulnerable to Gibbs's criticism of Becker et al. that according to their exposition there cannot be a "bum rap" (Gibbs, 1972). First, according to the probabilistic configuration the probability of being labeled as deviant for the norm infringer is higher than for the norm conformist. This, of course, is small comfort for an individual who happened to be caught in the smaller probability range and has actually been falsely accused and sentenced. Second, the victimologists tell us that there is a much higher probability for a person with a previous criminal record, for a professional criminal, and for a member of a deviant group or subculture, to experience a "bum rap" than for those who do not fall in these categories. This means that those who engage in non-normative behavior stand a higher chance of being falsely accused of a specific act, although in that particular instance they were innocent. It must be stressed, however, that the probability configuration of stigma does not land us into the Parsonian fallacy warned against by Simmons and Chambers (1965) of dividing societies into a majority of "law abiding citizens/subjects/party members/comrades" and a minority of "boat-rockers/bums/parasites/hooligans." Every configuration should relate to a specific norm or group of norms which the person or group is being labeled as infringing. Even the widest label with the most extensive halo effect does not relate to all the social roles and to the whole personality of an individual but only to part of them, so that a person who is labeled as deviating from one set of norms may still be regarded as nondeviant in relation to all the other social norms. Consequently, whatever the theoretical demerits of the structural-ist-functionalist school of thought in sociology, its exponents did contribute to the understanding of how non-normative and anomic behavior may interact with social stigma to form social deviance. I have also shown in chapter 9 of *The Mark of Cain* how the structuralists as well as the conflict theorists need the stigma frame of reference to help explain the formation and cohesion of the criminal and deviant groups and subcultures. Indeed the structuralists and conflict theorists are better able to describe the potential for and predisposition to deviance, whereas the symbolic interactionists and ethnomethodologists are in a better position to describe and explain the process of tagging the stigma of deviance and its socionormative consequences. The password in this area, as in many other areas of science, should be a wholistic synthesis and not an over-analytical either/or atomism—not just chance eclecticism, but an interdisci-plinary and integrated configuration of all the relevant levels of explanation. Consequently, Warren and Johnson's (1972) criticism that "labeling sociologists have paid inadequate attention to the question of 'core values'. . . and to the empirical relationship between deviant identities, deviant acts, acts of labeling and symbolic labeling" (p. 89) cannot be directed toward this configuration because it integrates all these factors.

The Myth of Primary and Secondary Deviance

One of the theoretical formulations of deviance which led some labeling theo-rists down a conceptual blind alley is Lemert's distinction between primary and secondary deviance. According to Lemert (1967):

> The notion of secondary deviation was devised to distinguish between original and effective causes of deviant attributes and actions which are associated with physical defects and incapacity, crime, prostitution, alcoholism, drug addiction, and mental disorders. Primary deviation, as contrasted with secondary, is polygenetic, arising out of a variety of social, cultural, psychological and physiological factors, either in adventitious or recurring combinations. While it may be socially rec-ognised and even defined as undesirable, primary deviation has only marginal implications for the status and psychic structure of the person concerned. Resultant problems are dealt with reciprocally in the con-text of established status relationships. This is done either through normalisation, in which the deviance is perceived as normal variation— a problem of everyday life—or through management and nominal controls which do not seriously impede basic accommodations people make to get along with each other.

> Secondary deviation refers to a special class of socially defined re-sponses which people make to problems created by the societal reac-tion to their deviance. These problems are essentially moral problems which revolve around stigmatisation, punishments, segregation and social control. Their general effect is to differentiate the symbolic and interactional environment to which the person responds, so that

early or adult socialisation is categorically affected. They become central facts of existence for those experiencing them, altering psychic structure, producing specialised organisation of social roles and self-regarding attitudes. Actions which have these roles and self attitudes as their referents make up secondary deviance (pp. 40–41).[1]

Lemert's claim that societal reaction is relevant only to the genesis of the persistent (secondary) deviant and his self-concept and not to initial deviance ignores the role of overt and covert negative expectations from the child within the family and in socializing agencies. I have shown that conflict situations within the family with the multiphasic expectations, reactions, and counterreactions of parents and their children, are important factors in the genesis of primary deviance and crime (Shoham, 1966). The dynamics of double binds in skewed family interaction as related to morbidity and the subterranean expectations of "badness" directed toward children as related to deviance has recently been empirically explored (Shoham et al., 1977). In *The Mark of Cain* I demonstrated how the expectations of "pollution," "badness," and promiscuity of a father toward his daughter in a Jewish North-African authoritarian family, as well as his derogatory reaction to her behavior and person, contributed to the daughter's predisposition to prostitution. My analysis of the life and career of Jean Genet (Shoham, 1970) portrays the stigmatizing expectations of the members of the peasant family from Le Morvan on little Jean Genet, the foundling bastard. Not only these expectations but also the reaction of the peasant family members to his mere presence and Genet's growing counterreactions contributed to his initial deviance. This initial deviance developed eventually into the professional thief, ideological homosexual, and habitual treason of the adult Genet. But this is precisely the career-of-deviance process, downgraded by Lemert (1967). It describes his primary and secondary deviance more realistically as the "maturing" process from initial to habitual deviance. Also the career process in crime and deviance as described and documented by Sutherland, Glaser, Cloward and Ohlin, and many others, has received ample support from empirical studies.[2] Goffman (1962) was, of course, right when he stated that secondary deviation is simply an extreme grade of a conflictual adjustment to the expectations of others as well as to stigma, implying that a similar adjustment but of lower intensity exists in the case of primary, or initial, deviance. Indeed the spurious distinction between primary and secondary deviation might have been linked to Schur's statement (1975):

> Often when it is argued that some deviance cannot be explained by labeling, the critics have lost sight of the distinction between primary and secondary deviation and think only of discrete or initial deviating acts of particular sorts. Actually, in some instances negative labeling does seem to come close to "causing" initial, or primary, deviation, as when an act of deviation appears to represent a kind of behavioural compliance with the prior expectations of significant others. Labeling

analysis does not, however, require that it be possible to specify negative labeling as a necessary condition for any single deviating act. No
labeling theorist has advanced such an argument, and it seems in no
way necessary for recognition of the vital significance of labeling, in
the broad sense of social definitions, of whatever sort, in shaping what
we have called the "varieties of deviant experience" (p. 448).

My configuration of deviance is probabilistic and it cannot include any "necessary conditions." However, in *The Mark of Cain* I showed how some negative
labels transmitted within the adoptive family contributed significantly to the
initial deviance of Genet and how the labels of promiscuity sent toward the
Jewish North-African girls by their fathers predisposed them for the initial
recruitment into prostitution. The attitude of the relevant others toward a
person and especially toward a child and their reaction to his behavior are relevant both for the initial recruitment (a phrase held in low esteem by Lemert)
into deviance, as well as for the maturation of a habitual deviant career.

The Stigmatization

Edwin Schur's (1971) review of the phenomenological and ontological literature
and its relevance to the labeling frame of reference relate to some of my own recent works, which also have some ontological undercurrents of the stigma premises. In the first chapter of *The Mark of Cain* I proposed a profile of low and
high susceptibility to labeling. The high effectiveness profile was mainly related
to a stigmatized person who is other-directed and sanction-oriented, that is, com-
plies to norms mainly out of fear of punishment or reprimand. The low effectiveness profile was largely related to an inner-directed stigmatized person with a
moral attitude toward social norms. This stigma susceptibility profile can be enlarged and improved by my recent exposition of object relationships based on
existential and ontological premises (Shoham, 1978b). The gist of this exposition relates first of all to the two opposing vectors which constitute the scaf-
folding of the personality core. These are *participation* and *separation*.
Participation refers to the identification of a person's ego with another per-
son(s), an object, or a symbolic construct outside himself, and his striving to
lose his separate identity by fusion with this other object or symbol. Separation,
of course, is the opposite vector. I use these opposing vectors of unification-
fusion and separation-isolation as the main axis of my theory in conjunction
with three major developmental phases. The first is the process of birth. The
second is the crystalization of an individual ego by the molding of the ego
boundary. The third phase of separation is a corollary of socialization when
one reaches one's ego identity (Erickson, 1956). The strain to overcome the
separating and dividing pressures never leaves the individual. The striving to
partake in a pantheistic whole is ever present and takes many forms; if one

avenue toward its realization is blocked, it surges out from another channel. Actual participation is unattainable by definition. The objective impossibility of participation is augmented by the countering separating vectors, both instinctual and interactive. At any given moment of our lives there would be a disjuncture, a gap between our desires for participation and our subjectively defined distance from our participatory aims. We have denoted this gap the Tantalus ratio which is the relationship between the longed for participatory goal and the distance from it as perceived by ego.

If the separation vector within a given personality type is more potent than the participation vector the personality type would tend to be *separant*, whereas in the opposite case the personality would be more *participant*. The dimensions and traits which characterize the two polar personality types are presented in table 9-1.

The high effectiveness of stigma profile would be the separant personality type whose dimensions appear on the left-hand side of table 9-1, whereas the low effectiveness of stigma probability profile, which is the participant personality type, appears on the right-hand side of the table. The description and proposed measurements of each individual dimension in the profile are as follows:

In the interactive dimension stimulus hunger characterizes the separant; stimulus aversion, the participant. This conceptualization is based on Eyesenck's (1967) research finding concerning his extrovert-introvert personality continuum. His extrovert is characterized by sociability, impulsiveness, activity, liveliness, and excitability; his introvert, by diametrically opposite traits. Of special importance are Eyesenck's findings concerning the "excitation" and "inhibition" of his polar types. An excited cortex will exert a restraining and inhibiting hold on behavior, whereas an inhibited cortex would loosen the rein over the individual with a resultant increase in behavioral excitation.

Table 9-1
Personality Types, Dimensions, and Traits

Separant		Participant
	Interactive Dimension	
Activist		*Quietist*
Stimulus hunger		Stimulus aversion
Reducer		Augmentor
	Ontological Dimension	
Object inclusion		*Self exclusion*
Field dependence		Field independence
Sharpener		Leveler

Eyesenck has shown that his extrovert is hungry for stimuli, that is, he is sensation seeking, whereas his introvert displays stimulus aversion. The more other-dependent separant would be stimulus hungry and hence more dependent on stimulation by and expectations of his relevant others, whereas the more quietist participant striving for inaction, that is, a state of nonstimulation, would be less likely to be dependent on the expectations of others and hence less susceptible to stigma. This might be linked to Eyesenck's finding that the introvert reacts favorably to sensory deprivation. This finding could be linked to the separant need for activity and the stimulation of the object, whereas the participant seems to suffer from stimuli which catapult him away from the coveted state of inaction. The stimulus hunger and stimulus aversion is readily measured by Eyesenck's Maudsley Personality Inventory and other instruments.

Another character trait relating to the interactive dimension of the personality is Petrie's ingenious experiments on those who increase subjectively the size of the stimuli (augmenters) and those who decrease it (reducers). Petrie's instruments consist of a block of wood divided by measured intervals and an elongated piece of wood which widens toward the end. The subject, who is blindfolded, first rubs the piece of wood and then the block. He then has to point out the place on the widening piece of wood which seems to him to have the width of the block. The reducer points out the width of the piece of wood which is narrower than the block, whereas the augmenter points out the width which is wider (Petrie et al., 1960).

The augmenter would tend to be less object and other directed and therefore less susceptible to stigma than the reducer who would be seeking more excitation and more attention from exciting others and hence would be more attentive to their expectations and labeling. The two interactive dimensions of the separant would depict him as aiming to devour the object and incorporate it into himself, whereas the participant wishes to exclude and isolate himself from the object.

The second ontological dimension relates to the object inclusion of the separant and the object exclusion of the participant. The separant would display a higher field dependence than the participant who would tend to be field independent. These two concepts, as well as Witkin's and his associates' later study, *Psychological Differentiation* (1962), relate to the object, setting an environmental perception while performing the task. The field dependent displays a low psychological differentiation because he is dependent on his performance on cues stemming from the overall gestalt and the background set of the situation. In other words, performance here is dependent on the configuration of the surrounding object. On the other hand, the field independent and the one who displays higher psychological differentiation relies on his own cognitive cues and not on the outward gestalt of the object. The field dependence and independence is measured by the rod and frame test (Witkin et al., 1966). Consequently the separant field dependent, that is, object and other dependent, would be more susceptible to stigma than the participant field independent. A somewhat related test is George Klein's sharpener and leveler dychotomy (Klein and Schlesinger, 1950). The separant would tend to be more of a sharpener trying to pinpoint details of the object, displaying thus an intolerance of objective ambiguity, whereas the leveler would be more of a participant displaying tolerance of objective ambiguity. The leveler/sharpener personality traits can be measured by instruments developed by Klein and Schlesinger.

My hypotheses as to the stigma effectiveness personality profiles have not as yet been empirically tested, and I am well aware of the methodological problems involved in setting up the proper research design to test these hypotheses.

The mechanisms of stigmatization presented in *The Mark of Cain* have also been vindicated by my observations and some research findings. Projection still seems to be the main fuel pushing stigmatizers to besmear their fellow human beings. Some of my colleagues who never added the names of their assistants as coauthors of their papers, although they did most of the work, were ever accusing somebody of plagiarism; others who were less than honest in their financial dealings had many stories about Professor X and Dr. Y. appropriating research funds, and one colleague who used to bring his mistress to conferences abroad always had stories about his adulterous dean. In a similar vein Simmons and Chambers (1965) found that people who were more liberal tended to resort less to negative stereotyping, that is, to stigma, than people who were more conservative. The latter had to project outwardly through stigma their repressed aggression against the normative system. The stigmatizing projections operate by some of the principles of the objective measurement techniques. In the Rorschach test and Thematic Apperception Test (TAT), for instance, one has to keep the objective stimuli at varying levels of ambiguity in order to induce the person's projections to soar outward. In like manner the projections of stigma would be more prominent in cases where the predisposing factors within the configuration are amorphic and ambiguous. In mental illnesses, therefore, in which the diagnostic criteria are rather vague, labeling plays a much greater role (Fabrega and Manning, 1972) than in physical illnesses, the syndromes of which are more concrete. In like manner stigma plays a greater role in labeling juveniles as "in need of care and protection" or "in need of treatment" when they are not accused of having committed a specific delinquent act (Cicourel, 1972) than in cases of older delinquents who are brought to juvenile court after a specific infraction of the law. This is also apparent in the differential role of stigma in cases where the criteria for the quality of performance are concrete or amorphic. In the evaluation of a good or bad factory worker, for instance, where the criteria of performance are more or less clear, stigma plays a lesser role than in the public evaluation of an artist or painter. In the latter cases the criteria of excellence are vague and sometimes obscure, so that labeling and clique affiliations are many times the main criteria for the judgment of excellence or worthlessness.

The complementarity of roles between stigmatizer and stigmatized hypothesized by me in *The Mark of Cain* has also received some further empirical support. Mary Owen Cameron (1964) reports that the arrest and the body search of the occasional shoplifter together with the formal report of the store detective staff forces him to regard himself as a thief. Schur (1971) describes the "role engulfment" of the deviant by the roles assigned and labeled on him by the stigmatizers. Consequently "as role engulfment increases, there is a tendency for the actor to define himself as others define him." This, no doubt, brings to the fore my analysis in *The Mark of Cain* of the making of Jean Genet.

The Degradation Rituals

Once a person has been labeled, the halo effect of stigma makes his proficiencies and his previously acclaimed wisdom tainted with derogatory labels and hence downgraded. As Schwartz and Skolnick (1962) have demonstrated, just being accused of a deviant or criminal act although subsequently cleared or acquitted of it, starts the positive feedback cycles of degradation. Two recent Israeli cases highlight these harsh degradation ceremonies of mere accusations which proved later to be unfounded. The first case is of a high public official who was accused of corruption and was found not guilty after a long trial. His daughter, an accountant in her early twenties, recounts:

After I got the telephone call that my father had been arrested for taking bribes I drove to the police station totally confused: I was always proud of my father, of his important job and of his integrity, but on the way to the detention centre I started to doubt the innocence of my father. How do I know he is innocent? These things are known to happen. When I reached the police station the officer in charge told me that my father was an extraordinary criminal and that he was accused of taking a bribe of half a million Israeli pounds. I got a shock. A moment earlier I had been young and cheerful and all of a sudden I was a tired woman. I remember saying to myself that we shall never get out of this mess. I knew that the mere experience of closing my father up like a criminal turned him into a nonentity. It made me bitter. I started to see the world in a different light. I couldn't sleep. I couldn't eat and I couldn't work. A thick shadow descended on me and deprived me of the joy of life and of my youth. I had the feeling that they had taken the person who was most dear to me, and had crushed him into a zero. I shall never be able to get rid of this shadow even now that my father has been acquitted. God knows when I shall be able to rid myself of this show.[3]

The second case is of a student at Tel Aviv University who was accused of murdering his girlfriend. After forty-seven days of detention and interrogation by the police, the real murderer was found and the student was released. In his action for damages against the state the student claimed that two and a half years after his false arrest he still could not find work because of his stigma and he was still deemed socially undesirable by many people.

> The whole affair is still not closed for me. I relive it every day and every hour. I cannot walk in the street without people pointing at me and whispering behind my back. I try to lead a normal life and to rehabilitate myself economically and socially, but part of the public still sees in me a negative and immoral character. I am being ostracized because many people cannot rid themselves of the image of the murderer which was branded on me by the television and the press. When I applied for a job as a teacher of history in a school the principal told me that he was afraid to employ me because of the bad influence I might have on the pupils. The manager of a department store to which I applied for a job told me that he knew that I was a good guy and he believed I did nothing wrong, but my name might frighten away the customers. Only 10 percent of the friends I had before my arrest are still my friends, and my wife left me because she couldn't stand our social ostracism. When I go out with a girl our dating lasts till her parents find out who I am and then the girl doesn't show up any more. I know that the mark of Cain is branded on me but I want the state to declare publicly that the police erred. It is impossible to estimate my suffering and damages. I therefore claim from the state a token compensation which will help clear my name.[4]

Stigma and the Deviant Career

As pointed out in chapter 9 of *The Mark of Cain*, stigma helps to push the criminal and deviant toward his peers in deviance and crime, landing him ultimately in the deviant and criminal cultures where his stigma is not derogatory any more because every member of the group has it. However, one should stress that in this process stigma is just one vector within a dynamic configuration which molds the individual's deviant career. An exaggeration of the role of stigma can be observed in the description by Jack Young (1971) following a lead from Leslie Wilkins of the dynamics of the amplification of deviance. The positive feedback cycle starts, according to Young, with such attitudes of the police as the following toward cannabis users: "Never in my experience have I met up with such filth and degradation which follows some people who are otherwise quite intelligent. You become a raving bloody idiot so that you can become more lovable" (Devlin, 1970). Young describes the positive feedback cycle as follows:

1. The police act against the drug users in terms of their stereotypes.

2. The drug-user group finds itself in a new situation, which it must interpret and adapt to in a changed manner.
3. The police react in a slightly different fashion to the changed group.
4. The drug users interpret and adapt to this new situation.
5. The police react to these new changes, and so on.

This gives the impression that the whole life-style, self-concept, and group affiliation of the drug users are the results of a dyadic interaction between them and the police. This unduly inflates the role of a labeling dynamic which in its proper dimension is rather significant and relevant.

The narrowing of the normative socioeconomic opportunities with each consecutive arrest or deeper induction into a deviant group and the corresponding widening of the non-normative opportunities as described by Cloward and Ohlin (see Shoham, 1970) create a "deviance corridor" (conceptualized by Rubington and Weinberg, 1968) which leads a person deeper and farther into full-fledged membership of the criminal and deviant subcultures. Stigma is, of course, an important dynamic in this process because a tag of deviance or conviction once branded on a person is very difficult to wash off. It makes for the deviant's rejection from the normative structure and his adoption of a deviant self-image. This is especially true if the deviant, criminal, or mental patient has spent some time in a total institution like a prison or a hospital for the mentally ill (Sykes, 1961). This accelerates the process of isolation from the law-abiding, or normal, society, deeper embeddedness into the deviant sick roles, and a further entrenchment in the deviant groups. However, the deviants may sometimes devise some situational and self-concept defenses that may help them shield themselves against stigma and keep the appearances and self-concept of nondeviants. One instance is the outward facade, language, and setting of an illegal abortion clinic which help the staff and patients appear and feel as if they were engaged in a legitimate medical operation (Ball, 1975). The classic study by Al Reiss (1961) demonstrated how by means of rationalizations and defense mechanisms male prostitutes could still keep their heterosexual self-images.

Of special interest is Gideon Fishman's (1977) study of sixty-three inmates of a juvenile delinquency treatment center in Ohio. In discussing his findings he says, as follows:

The question that is raised by our findings is: Do all boys who are processed through the juvenile justice system develop a negative, or a delinquent self identity? The data presented here clearly show that this is not the case. The second question, realizing that some boys actually did perceive themselves as delinquents, is whether the offense rate of those was higher than that of juveniles who did not have a delinquent identity? The findings dispute this as well. The overall adjustment rate in the community, including future involvement in crime, was not associated with the labeling effect. The single variable that was significantly related with the labeling effect was the length of recommitment (which also indicates the seriousness of the offense committed after release from the institution). However, the relationship here contradicted expectations. The more serious offenders, those who were recommitted for longer terms, were not those who seem to have experienced the labeling effect but rather those who were not affected by the labeling process, at least according to the youth's own perceptions.

The possible explanation of these findings would suggest four hypotheses. First, the labeling effect is differentially felt, and sometimes is not felt at all, by juveniles who have been processed through the juvenile justice system. Second, those who do experience the negative labeling effect are not always adopting a criminal mode of behaviour. Third, awareness of the labeling effect may indicate sensitivity to informal social controls and awareness of the "significant other," who is a member of the law-abiding population. Fourth, lack of awareness as to the existence of the labeling effect may suggest a lack in sensitivity to informal social controls and the irrelevance of the law-abiding reference group.

These hypotheses would lead us to offer a revision of the traditional labeling hypothesis. Thus, it should be pointed out that juveniles who have been formally processed through the court system, who fail to recognise that labeling has occurred and thus exhibit closure to the influence of law-abiding reference groups and their informal control power, will engage in continuous criminal behavior. On the other hand, juveniles who have been processed through the court system, who perceive the fact of being negatively labeled and hurt, and who thus indicate acceptance of community controls, will try to stay away from adopting a criminal way of life.

The implications of these findings could reach beyond the refinement that it offers to the traditional labeling perspective. It points out that labeling is not to be universally perceived as having a negative and devastating effect on the juvenile. For certain boys, labeling can, indeed, serve as a control mechanism that regulates their behaviour. For them, the stigma that results from the labeling process is a signal as to the tolerance limits of the community (pp. 45-46).[5]

Fishman's sample was small and his findings have to be replicated and reassessed in different locations and different cultural settings. If reconfirmed, Fishman's findings could induce us to indeed reassess the role of stigma in the development of the criminal and deviant careers.

The Labeling of Mental Illness

The sociological approach to the genesis of mental illness with its stressing of the importance of the breakdown of human communication as a predisposition to mental aberration (Scheff, 1967) highlighted the importance of stigma in the formation of the self-concept, roles, and images of the mentally ill. Moreover, some scholars find a close similarity between the core mechanics of social deviance and mental illnesses. Scheff, for instance, regards social deviance as the main dynamic underlying mental illness. According to Scheff (1966): "The culture of the group provides a vocabulary of terms for categorizing many norm violations: crime, perversion, drunkenness, and bad manners are familiar examples. Each of the terms is derived from the type of behavior involved. After exhausting these categories, however, there is always a residue of the most diverse kinds of violations for which the culture provides no explicit label" (pp. 33-34). Consequently, the mechanisms of stigma in social deviance apply mutatis mutandis, to mental illness. The role of stigma in accelerating and deepening mental illness, similar to its role in forming the deviant career, has been pointed out by Scheff (1966) as follows:

> In a crisis, when the deviance of an individual becomes a public issue, the traditional stereotype of insanity becomes the guiding imagery for action, both for those reacting to the deviant and, at times, for the deviant himself. When societal agents and persons around the deviant react to him uniformly in terms of the traditional stereotypes of insanity, his amorphous and instructed rule-breaking tends to crystallize in conformity to those expectations, thus becoming similar to the behaviour of other deviants classified as mentally ill, and stable over time. The process . . . is completed when the traditional imagery becomes a part of the deviant's orientation for guiding his own behaviour (p. 82).

Nunnally (1961) has demonstrated that the mentally ill are regarded with fear, distrust, and dislike and, as with social deviance, their whole person is engulfed with a negative halo effect and their public image is that of being "dirty, unintelligent, insincere, and worthless." Scheff (1968) also demonstrated artfully how the patient who is confused, insecure, and powerless is totally influenced by the "Great White God," the omnipotent and omniscient therapist. As psychiatrists and psychologists are notorious labelers, the patient is more than willing to oblige "the Great Man," adopt the label and act accordingly. The stigmatizing effects here in producing the symptoms of mental illness are even more pronounced than in the covert stigmatization of the young Genet by the peasant family at the Le Morvan and the labeling of the young Jewish North African prostitute by her father. The stigma of mental illness is also used as a device of relative achievement. Among my colleagues in academia a scholar's esoteric yet brilliant book would be dismissed as the "hallucinations of a madman." I was present recently at an excellent lecture by a scholar who was known to be a dull lecturer. I overheard one of the lecturer's colleagues explaining away the brilliance of the lecturer by the fact that he had undergone intensive psychiatric treatment; "so much treatment and money," winked the "friend" of the lecturer "should produce at least one good lecture."

Some critics, like Walter Gove (1970), for instance, reject the extreme labeling approach to the genesis of mental illness because societal reaction in itself and by itself cannot explain the etiology of schizophrenia.

> The available evidence on how people enter the mentally ill role indicates that the societal reaction formulation, at least as stated by Scheff, is false. The evidence is that the vast majority of persons who become patients have a serious disturbance, and it is only when the situation becomes untenable that action is taken. The public officials who perform the major screening role do not simply process all of the persons who come before them as mentally ill but instead screen out a large portion. If the person passes this initial screening, he will probably be committed, and there is reason to assume the process at this point frequently becomes somewhat ritualised. But even here a number of persons are released either through the psychiatric examination or the court hearing.

Here again the fault lies in the extremity of the labeling approach and the exclusiveness which its proponents claim for stigma as the main or even sole dynamic of mental illness. As with deviance and crime the more realistic approach is to see the societal reaction as one dynamic within a configuration which also includes behavioral disturbances and functional maladjustments as predisposing factors toward morbidity. Also, in a recent study my colleagues and I have shown the importance of some skewed family interactions, such as double-binds, in predisposing a child toward schizophrenia the way conflict situations in the socialization process predispose a child toward deviance and crime (Shoham et al., 1977). We also share Gove's (1970) criticism of the concepts of primary and secondary deviance as applied to mental illness. Indeed, in our study of schizophrenics we have demonstrated the role of scapegoating and stigma in the genesis of the initial stages of morbidity (Shoham et al., 1971), whereas the role of stigma of a mental patient in deepening the morbid cycles of mental illness is well documented (Bursten and D'esopo, 1967).

The gist of the criticism of the labeling frame of reference by the "new criminologists" is as follows:

> We have suggested that the social reaction perspective falls far short of a "theory" of deviancy. In trying to correct the limitations of the structural approach of Merton and others, it has ignored the structure of power and interest. But a relevant theory of deviancy must treat the causal variables—motivation and reaction—as determinate and as part of a total structure of social relationships. If we examine the creation of deviancy and reaction in this way, we do not end up with a completely indeterminate picture: we see that the institution of private property, in a stratified and inequitable society, divides men from men as owners and non-owners. It is in the light of this division that the activities of thieves, police, magistrates and property-owners become explicable. Again, in a sharply competitive industrial society

with a high premium set on technological innovation, big business creates, fosters and cynically condemns industrial espionage. A society which expands its higher educational system at a phenomenal rate and is unable to provide interesting or materially rewarding jobs is likely to be faced with a problem of student militancy on an ever-increasing scale. In all these cases of deviance—thieves, industrial spies and student rebels—no explanation is possible without a detailed social history of the constraints, aspirations and meanings which inform and activate the actors. And in all of these above respects, social reaction "theory" must be found to be lacking (Taylor et al., 1973, p. 170).[6]

The dogmatic value-laden argument of the new criminologists is that if the labelers are the capitalists, industrialists, and industrial spies and the labeled are the downtrodden working classes, it is "bad." However, if the labelers are the working classes and the labeled are the exploiting capitalists this presumably would be "good." Also if a psychiatrist in New York or London labels a patient as mad it could be motivated, as per the new criminologists, as a class bias, but they did not even hint at the meaning of the stigma of madness branded on political dissenters by state psychiatric clinics in Soviet Russia. The problem here is that Taylor et al. apply shutters to their critical gaze at the labeling frame of reference. Nobody claims that the class system and power inequalities do not contribute to stigmatization and hence to deviance. Of course they do! But only as factors in a configuration which includes stigmatization within the family by parents and siblings, by rivals, by other socialization agencies, and by other social institutions. The new criminologists label the labeling frame of reference as unsatisfactory because it does not single out the capitalist system as the sole candidate for the label of badness. The business of science is not to attach labels but to try and study in as value-free a method as possible how these labels are branded and what their psychosocial consequences are. This study cannot be confined to one social institution or one segment of society chosen by some value criteria. It must engulf all social institutions and all segments of society in order to identify the relative importance of labeling in the etiological configuration of social deviance. We fully subscribe to Goode's answer to the neo-Marxists' criticism of the labeling premises:

> The forms of behaviour that Marxists and radicals consider—those they criticize labeling theorists for ignoring—oppression, exploitation, racism, sexism, imperialism, certainly do far more damage to human life than most (or any) acts of obvious deviance. And yet behaviour that falls under their umbrella is not generally regarded as deviant. Many of us might feel that they should be condemned by the public. Some no doubt feel that a theory, like labeling theory, should not be taken seriously if we can't call such actions deviant. But the fact that they are not deviant in the public mind should excite our curiosity. Deviance is not centrally about oppression, although it overlaps with it in important ways. Oppression is certainly a basic feature in some

forms of deviant behaviour, just as the quality of deviance is entirely lacking in much oppressive behaviour.

This divergence leads to the issue of how definitions of deviance favorable to those in power manage to win out over definitions that would threaten established ideological and material interests. As Marx and Engels pointed out over a century and a quarter ago in "The German Ideology," the ruling class tends to dominate a society's intellectual and ideological life, its notions of true and false, of good and bad. Consequently it often happens that the relatively powerless in a given society, the economically deprived, are more likely to have their behavior defined as deviant and are less capable of resisting an imputation of deviance than the affluent and powerful. Thus, the study of deviance often parallels the study of powerlessness. Why this essentially Marxist idea should enrage the Marxists is puzzling (Goode, 1975).[7]

We may conclude therefore, that in spite of the massive criticism against the labeling frame of reference, some of which is justified, it still stands largely vindicated.

Notes

1. Edwin M. Lemert, *Human Deviance, Social Problems, & Social Control,* © 1967, pp. 40-41. Reprinted by permission of Prentice-Hall, Inc., Englewood Cliffs, N.J.

2. See E.H. Sutherland and D.R. Cressey, *Principles of Criminology* 9th ed. (Philadelphia: Lippincott, 1974), chapters dealing with differential association and the behavior systems of crime.

3. From an interview in *Ma'ariv* on July 29, 1977.

4. From an interview in *Ha'aretz* on June 12, 1977.

5. Gideon Fishman, "Can Labeling Be Useful?" in P.C. Friday and V. Lorne Stewart, *Youth Crime and Juvenile Justice*, New York, Praeger, 1977, pp. 45-46. Reprinted with permission.

6. I. Taylor, P. Walton, and J. Young, *The New Criminology*, London, Routledge & Kegan Paul, 1973, p. 170. Reprinted with permission.

7. Erich Goode, "On Behalf of Labeling Theory," *Social Problems* 22(5) (June 1975): 577-578. Reprinted with permission.

10 The Young Offender and the Tug-of-War between Ideologies on Crime Prevention

Inkeri Anttila

Young Offenders in Penal Legislation

In Finland, as is the rule elsewhere, young offenders have in some respects been in a special position for centuries; the criminal justice system has only been applied to offenders who have reached a certain age. The trend has been toward having two or even three age limits which regulate partial or full criminal responsibility.

The special legal status of young offenders was greatly emphasized when special sanctions and a separate criminal procedure were created. This type of separate system developed in many countries at the end of the nineteenth century or in the beginning of the twentieth century (Platt, 1969). The juvenile court system spread from the United States to a number of countries, and a competing child welfare system was created in Norway. These two models, often regarded as opposing, have in fact much in common. In both models young people form a separate group for whom special sanctions and special procedures are to be used. In the juvenile court system certain age groups are kept within the criminal justice system, while in the child welfare system they are placed under the supervision of welfare officials. However, the factual content of both institutional and noninstitutional sanctions was very similar, in spite of slightly different terminology (Scandinavian literature on the subject includes, for example, Nyqvist, 1960; Stang Dahl, 1974).

The Golden Age of Treatment Optimism

When the special legislation on young offenders was first planned in Finland about forty years ago, the other Scandinavian countries served as a natural model. The first Young Offender Act, which is still in force in an amended form, was passed in 1940. The main principles of this act were as follows (the content of this act and of previous proposals for reform is discussed in Joutsen, 1976):

Editor's Note: This chapter was submitted in February, 1977.

The criminal justice system was applied to offenders between fifteen and twenty-one years of age. Offenders under fifteen years were left to the control of child welfare authorities.

Nonprosecution and absolute discharge could be applied to offenders between fifteen and eighteen. In these cases the prosecutor or the court notified the child welfare authorities of the matter for possible control measures.

Fifteen to twenty year olds sentenced conditionally were, in contrast to the provisions concerning adults, as a rule placed under supervision.

Some offenders between ages fifteen and twenty-one were sent to a juvenile prison instead of an ordinary prison; the decision was made on the national level by a special organ, which included not only lawyers but also experts on penology and psychiatry. For an offender sentenced to juvenile prison, the term of imprisonment was lengthened by a term set in legislation.

With the exception of minor cases, a personal history report was prepared for the use of the court for each young offender in order to clarify the "reasons for the crime."

In the public debate of the 1940s, the new system was felt to be a great step forward. It was believed to be particularly important to divide offenders into different groups for which different sanctions could be used. The new system of supervision for conditionally sentenced young offenders was regarded as especially promising. The juvenile prison's role was also emphasized as an institution of training and education, vastly different from ordinary prisons.

As late as the 1950s, the new act was held to be very progressive and significant. The poor results received from the supervision of conditionally sentenced offenders were regarded as temporary, and could be offset by the use of sufficient resources. The collapse of the great hopes for the juvenile prison was blamed primarily on the poor prognosis of young offenders sent to this institution. As far as is known, no one questioned the necessity for a special system for young offenders, not in Finland nor anywhere else in Scandinavia. The opinions of the time reflected strong treatment optimism, which emphasized the responsibility of the social welfare authorities. One saying that was often repeated was that a young person's offense was always a symptom of a personality disorder that should be cured as early as possible.

However, the 1940s and the 1950s were not totally lacking in reform. The first committee appointed by the government to reform the legislation on young offenders began its work as early as the end of the 1940s. The report led to some minor reforms dealing with the term of imprisonment in juvenile prison. These reforms served to emphasize the treatment ideology: the decision on the length of the term was now left to the enforcement stage, while previously the decision was made automatically on the basis of law. However, in practice the reform led to a moderation of the system.

The Period of Criticism: The 1960s and 1970s

It was not until the 1960s that the criminal policy climate in Finland changed. In part, this was due to the attention that was being paid to new criminological research. In particular, studies of hidden criminality and studies of the effects of prisons deserve to be mentioned. The joint Scandinavian hidden criminality studies, which were carried out at the beginning of the 1960s with army inductees, had a significant effect on decision making in Finland. Reports on these studies are included in Anttila and Jaakkola (1966), Stangeland and Hauge (1974), Werner (1971), and Greve (1972). The results seemed to show that at a certain age it was statistically normal to commit offenses, and thus also suggested that committing an offense was not a symptom of a deviant personality. They seemed to cast doubt on the current doctrines on the need for treatment. It was argued that the attempts to uncover criminality at an early stage and the idea of relating treatment efforts with these attempts were based on false premises. Even though committing an offense at a certain age usually was a passing phenomenon, those who were caught—and especially those sentenced to institutions—repeated their offenses. (Bengt Börjeson's book, *Om påföljders verkningar* (Reactions following the consequences of crime), was especially instrumental in arousing public debate.) The step from this to the labeling theory was short: it was asked whether or not society should react to offenses as leniently as possible instead of as harshly as possible, as the process of being labeled as an offender seemed to make the difference between those for whom criminality was a temporary phenomenon and those who became recidivists.

During the same decade studies were also carried out in Scandinavia, especially in Norway, on prisons and their effect on inmates (Galtung, 1959; Mathiesen, 1965). The experiences of inmates and the observations of outside sociologists seemed to demonstrate that the institution lessened instead of increased the possibility of resocialization after release. The old beliefs about contagious criminality received new support. As a means of counteracting prison culture, it was proposed that the use of conditional sentences be increased and that short-term solitary arrest be adopted.

Other Scandinavian studies compared traditional prisons with some treatment institutions used for offenders. (One of the first was Christie, 1960. Several pamphlets were published on the question in the Scandinavian countries during the 1960s.) It was clearly demonstrated that compulsory treatment in an institution was no better than a prison sentence. As a matter of fact, in some respects it could be worse, as the legal principles traditionally connected with the criminal justice system were by no means always taken into consideration when sending someone to a treatment institution or when setting the length of the treatment. The implication drawn from this was that inefficient and unjust compulsory treatment should be abandoned and replaced with manifest punishments.

During the 1960s, which in general were typified by a spirited discussion of the goals and methods of criminal policy, attention was also paid to the problem of the cumulation of sanctions. It was demonstrated with examples taken from law practice that the same offense often resulted in a number of negative sanctions, some of which were called punishment, others treatment, and yet a third group, administrative sanctions. As the cumulation of sanctions was often based on random factors and was rarely, if ever, planned, demands were raised for a full investigation of the matter and a reform of legislation. (Viewpoints touched upon in Scandinavian criminological debate are to be found in Anttila, 1966.)

The new thinking is reflected in the mid-1960s in the report of the commission appointed by the Ministry of Justice (Committee Report 1966:A 2, in Finnish only). The commission noted the prevalence of hidden criminality, the dangers of becoming set in a pattern of crime, the errors of treatment ideology, the contagious criminality in prisons, and the injustice of the cumulation of sanctions. The commission primarily wanted to reduce the use of unconditional imprisonment for young offenders. A controversial proposal of the commission involved replacement of long-term imprisonment with weekend arrests. The commission also wished to reserve the juvenile prison solely for those special cases where treatment was needed, and even in these cases, no indeterminate sentence was to be allowed.

The commission did not, however, propose a curtailment of the special system for young offenders. Nor was this done by another committee which continued the work a few years later (Committee Report 1970:A 9, in Finnish only). Possibly the most significant proposal produced by the latter committee was the suggestion of a radical reduction of prison sentences for young offenders by converting them to short strict-regime sentences. The proposals did not lead to new legislation.

The beginning of the 1970s brought some new features to the discussion. As in classical jurisprudence, the emphasis was placed on the offense instead of the offender. Punishment was to be proportionate to the criminal intent or recklessness of the offender manifested in the offense. It was not to be determined on the basis of the personality of the offender or on any supposed need for treatment. The significance of equal and uniform legal practice was emphasized. General deterrence was now regarded as the main goal of the criminal justice system; this goal was to be reached through a system where the punishments would be as light as possible, but the risk of detection was essentially raised. (For a discussion of the outlines of the new trend, see Törnudd, 1975.)

This new ideology has also been apparent in Finnish legislation. The number of recidivists simultaneously incarcerated in preventive detention fell from 300 to under 10. With another reform, the higher sentence scales for recidivists were removed, and instructions on sentencing were included in the penal code to unify sentencing parctice. (The Act on the Incarceration of Dangerous Recidivists in preventive detention was amended April 23, 1971, and the entire penal law chapter on recidivism (chapter 6) was reformed on June 3, 1976.)

Another trend of the 1970s emphasized the necessity of separating coercion and social service. Coercion was seen as an essential element of the system of penal sanctions. Social service, on the other hand, was something that the state was obliged to arrange, but only on a voluntary basis. Thus, for example, the compulsory supervision of prisoners released on parole could no longer be defended with reference to the need for treatment and care. Instead, supervision was interpreted as an "afterpunishment." In 1972, the Committee on Probation and Parole proposed that the parole period be shortened radically, compulsory supervision be abandoned, and social service activity be noticeably increased (Kriminaalihuolto Komitean mietintö, 1972). Of the proposals, one has been realized. In 1976, the period of parole was considerably shortened, which has automatically lessened the significance of compulsory supervision. The Statute on the Enforcement of Sentences was amended on December 3, 1976.

A separate and highly evolved system for young offenders no longer seemed to be compatible with the new ideology. As a consequence, the legislation on young offenders has been the focus of continuous attention during the last few years. A working group of the Ministry of Justice prepared several proposals for reform from 1973 to 1975. However, these did not lead to any new legislation.

The Present Situation

At this writing, a new development is to be seen. The newest plans for reform are included in two recent proposals. One of these was published in March 1977 in the report of the Penal Law Committee planning a total reform of penal legislation. The other is a separate proposal by a so-called one-man committee (Rikosoikeus Komitean mietintö, 1977). The former committee is concerned with long-range planning, while the separate proposal can be carried out within the next few years.

A common feature of both proposals is that they aim at doing away with the special legal status of young offenders. This is primarily explained by the ideological shift outlined above. In addition, some other factors may have influenced the proposals. For example, the penal sanctions have in general become less severe. Nonprosecution and absolute discharge, which previously were possible for offenders under eighteen, can now be used for all offenders. Also, the prerequisites for the use of a conditional sentence have been eased. The use of imprisonment at hard labor has been completely dropped from the system. Thus, the traditional arguments for humaneness no longer necessarily demand a special system for young offenders.

During the past few years the whole prison system has also been reformed. The scope of open institutions has been broadened. The prisoner's contacts with the world outside, as well as the facilities for education and leisure time activities, have been increased for all age groups. Young offenders no longer need special provisions.

In the following, the main features of the reforms will be reviewed on the basis of the short-range proposal. Most of its proposals are also included in the report of the Penal Law Committee. The separate proposal contains, among others, the following proposals for the repeal of present provisions:

The special provisions on nonprosecution and absolute discharge for young offenders would be repealed.

The prerequisites for conditional sentences would be the same for both young people and adults. Young offenders could no longer be placed under supervision (probation). The suspended sentence would simply mean what it now does for adults: the enforcement would be suspended for a certain period and the sentence would be enforced only if a new offense is perpetrated.

A special juvenile prison would no longer be needed; the same imprisonment sentences would be used for both young people and adults. However, a new provision would be included according to which an offender under eighteen at the time of the offense could be sent to prison only when "the general obedience to the law demanded by general deterrence" calls for this or when there is another exceptional reason.

The personal history reports for offenders over eighteen shall be abandoned. In the Young Offenders Act of 1940, the personal history reports are regarded as an expression of modern criminal policy, as they could be used to give every offender an individualized sentence. Today, criminality is no longer compared with an illness for which one must find a cure, and the court's task is not regarded to be the formulation of a diagnosis. The personal history report system also has noticeable drawbacks, as the family and acquaintances of the offender are made aware of the offense.

In the proposal the personal history reports are, however, retained for the youngest age groups, those fifteen to eighteen, principally for achieving a certain coordination with the provisions in the Child Welfare Act. Personal history reports for older offenders would be compiled only when the court orders this for exceptional reasons. Psychiatric examinations of the sanity of an offender would of course still be carried out when needed.

According to the proposal, the following provisions would remain:

> Offenders between fifteen and eighteen at the time of the offense would still receive the traditional general mitigation. The maximum of the punishment scale would be the same as it is at present—three fourths of the normal maximum. The minimum would be fourteen days in prison or one day plus a fine. The special rule excluding the use of life imprisonment for young offenders under eighteen years would remain in force.

> Even though juvenile prison as a separate sanction would be abandoned, the prison administration would still reserve certain institutions mainly for juveniles. The youngest prisoners, as well as those young prisoners who are in need of special education, would probably be sent to these institutions. On the other hand, a young offender could be sent to an ordinary open prison when this seems suitable. The placement would be entirely left to the prison administration, as would the release on parole.

The proposals also include two new categories of punishment, both of which would apply to both adults and young people. These would be a punitive warning and punitive supervision.

A *punitive warning* would be an alternative especially to conditional sentences, but also to fines when these are unsuitable because of the financial circumstances of the accused. It would be a serious admonition given by the court, used principally for first-time offenders. It would be noted for some months in the criminal register.

Punitive supervision could, by order of the court, be connected with a conditional sentence. It would involve reporting to the police one to six times a week for a period of one to three months. This sanction would not involve any treatment; the offender would simply "check in." If the offender neglects to report to the police his conditional sentence can be enforced.

Some Conclusions

According to the ideological background of the reform, compulsory measures directed at a young offender over fifteen would be concentrated in the criminal justice system. The punitive elements of the system are deliberately made as manifest as possible. The severity of the sanction should be related to the offense and the criminal intent or recklessness apparent in it, not to the personality of the offender or the supposed need for treatment.

Under no circumstances should the system hinder young offenders from obtaining treatment in the institutions, for example, psychiatric care, psychological therapy, and vocational guidance. However, the length of the sentence would not be based on a supposed need for treatment but on the offense and the guilt shown therein. In the same way, one would clearly differentiate between the noninstitutional sanctions and the treatment, given only on a voluntary basis. Social welfare authorities could in the future concentrate on the support and assistance that are an essential part of their field, and would not be as greatly burdened with control policy. This would emphasize the independent position of social welfare.

If the reforms are carried out, this would complete the cycle: young offenders would be returned to the general penal system. Only the general mitigation of punishments and the limitations on the use of prison for offenders under eighteen years would remain. In other respects, one and the same system would concern all offenders over fifteen years of age.

11

Criminology: A Turning Point in its History

Jean Pinatel

The death of Karl Otto Christiansen occurred at a turning point in the history of criminology. Will it be swallowed up by social pathology? Can it abandon the empirical inductive method in the experimental stages in favor of anticriminological dogmatism? Is it strong enough to help revive the challenge of criminality? These are the main problems which face us today and which we must confront without recourse to the science and wisdom of our too soon departed friend.

Fashion in criminology is dominated by the inclusion of criminality in the vast and disparate whole of deviant behavior. From here to the assimilation of criminology into social pathology is but one step. This step, however, is not taken without hesitation by true criminologists.

In the presence of this tendency, it is fitting to turn to the beginnings of scientific criminology. From the outset, there has been a question whether to define crime as an objective reality. From this point of view, there was much temptation to keep to the legal definition given in penal law. It was a temptation to which the first criminologists did not succumb. After much hesitation and controversy, in which Durkheim (1938) and Tarde (1924) opposed each other and which D. LaGache (1950) later cleared up, it was finally agreed that crime—a very wide concept which was considered synonymous with misdemeanor and breach of the law—is an aggression against group values arousing in the members of that group an emotional reaction leading to punishment. Precision was brought to this definition in 1885 by Garofalo. This precision rests on the distinction between natural crimes, which offend the elementary feelings of pity and integrity to be found in all groups, and conventional crimes, which relate to values which can vary according to time and place. The fundamental object of criminology therefore appeared to be linked to the concept of natural crime. Breaches connected with homicide and violence, theft and related conduct, rape and sexual aggression, belong at this fundamental criminal level.

The definition thus given and the precision thus introduced have brought criminology out of the commonplace, where it had belonged until the first scientific studies were undertaken. It has indeed been proved that natural crime is distinct from conventional crime, is always defined as an aggression against values and arouses this specific social reaction, namely punishment.

Nowadays, one should be even more restrictive. It is only possible to speak of crime if the following three conditions are present: (1) the act in question must have been condemned, under various methods, throughout the history of penal law; (2) it must be considered a breach of the law by the groups which constitute the modern state; (3) its accomplishment must have been experienced as an offense by its perpetrator, who must have made a special effort of subjective autolegitimization in order to envisage performing the act.

The combination of these three conditions brings one into the area of the fundamental criminal level, that belonging properly to pure criminology, as distinct from social criminology. To the latter, which has the task of approaching problems of social pathology from a criminological point of view, belong the various forms of deviant behavior (alcoholism, drug addiction, sexual deviations, suicide, vagrancy, and prostitution) as well as practices arising from the domain of social discipline (road accidents, work, financial fraud), or sexual and family morals (abortion, adultery). This contribution of social criminology is of a differential nature and must allow the more or less prominent criminological aspect, which exists in these phenomena of social pathology, to be brought into focus.

The obstruction encountered by social pathology goes hand in hand with the vogue from which anticriminology has benefited during recent years. Everything has already been said about this movement of ideas on the political and general planes. However, the clinical views of anticriminology—which were exposed by Denis Szabo, based on the work of Michel Philipson, at the Twenty-sixth International Conference on Criminology (1976)—have not been stressed.

Anticriminology claims that it is no longer necessary to look for the causes of delinquency, but rather its significance. What counts is to grasp, through empathy, the delinquent's point of view. This attitude is by no means new to criminology. It was the attitude of De Greeff (1946), the great Belgian scholar whose work dominates contemporary clinical criminology. To him goes the credit for declaring that the delinquent should be approached in total sympathy, enabling, "without, however, showing approval, the understanding of his own line of conduct, thereby establishing a certain communication between the examiner and the examinee." But what distinguishes De Greeff's criminological attitude from that of anticriminology is partly the short phrase "without, however, showing approval," and partly the fact that comprehension is not sufficient, that, after having placed oneself on the axis of the responsible "I," one must then "apply scientific concepts to the experienced phenomenon," in other words, endeavor to find the explanation for criminal conduct.

De Greeff (1946) made his theory more specific by saying that the criminal, like all people, is seeking that which will remove him as far as possible from pain or suffering, that his act therefore corresponds to his most balanced state, and that he could not refrain from doing what seemed best to him. "And it is precisely this", he added, "which constitutes the problem of criminogenesis. How is it that this man seeks his good in what appears to us as an aberration?"

One can thus see that what separates clinical criminology from anticriminology from the start is a moral attitude and a scientific attitude. On the one hand, unlike the anticriminologist, the clinician does not identify with the delinquent. On the other hand, the course of criminology, as opposed to anticriminology, does not limit itself to comprehension, but tries to discover the objective explanation of criminal conduct.

The moral attitude which is fundamental to the criminologist is proscribed by the anticriminologist. What he will try to define are, based on the perceptions of the criminal, the emergence, the transmission, the perpetration, and the modification of the sociocultural significance of his act. The role of anticriminology is to take the part of the subject of its study, to know the delinquent and to understand, throughout his perception, the significance, the scope, and the meaning of his delinquent behavior. It is here that clinical criminology is radically opposed to anticriminology. In fact criminology, according to the excellent formula of D. LaGache (1950), is to morals what psychopathology is to psychology. That is, clinical criminology is above all a moral pathology. "One can only study a problem of criminogenesis," said De Greeff (1946), "if one considers that there is such a problem, and that the crime whose genesis is being studied is truly a crime. The man who wants to study theft can do so only if he considers theft to be really wrong".

But anticriminology does not merely take the side of the delinquent. It also takes the side of the class to which the delinquent belongs. What it wants to emphasize are the relationships of dependence, exploitation, manipulation of the weak by the strong, of the wage earners by the property owners. Thus, the political and economic principle of class struggle is introduced into the proceedings of anticriminology. It follows that there is no possibility of establishing a scientific method based on the observation of facts, the hypothesis arising from these facts, and its verification.

This antiscientific attitude is found in connection with the actual performance of the act. Here, anticriminology suggests that the performance of the act does not result from an objective motive or from a strong determination, but rather from spontaneity, liberty, and subjectivity of action. In so suggesting, this attitude introduces the theories of the old schools of penal law, and the perspectives of existentialism. For criminology the performance of the act is simply one person's response to a situation. The experience of this response is for him based on several factors. For, to quote De Greeff (1946) again, "the 'I' is by no means the man: what goes on in his consciousness 'is minimal compared with what goes on in himself'; the 'I' is no more than the moment when a number of mechanisms become conscious, allowing the emergence at this point of confrontations, comparisons, judgments, choices, which are not necessarily in harmony with the whole being". At this point it could be suggested that the experimental stage of anticriminology is simplistic. To limit oneself to discovering the significance of an act, to identify with its perpetrator, to proscribe any moral attitude, to take the part of a social class, to reduce the performance of the act to spontaneity, liberty, and subjectivity of action, all this comes from a philosophical-political point of view which is cut off from reality, from general ideas that have no empiric basis.

The danger of this dogmatic approach taken by anticriminology is that it tends to leave in the dark and to neglect a large part of criminal reality. Therefore, there is a preference, in clinical criminology, for the approach which was always that of Karl Otto Christiansen and which has recourse to an empirical process in order to observe and gather facts, to group and systematize them, and to extract from them working hypotheses which will in turn be scrupulously checked. In applying this inductive method, he set aside his own beliefs, his prejudices, his ideology, in order to concentrate exclusively on facts. This is the path he followed in his splendid research on delinquent twins.

Is there an area in which this scientific precision can be moderated? In particular, is it possible, faced with the challenge of criminality, not to become involved in criminal politics, even in the absence of established facts?

For my own part, I became aware of the challenge of criminality on the occasion of the International Conference on Criminology, held in Montreal in 1967, at which I realized the stress felt by the most highly qualified specialists in the United States in the face of the formidable growth of criminality in their country. On my return to France, I was struck by the fact that our rapid economic development, together with urbanization and the living conditions it entails, was Americanizing our country. I then had the feeling that French criminality would model itself on American criminality in years to come. Since then I have continually pronounced my conviction. In 1969 I stated the following in a report I presented to the European Council on Criminological Research in France (Pinatel, 1970):

> From the general point of view of the situation of criminological research in France, the question arises of knowing what its future will be. The answer can be given with precision: the future of our criminological research depends on the development of our criminality. In France, as in most other European countries, criminality has remained until now a minor phenomenon, except in times of unrest. The low level of criminality did not bring about, on the governmental plane, awareness of an important social danger. It was therefore enough to allow the traditional penal administration to operate. But at the moment, continental Europe is getting closer to the American model. This is true from the point of view of economic and social development and is equally true of criminality. Adolescent violence, the first appearance of drug addiction, the development of organized crime and its techniques—its manifestations fluctuating and fragmented —make possible the prediction that criminality will, within a few years, constitute a grave danger to society. We should already organize ourselves against this menacing danger on the basis of coordinated research.

This conclusion was also adopted by M.A. Benton, controller of penitentiary activities in the United Kingdom. But the late Karl Otto Christiansen often said: "Perhaps Pinatel is right. However, I think that we should study more closely and in greater detail the evolution taking place in Europe before we begin to organize the struggle against criminality as it exists in the United States."

In 1971, wishing to alert public opinion, I published *La Société Criminogène*. Sadly, it came too late and appeared at the same time as highly publicized, terrible and dramatic criminal acts drew the attention of the French public harshly to the criminal problem. Five years later, a committee on research into violence and delinquency was set up in France at the highest governmental level.

I have brought up these facts only in order to illustrate the difficulty of criminology's position faced with the challenge of criminality. From a strictly scientific viewpoint, Karl Otto Christiansen was undoubtedly right. In 1969, the truth of my intutition had not been proved; there was merely a collection of signs predicting future development. But should we wait for the situation to take an irreversible turn before suggesting a criminal policy? If criminology remains a merely factual discipline, it risks being quite useless to criminal policy. This is why there is one area, in which Karl Otto Christiansen was much interested, which merits greater attention: that of future research on the evolution of criminality.

The conclusion I wish to draw from this short survey of the main problems existing today in criminology is a double one. On the one hand, it is incontestible that the dogmatic method should not be allowed in either general or clinical criminology. To accept facts as they are, this is the sole attitude of the criminologist—an attitude followed by Karl Otto Christiansen. This will lead to the recognition of a pure criminology, one which cannot be reduced to social pathology.

But on the other hand, the problem arises of the relationship between research and action, between pure criminology and criminal policy. Should we, because of the inadequacies of our predictive techniques, and the slowness of our research, wait for the situation to develop in one direction or another before proposing a criminal policy? Scientific rigidity is leading inevitably toward this restrictive attitude. But then what is the practical use of criminology?

I believe that the duty of the criminologist is to take a stand, at the risk of playing Cassandra, when he is convinced that dangerous development is approaching the domain of criminality. However, it will be said that it is contradictory to advocate a stand in this case, and to condemn the dogmatic attitude in the experimental stages of anticriminology.

I think that an important distinction should be made here. What I think is open to criticism in anticriminology is the tendency to attach a scientific image to an approach based essentially on ideas, and on a preconceived ideological system. On the other hand, intervention in criminal policy, based on anticipated facts, does not make the same scientific claim. Criminal policy is both an art and a science. As an art, it permits the use of intuition where there is no certainty.

The personal gratitude I feel toward Karl Otto Christiansen is that he allowed me to clarify my position on these difficult problems, and perhaps to contribute by these reflections to the clarification of others' positions.

12 The Criminal Justice System and Public Opinion

Philippe Robert

One of the salient aspects of contemporary criminology is its increasingly frequent recourse to procedures drawn from the sociology of representations (Henshel and Silverman, 1975). If one tries to see clear in the abundance— promising but confused—of budding attempts, this observation has two rather troubling correlates.

First, it is far from apparent that all those who opted for this path have specified beforehand what it was capable of contributing, in what way its utilization was likely to be legitimate and fertile. One sometimes gets the feeling that a certain criminologist's recourse to the procedures of representations in sociology rests on the illusion of finding answers that are simply not there, that could not be there. What such a path could actually offer is often left aside.

Second, the manner in which this recourse operates is often inadequate; an insufficient conceptualization therefore extends itself into a crippled methodology. And the result is distressing. Where false consciousness about public opinion might have been shaken up, it is merely reinforced—another abdication to the deceptive charms of so-called common sense.

Nonetheless it seems plain to me, after several years of research on this theme, that what the sociology of representations has to offer represents one of the most promising paths among those opening up to contemporary criminology. But this potential fecundity requires our throwing sufficient light upon the *why* and, correlatively, upon the *how* of such research. A sufficient amount of work on the subject exists to reasonably attempt such an exercise.

It also seems to me that this double effort at reflection, partly problematical, partly conceptual and methodological, is particularly appropriate for honoring Karl Otto Christiansen whose scientific career, I think, bears two lessons for us: he knew how to be a pioneer in a variety of very different sectors of criminology; yet in these various domains, he maintained equal quality and equal rigor in carrying out his research enterprises. This is the same pair of characteristics that had struck me during one of my first discussions with Karl Otto Christiansen which concerned—if I recall correctly—the different forecasting methods in criminology. It is this memory that comes back to mind as I

Translated from the French by Brooke Maddux.

attempt—in the altogether different domain of representations research in criminology—to specify successively:

What it is legitimate to expect from such research.

The conceptual and methodological difficulties most frequently encountered.

Some basic principles for carrying out such research correctly.

Criminology and Representations Research

Reading the countless studies on representations in criminology, one gets the impression that their authors are participants in the quest for a new legitimacy of the criminal justice system. They seem to take their stand in accordance with the expectations of those they work for, indirectly or directly, the legislator, the administrator, or the judge. These last note the existence in the majority of our countries of a pervasive sense of crisis in the penal system in need of remedy.

For several years, it was thought the cure-all might be found in social engineering or technological criminology. But this effort has now proved unsuccessful. This school of criminological thought was guilty of an epistemological laxity which allowed it to accept as postulates all the commonplaces and *idees recues* concerning the penal justice system, whereas it would have been better to regard them as mere hypotheses to be tested through investigation. In this way, such a research trend eliminated the object of its research. To the basic premises, the result added only esoterism or mere "recipes." Common sense assertions—even dubious ones—were simply restated in complicated terms; or one settled for a patch job despite a steady worsening of a crisis affecting the level of the penal system's social function while affecting little, or only on the rebound, the level of its functioning.

Faced with this undeniable ineffectiveness, the more perspicacious decision makers have, more or less plainly, modified their diagnosis; behind the crisis in the criminal justice system, they think they detect a crisis of legitimacy. This makes it tempting to ask the criminologist to provide the foundations for a new legitimacy. And, to this end, he is encouraged to reveal what, with regard to penal matters, is the state of public opinion. We would only need afterward to translate into laws and judgments this state of opinion, and penal justice will have been brought into step with the times in one fell swoop, wedded the form of its era and seen its legitimacy fortified or recovered.[1]

Evidence of this expectation may be found in the manner that various penal law reform commissions seek, throughout the world, to utilize a familiarity with opinion. This is done, not for the purpose of discovering—just one element among others—the various kinds of attitudes and expectations about penal law, the informal substructures of certain social control mechanisms of crime, but in order to have access to a sort of average opinion as a yardstick for shaping the law.

But such a demand presupposes that public opinion is unified. It leads the researcher—if he allows himself to be thus "pushed around"—to postualte a model of *consensus*. It locks him into the old postulate of judicial ideology that defines the law as the expression of the general will.

To expect this from research studies on representations is to take out a guarantee on the mediocrity—and the uselessness—of such research, because one is postulating what can only constitute one of the hypotheses of such a procedure. So the considerable value to criminology of an investigation into social representations must be sought elsewhere.

Little by little, social control of criminality is emerging as an autonomous object of study for the criminologist. In the last decade, the interest taken in this theme was really limited to making it a privileged variable in the explanation of the etiology and genesis of crime. We have more recently come to understand that it can only be truly studied if we concede it the status of a specific object of study (Robert, 1973, 1975).

But the mistake has often been made of centering all attention upon the mechanisms and institutional agencies of the social control of crime. And the penal system was hence considered as amounting to a more or less complex ensemble of institutions or agencies sustaining systemic relations between them. With attention restricted to this institutional complex, the danger of returning to or remaining ensconced in a pure functionalism is evident. These institutions of criminal justice, however, are just the tip of the iceberg. To understand the whole of this process of social control of criminality, we must prove ourselves capable of sounding the far greater mass which remains submerged. To put it differently, not only is social control of criminality not entirely institutionalized, but the functional portion is too often neglected. This is why the knowledge of social representations is indispensible.

First, the concrete functioning of the penal system heavily depends upon the representations of law, crime, the criminal, and justice that circulate in the society (Robert, 1977).

In order to reach the repressive institutions, the facts and their circumstances have to be sufficiently visible or someone has to call the police. Visibility depends on objective conditions which vary considerably with the case. There is no need to be a scholar to realize that some people spend the better part of their lives shielded from indiscreet glances while others live almost permanently uncovered; the latter's illegalities are more visible than the former's. And this visibility is strongly linked to the status (particularly professional) of the agents, and, finally, to their place in the social structure. But visibility is not all there is to it. The facts that the repressive agencies actually discover on their own initiative are not the most numerous.[2] When you come right down to it, most information that reaches the penal authorities does so through outside sources. Naturally, this calls into play the objective conditions of reportability. Certain offenses—untowardly called "victimless"[3]—such as those with a consensual or conspiratorial nature, are less likely to be denounced either because no one recognizes himself individually and personally as a victim, or because the victim is prevented from appealing to the repressive mechanism. This applies to a good part of organized crime and big business criminality. The opposite is true, however, in attacks on individual property, from car theft to armed robbery, which have a maximum chance of discovery by the police for the simple reason that insurance companies often require this step prior to the declaration of loss. But reportability also calls into play other less apparent but equally influential mechanisms. The decision to notify the police about something finally depends to a great extent upon one's representations of the offenses (Do we consider the behavior which we have witnessed or been a victim of a "genuine violation"?), of the delinquent (Do we classify the offender among the "real delinquents" appropriately ascribable to penal repression?), and lastly of the penal system and its adequacy (What is it supposed to do, able to do?). In short, police knowledge of an event often depends upon:

Objective conditions which vary with social standing, such as greater or lesser visibility or the circumstances pushing for or against reportability.

Representations of the offense, of the delinquent, and of the adequacy inherent in each control apparatus, including the system of criminal justice.

The influence of representations on the functioning of the penal mechanism does not come to a halt with this preliminary but fundamental phase. A few studies (Chamboredon, 1971; Robert et al., 1976) have shown that the penal justice system operates upon the raw material it discovers or with which it is supplied by a sorting and elaboration leading to the final product. This product takes shape through the successive phases of this systematic process. Constantly coming into play are, in particular, the representations forged by the operators of the penal system, that is, their professional ideologies.[4]

But these representations, which significantly condition the functioning of penal justice in the sense that lines of conduct are a combination of attitudes and situational constraints, do not occur through spontaneous generation. In the final analysis they depend on the structure of the penal apparatus, its functioning, and above all, its production. Representations of the criminal justice system show the existence of powerful stereotypes that rest upon the production of a standard image of the finished product. It may also be observed that the apparatuses of ideological production (the press, for example) diffuse such stereotypes and similar standard images. And the existence of this ideological colonization nourishes the mechanism through which the penal system progressively constructs its object. Among the data and individuals that make up the initial raw material, certain elements are selected and others are rejected. Then, those which have been conserved are reconstructed according to the internal logic inherent to the system and to its social function. Its intervention—made possible in fact by the situational constraints and the representations of external intervening parties, elements which far from being aleatory differ significantly according to the social structure—appear with the ineluctable attributes of fate. By virtue of this operation, the standard images of the clientele of penal justice and the adequacy of this apparatus to one intervention or another are edified. It so happens that it is this finished product which partially emerges and thus it is the most visible. It is easy to understand the place reserved for it in the production of representations of the offense, of the offender, and of the penal system.

Even so, these representations are not a photograph. Everything in the penal apparatus is not equally visible or equally comprehensible. Furthermore, visibility and esotericism also vary with the situation of the different social classes, class fractions, categories, and strata. We should add to this the existence of intermediaries, ideological entrepreneurs who inform, form, and deform. And we should also take into account the fact that penal justice has a long history, so that any change today will take a long time to erase the traces of yesterday. It must not be forgotten either that the penal system cannot be represented in isolation, that its image must be inserted into certain conceptions of the world, visions of life in society. Last, in the determination of the actual lines of conduct of the different pertinent social groups, attitudes must interact with various situational constraints.

All these considerations explain why the representations of the penal system that may be forged have their own consistency and a certain relative autonomy with respect to the system's functioning. Yet it must be remembered, on the other hand, that representations, for their part, condition to a considerable extent the functioning[5] and the production of penal justice. Thus a thorough knowledge of the penal system can only be enlarged through the examination of social representations.

The reality of the penal apparatus is not restricted to what this apparatus is today, even if the weight of history is taken into account. It also resides in the contradictions, conflicts, and expectations which may be observed in relation to this reality. It seeks its definition within a constantly unstable and permanently threatened equilibrium, in a dialectic of the instituted and the instituting. And this necessity—in view of a sound knowledge of the penal system and its social function—for situating it historically in an unstable present between a past and a future makes an investigation of representations of still greater urgency. This investigation must be carried out with relevance, which is no easy task. The question, although important, can only bear fruit if a multitude of precautionary measures are taken.

The Difficulties

How do we attain these representations of the penal system? Why, of course, I can hear the reader say, you are talking about so-called public opinion. But here we are exposed to all the false certainties of common sense, to those old mistaken ideas that serve as a basis for superstitious beliefs and that undermine any effort to get at the truth.

Few are those who harbor any doubts about the state of opinion concerning whatever is penal. Quite the contrary, the word is on every tongue and invoked at the drop of a hat. One might well lay down arms before such assurance. But the doubt arises from seeing that few agree on the content of an opinion that each, nonetheless, declares unique.

One ends up wondering if—despite the best intentions—he who speaks emphatically about public opinion is not just decking out in this garb his own idiosyncrasies, the chit-chat of his friends and acquaintances, or the opinion of his newspaper or television station.

And since nothing can halt technical progress, many people believe they can now discover public opinion in the opinion polls—so fashionable at the moment—published regularly in daily newspapers.

Alas, public opinion does not exist, or exists only as an attempt to create a false consciousness out of nothing. Beneath the deceptive veil of public opinion so dear to common sense, we must seek in depth what representations circulate in the society with respect to the penal system. The majority of productions which concern our purpose, whether research or polls carried out by commercial groups, employ a quantitative methodology. There are, however, a few which opt for qualitative procedures. And this distinction facilitates the exposé of the difficulties or traps which must be avoided, but this is not always (or even frequently) attained in practice.

The Pitfalls of Quantitative Procedures

We shall concentrate our attention successively on four points: the first two concern data gathering and focus on the construction of the gathering implement and on the selection of persons to be questioned; the other two are more concerned with the exploitation of this material, they aim at the problem of their transformation into variables and that of postulates for interpretation.

Sampling and Representativity. When recourse is had to a quantitative procedure—highly standardized and applicable to a large number of subjects—the ambition most frequently pursued is one of representativity. A population of respectable size with the characteristics of a sample is used. If by chance this is not done—either because one wishes to test certain implements and treatments

(Robert and Faugeron, 1973a) or because the obstacles encountered are insurmountable—it is essential to know enough to limit one's ambitions and, above all, one's interpretation. Several problems then traditionally pose difficulties.

We will not go into all the intricacies of the various sampling techniques. (In this domain, purely random sampling is rarely done.) We shall simply call to mind some of the predominant pitfalls for our field.

A sample is never worth more than its theoretical basis of determination[6]. A national sample, for instance, generally refers back to the last known census. One then comes up against a time gap because censuses are rare and take a long time to analyze and underrepresent categories with no fixed abode or whose lodgings depart from the norm (temporary quarters, tenements, room or dormitory set-ups). This can present problems if, for instance, one is interested in a possible penal experience the interviewees may have had; we know that the clientele of the penal system is concentrated in certain sectors of society.

It is important to remember that representativity also stops at our own preestablished limits. Most of the polls on the penal system in the United States actually concern only the age group over eighteen or even over twenty-one (Hindelang, 1975). Nor does representativity go any further than the limits of the variables one controls. In the quota methods, for instance, generally only the sex, age, socioprofessional category of the family head, the size of the locality, and the region are controlled. The field must also have been responsibly covered and its representativity verified. In the case where no public or university polling organism exists, one is most often obliged to go through a private firm which operates under a rule of maximum profitability. The quotas may be globally respected, but important variations in the subquotas are frequently observed. So it is a usual occurrence—if a close eye is not kept on things—to find underrepresented the manual workers, rural dwellers, and young people—categories with a reputation for being difficult to find or to question. This may be of slight importance when it comes to selling margarine, but it is a very different story when the investigation bears on penal questions that are so intimately related to norms and mores. In order to remedy these distortions, the sample is often "adjusted," which means each question is corrected by a coefficient (inferior or superior to 1) to bring it into line with the distribution of a perfect theoretical sample.

Here we uncover a whole series of hidden vices which weigh down the polls on penal justice and, sadly, are not always missing from studies with more scientific pretentions. It would be a mistake to dismiss this as a mere obsession. Certain of these vices can, under certain circumstances, totally and radically disqualify the results. Moreover, it often takes weeks or even months to avoid or correct them. In our field, haste is the mother of many a flaw.

The Data-gathering Implement. Here, the problems are more visible and just as frequent. Of course, it has been said that there is no such thing as a good questionnaire—just some less bad than others. But where penal system representations are concerned, the instruments encountered are frequently detestable. And if the commercial polls published on this problem are close to being in just plain bad faith,[7] there are unfortunately countless scientific studies which fail to distinguish themselves clearly from these deplorable examples.

There are five principal difficulties which must be confronted. The first two are classic in the art of the questionnaire. First is the inference effect instigated by the form of questioning ("yes" inference) or by recourse to stereotyped formulations.[8] Second, induction effects are often observed which arise from the arrangement of the questionnaire (contamination for instance).[9] Three other perils, less apparent but perhaps graver still, must be added. Quantitative research projects concerning aspects of the penal phenomenon are often launched without ensuring beforehand that the aspect of the penal phenomenon under investigation enjoys sufficient visibility. This concept (Robert and Faugeron, 1973b; Robert and Laffargue, 1977) is fundamental for our purposes. Contrary to popular opinion, especially if one confronts penal problems as a jurist, most are barely visible. To pose questions on objects which lack sufficient visibility draws an aleatory response in the best of cases, and most often an induced one. No opinion is gathered. Rather it is created by awkward questioning (Cannel and Kahn, 1959). And the traditional trial questionnaire, even if administered with care, falls short of determining visibility decisively. Other methodologies with a more qualitative style are required. Their prior application would present the additional advantage of remedying a very frequent lack of pertinence in the formulations. Just as the researcher is often tempted to force the emergence of an object of representations devoid of visibility, he tends often in the same way to formulate his question in a manner which seems relevant to him but which is not to the individuals questioned. A very important point, and one which has been remarkably pointed out by Kutchinsky (1972), is neglected here: representations of law, crime, the criminal, and penal justice generally possess a very mediocre cognitive dimension and one which contrasts with their affective-normative intensity. To organize a questionnaire around an essentially cognitive grid therefore amounts to removing the better part of its relevance. And here again, no test can ensure against mistakes. The quantitative investigation must take root in ground cleared beforehand by other procedures. And finally, questionnaires often err in the penal field on the level of their comprehensibility and universality. Admittedly, this is a delicate point. But how much better armed is the researcher who, instead of throwing himself from the outset into a questionnaire procedure, takes the time to probe the heart of the verbal material he has previously gathered from less standardized approaches of a nondirective nature. And as an additional boon, he then knows how to arrange the batteries of questions in order to eliminate certain ambiguities or to go beyond the various stereotypes.

The difficulties concerning the data-gathering implement are not limited to these questions: they extend even further to questions of criteria (characterizing the population) which are still less likely to attract attention. Very often, no effort is made to complete the questionnaire other than by a "classic" set of such questions. In actual fact, the selection of these criteria and the status each one may appropriately be attributed cannot be determined in the context of a purely methodological reflection, ordered in its entirety according to precedents, usages, and possibilities. They depend upon a hypothetical conceptual reflection.

From the Data to the Variables. Here we come to an absolutely crucial point in the study of penal system representations. There is a common tendency in practice to confuse opinion and attitude. This is what comes of according an autonomous value to each answer. It makes us forget that we are dealing with a pure manifestation of opinion. It is as if we presumed to study the movement of the tides and did nothing more than gather the foam off the top of the waves. An opinion expressed at a given moment is actually strongly contingent upon the situation in which it is expressed. It therefore depends upon the interviewer-interviewee relationship, the impression one is trying to give of oneself, the latest news bulletin, the mood of the moment. This said, it should also be added that the same answer can have different, even opposite, meanings. This is the trap in the case of apparent homologies.[10]

A manifestation of opinion interpreted in isolated fashion means nothing on its own, except perhaps as a mystification. Only the interpretation of a group of answers, the interrelations of which have been explored, is meaningful. In more theoretical terms, this simply means it is taboo to work directly on the data gathered, to treat each piece of data separately and successively, and to attempt to explain each one directly by a simple relationship to the criteria. It is necessary to study these data in such a way as to extract the dependent variables. Afterward an attempt may be made to explain the variables by the criteria. This remark has consequences for treatment methods because it leads to disqualifying the nonetheless common procedure of cross sorting data and criteria. Here, too, we are gathering only elementary data. The criteria are usable only after they have been the object of an internal arrangement, of a construction of real criteria variables. And this cannot be accomplished unless there already exists a clear hypothetical conceptual scheme of the possible explanatory relationships.

We are confronted here again with a key problem: it is impossible to carry out a relevant piece of work on the representations of the penal system without first undertaking such a theoretical elucidation. Of course, we are perfectly aware that similar research rarely proceeds by a strict hypothetical deductive scheme, but rather by an inductive procedure. This is precisely why it is indispensable to make a first effort at hypothetical conceptual elaboration, even if only to clarify the sequence of concepts and their implementation, which calls for an attempt at theorization. In its absence, an inductive procedure is doomed to fall into empiricism. And this has a most precise significance to representations; it forces us ineluctably to surrender, hands and feet tied, to the most stereotyped of common-place clichés— the exact opposite of an attempt to bring out representations. The absence of this prerequisite (a hypothetical conceptual theorization) also makes it impossible to proceed correctly with transformations of data into variables, be they dependent or explicative.

Without theorization, there is no way to grasp why and how it is possible (and necessary) to go from opinion data to attitude variables and representations. In its absence, it is impossible to see why the ideological zone that has just been reconstructed only becomes truly comprehensible via a complex process in relation to the social structuring. With this in mind, one must not settle for "explaining" ideology by ideology, or neglect the complex (and dialectical) processes which exist between this instance and the social structure in its historical development. For example, the strong correlations observed between representations of the penal system and political and religious attitudes are not mutually explicative; they merely reflect common adherence to different sorts of ideological configurations.

Such an attempt at hypothetically conceptual clarification should also make it possible to surmount another difficulty attached to quantitative procedures.

Postulates for Interpretation, or, One and the Multiple. Research studies on the representations of penal problems very frequently suffer from the clandestine existence of implicit postulates, the plausibility of which appears dubious. It would be worthwhile to move to the status of research hypotheses which could be confirmed, invalidated, or modified.

Such research is heavily weighed down by a frequent and implicit hypothesis of consensus. The strength of this hypothesis derives from the fact that we are working in a strongly normative domain. Take for example the assertion of law as an expression of the general will. As a zone of intersection between the political and the ideological, law feeds upon an ideology of consensus. To borrow Ferrero's (1945) expression, it is one of those choice areas where one may perceive "the guardian spirits of the polis" who sustain power more mightily and continuously than naked force. This phrase is likely to wear itself out quickly from overuse ("You can do anything with bayonets," said Talleyrand, "except sit on them") such that the everyday conception of power is closer in meaning to what the jurists call legitimacy and the sociologists, ideological impregnation. The unfortunate consequence of this state of affairs resides in a tendency to postulate a consensus which is precisely what is presumed to be tested. This was the error of the initiators of the criminality index method and of most of their followers (Weinberger et al., 1976).

Such imprudent and useless postulation leads too easily to reasoning in terms of a majority or average, taken as manifestations of this famous consensus presumed to be there although no one has bothered to verify its existence. In so doing, we run the risk of talking about inconsistent majorities, such as those created when we stop at apparent homologies and illegitimately regroup divergent attitude structures. Similarly, before talking averages, it is necessary to make sure that the distribution of responses does not deprive it of all significance. Otherwise, it would be like taxing with average density a region composed of a big city surrounded by a desert.

Even if they are not totally irrelevant, these arithmetic notions do not mean consensus. What is the concrete significance of this term? We cannot, of course, equate it with unanimity, especially in a society as complex as our own. But the notion of majority is just as unsatisfactory. What cutting-off point should we select? Half-plus-one, for instance, can signify an opposition of two halves of the population that is the exact opposite of consensus. And any other cutting-off point would be purely arbitrary and devoid of any particular sociological significance. Furthermore, if along with a majority (more or less sizable), there exists one or several minorities unified along radically different positions, we cannot speak of consensus; the situation will be one of conflict, of confrontation between majority and minority fractions. In order for there to be consensus, no collective alternative must be found in opposition to a point of agreement unifying a majority. We would still be entitled to treat as consensus the fact that a fraction is ideologically unified on a question as long as outside this fraction, all other positions are atomized. However, whatever the numbers, there will be no consensus if two or more collective positions enter into opposition with each other.

Thus it is impossible to make a decent study of penal system representations if one starts with a consensus postulate that must be tested, or if one settles for notions like arithmetic majority or average, which are likely to be deceptive and which, furthermore, have no particular significance in the ideological domain.

The Pitfalls of Qualitative Procedures

A certain "quantophrenia" has led to considering highly standardized procedures of the quantitative variety as the royal road in the exploration of penal system representations. Such begging of the question, moreover, constitutes in itself one of the major difficulties of this undertaking. There are, however, a certain number of research projects adopting procedures of the qualitative type. But this path is not exempt from a certain number of difficulties. Here, too, we shall limit our examination to a few principal points fraught with practical implications.

Some time may be gained in the exposé if we simply go back to the most fundamental problem which is far from specific to qualitative approaches: the necessity for a prior hypothetical conceptual elaboration. I thought it preferable to treat this question in the section on quantitative procedures since the problem is most often encountered there. With this now thoroughly debated point in mind, two problems remain to be discussed. One concerns the gathering procedure; the other, exploitation of the data.

The Type of Interview. When one proposes taking on a problem of representations which has not yet come up with solid theoretical construction or proper scientific empirical research of sufficient breadth; or when the investigation is intended to bear upon an until now little explored social group or category; or finally, when one feels the need to probe more deeply a particular point concerning representations that the telescope of the broad quantitative investigations leaves in the fog—any one of these three hypotheses calls for inevitable recourse to qualitative investigation techniques. And there is no way of reducing this to the traditional trial test or the pseudo-exploration wrapped up in three months' time.

Even if prior efforts at theoretical elaboration have made it possible to avoid falling from an admirable empirical verification into a pure and detestable empiricism, the implements for relevant exploration of this field still require adjustment. It would appear indispensable to determine and analyze as precisely as possible the field of these representations, their various dimensions, and their organization; in other words, the mechanisms which structure them and the logical thought processes applied to the object of representations. To accomplish this, it is essential to gather discourses, not merely responses, to questions elaborated a priori by the researcher. It then becomes possible to work on material as global as possible, expressed in the language of the interviewees themselves. Such material lends itself to exploration of the links between the object of representations and other areas—meanings (which may be plural) and feelings. In short, we must allow the person being interviewed to determine on his own the pertinent field of his discourse without imprisoning him ahead of time.

Simple answers—limited, cut off from any context which might allow them to be interpreted other than in the imprisoning terms of the researcher's preconceived ideas—could not provide the data that the very nature of the study object demands. It is necessary to have an organized group of elements in contact with the object but fitted out with all kinds of extensions into other domains, even those situated a priori at a distance. These relations and extensions are indispensable if we are to fathom what, in the investigation, actually constitutes the object of research. It goes without saying that they vary according to the relevant social groups. The approach must hence make it possible to apprehend the greatest possible variety. Social groups have neither the same manner nor the same capacity for using language; the organization of the discourse is dependent on the way that mechanisms of ideological colonization operate.

Only open-ended qualitative approaches allow for the gathering of a discourse, although, it should be recalled, just because a procedure is qualitative does not mean it is open-ended, and simply because it is open-ended does not mean that it is necessarily pertinent. A difficulty often arises here. Certainly, there are many interviewing methods, and none of them pretends to be the absolute panacea for our purposes. We found ourselves using, for instance, in one specific case (Robert et al., 1976) a relatively structured qualitative method, the focused interview (Merton et al., 1956), although we employ it rarely in this area of research.

But just because there is no magic formula is no excuse for authorizing recourse to mongrel forms of interview and ones whose relevance has not been assured. Yet this is too often the case in criminal research. Many of the studies in this sector of research have opted for a qualitative procedure, either through well-reasoned conviction or out of sheer desperation confronted with the complexity and cost of large-scale quantitative investigation. But sometimes a vestige of regret leads to adoption of a fence-sitting position. The fact that it is often baptized *semi-directive interviewing* does not suffice to make fertile a hesitant procedure, a muddy methodology poorly linked to the hypothetical conceptual construct. Most of the time, the upshot of this is to lose the benefits of a veritably qualitative exploration without acquiring those of a quantitative study.

In actual fact, except for special cases where recourse to a particular type of interview is called for, it is logical to adopt a procedure which structures as little as possible the field of exploration proposed to the interviewee. Such a broad base must, however, remain relevant to the zone being explored. The goal is thus to induce in the interviewee an attitude of self-exploration of his practices, feelings, attitudes, and expectations with regard to the penal system. We hardly mean to suggest by this that the interview relationship is neutral or that the interviewer has no structuring effect upon the field of exploration. This relationship admittedly remains asymetrical, but the interviewer does not have a monopoly on the exploration as he does in the case of questionnaires with preformed responses.[12]

Outside of those special cases where it is justifiable to resort to a particular kind of interview, the in-depth exploratory interview of the nondirective type appears well suited to our purposes. And, whatever the case, it is essential to avoid falling into the trap of a mongrel methodology, be it overstructured or understructured, even if it is later baptized semi-directive interview where it ought to be called "badly done interview."

We have always found it striking, moreover, to observe that the studies which fail to avoid this pitfall are characterized by a very mediocre level of data exploitation, sometimes aggravated by an inefficient data-gathering technique which makes it impossible to subsequently arrange the material in a satisfactory manner.

Data Exploitation. The way in which interviews are analyzed is clearly closely related to the principle which led to utilizing certain information-gathering techniques rather than others.

Although there is no doubt that supple methods of sociolinguistic analysis are suitable in certain cases (Lascoumes and Moreau-Capdevielle, 1976), and that the linguistic analyses utilized by Raymondis and Le Guern (1977; see also Reasons, 1976; Henshel and Silverman, 1975) could sometimes prove extremely useful, the fact remains that, in the most general cases, the use of open-ended and little standardized information-gathering techniques requires an analysis without standardization or quantification.

As a product of self-exploration (although provoked) the discourse thus obtained cannot be considered as a closed system. It is situated on several levels of significance. Beyond apparent coherencies or incoherencies, beyond the manifest, exists a socioaffective logic which possesses its own coherency but which is not directly forthcoming.

The frequent ambiguity of the manifest and the plurality of pertinent levels of interpretation make it generally undesirable and even virtually impossible to utilize, for the exploitation of such material, formalized content analysis techniques of the Berelson variety, because one would then be obliged to presume the categories unambiguous and univocal. While it is true that frequency can bring to mind an ideological dominance of a stereotype, a statement which is rare or even unique can contribute equally as much to the analysis. Nothing may be considered a priori as irrelevant according to the basic rule laid down by Michelat (1975). Every contradiction, every slip, every unusual element must be taken into account as a symptom to be deciphered.

Such considerations show up in particular relief because of the importance of the interviewer-interviewee relationship; for the discourse is partially structured in response to the way the interviewee perceives the interviewer. (This does not mean that this relationship plays no role in the other type of interview, even the most closed. But the standardization of the material masks and dissimulates that the interviewee's dependency is, in this case, really maximal.)

Based on the manifest statement, an attempt is made to reconstruct the latent, that is, the logic which organizes the discourse and the significance that this logic implies.

It is only through thorough impregnation by the material and successive approximations that it becomes possible to reconstruct the underlying logic. We proceed with a first reading, then form a model interview by interview; next comes their rereading and transversal analysis, finally a return to the models of interpretation which have been sketched out, and so on, until we think we have obtained models which are sufficiently exhaustive and coherent.

It is obvious that such a method puts the analyst himself into the instrument of analysis. He is the one who operates the associations which serve as a basis for interpretation. And the only criteria of validity at our disposal will be, on the one hand, the coherence and exhaustivity of the interpretative schemes, and on the other, the reciprocal criticism of the analysts who seek thus to protect themselves from submersion into each other's personal idiosyncrasies.

No one pretends that this method is devoid of risk, but it will surely be agreed that at least its flexibility lends itself well to the type of exploration contemplated. Highly standardized procedures also have subtle pitfalls. But they cover them up more prudishly. Those who have sufficient practice with one or the other will bear this out. Besides invasion by idiosyncrasies, the worst and most frequent flaw is the lack of exhaustivity in the analysis. This causes anything that resists a first assault to be left aside. The flaw generally goes along with a mediocre interviewing procedure, because the procedure, for the researcher, is a similar one whether at the time of data gathering or analysis. If the researcher's attitude is one of "forcing" the material, it will appear at these two moments in the research.

Some Principles for the Study of Representations in Criminology

The lack of space does not permit me to indulge in an exhaustive examination; I prefer to confine myself here to two types of reflection, one concerning the hypothetical conceptual field, the other regarding principles of implementation.

Concepts and Hypotheses

If we question individuals, it is because their images of the penal system ought to make possible a reconstruction of the types of representations circulating in French society through the pertinent social groups in which these individuals are participants. It is this sociological reality which is of interest. In its absence, we remain in the realm of anecdote. Questioning individuals simply constitutes a detour for arriving at social knowledge. But in order to get there, we must somehow manage to reconstruct the types of social representations. How can this be done?

To different social classes, fractions of classes, strata or categories correspond different conceptions of the world (*Weltanschauung*). They include not only cognitive, affective, and normative elements, but also very generalized attitudes toward the social universe. These attitudes will tend to manifest themselves operationally by relatively stable organizations, responses, or behaviors in answer to stimuli coming from the social universe. They are, in fact, positions, ways of "being in the world." I shall not get involved here in the debate, which may be useless, on the nature of attitudes. I will simply say that the observation of regularities in collective behavior (verbal or not) leads to the presumption that there exists an intermediary or transformation variable that we call attitude. I am really talking, then, about a latent structure which makes it possible to account for relatively stable and organized positions within a certain social context. As organizing variables, these general attitudes instill a prestructuring effect upon specific fields of representations (relative to a social object). Elsewhere, the combination of collective practices and objective situations gives rise to conducts (regularities in real or symbolic behaviors) which generate behavior. It goes without saying that the conducts—as combinations of situational constraints, practices, and general collective attitudes—retroact upon attitudes and upon the vision of the world.

In any event, none of this comes to the researcher on a silver platter. Most generally, he gathers a discourse (or fragments of a discourse) on behaviors, conducts, attitudes, and visions of the world. The first data he obtains are characteristics which are fragmentary in relation to the image that the individual questioned has of the object (here, the penal system). These data must be organized. Two processes may be used to accomplish this. The researcher can begin by reconstituting the corresponding image for each discourse gathered and then seek to detect the specific attitudes (this is the procedure used on a small contrasted population when the images are first reconstructed before proceeding with the transversal analysis). Or he can make these attitudes emerge directly on the basis of the data (this is the direction of scale analysis in quantitative procedure). But in both cases, the idea is to succeed in determining a typology of models of representations. It is important to realize that a differential model (simplified figuration) is operating here. These types of social representations are structured according to specific attitudes.

It is then easy to grasp the necessity for combining quantitative and qualitative procedures in the sense that the latter make it possible to restore in all their diversity the structure of representations as well as their articulations; the former enable us to specify the typology of representations and its distribution within the population.

And one succeeds not only in presenting a typology of representations but also in tying it into the social structure. Specific attitudes toward the object that structure its representations are actually the traces of global attitudes specifying visions of the world.

Of course, it would be disappointing to leave things at that. These visions of the world are not spontaneous creations. We must explain them and therefore be capable of going back to the social structure. To accomplish this, it is necessary to introduce the concept of *ideology*, a central key in our investigation.

The use of this word is frequently accompanied by pejorative evaluations which make of it the antonym of truth; or else it is used to designate a group of ideas that might dominate a person's mind. But these idealistic conceptions do not explain why this ideology exists. The instance of ideology escapes apprehension as a formal unity defined as soon as it is named. If the apparatuses constituting politics—like the penal system—have an ideological production, it is plain that ideology itself cannot be considered as an abstract category or as a concrete object. The apparatuses—for example, the institutions of social control and in particular the penal system—have an ideological production in as much as they have an impact upon the level of practices and systems of thought, constituting them or reinforcing them. This is not to say that these apparatuses function in uniform or absolutely constraining fashion, since they are areas of conflict and naturally fraught with contradictions (corresponding, more or less directly, however, to structural contradictions). In the final analysis, ideology can only be apprehended through or via the bias of manifest behavior, particularly verbal, the meaning of which remains to be deciphered. Ideology may then be discussed in terms of an imaginary relationship to the concrete conditions of existence. This stated, the fact remains that the concept of ideology cannot be clearly explicated unless it is referred to the division of society into classes, each one of which is determined by its position within the forced division of work in the society.

But this nonidealistic acceptance of ideology must not turn into mechanicism either. The political and the ideological (the law capping them both) do not constitute mere epiphenomena. They dispose of a certain autonomy which is reflected in the existence of retroactive mechanisms.

It should also be recalled that the instance of ideology is not related only to the present state of affairs. We note frequent phenomena of hysteresis, of survival on the ideological level of a state of things which has, in actual fact, disappeared, which belongs to history. Furthermore, this way of turning back the clock of history is fine evidence of the autonomy of this instance.

In the last analysis, to the extent that we are dealing with the "imaginary relationship" of collective man to the social universe, as seen in the relations established between the various elements of this universe (the representations of these relations), ideology can only be grasped within a specific framework which is that of representations and social practices or conducts. We shall therefore go about studying this instance—so important in determining the informal substratums underlying the functioning and social function of the penal system—in the form of relationships established within a given representation between the various elements of the social universe.

Once the differentiated models of representations have been reconstructed, it is necessary to bring in the rest of the data gathered by the researcher in order to constitute criteria, that is, in order to account for the social structure. As stated previously, ideology cannot be studied as something in itself which needs only to be named. In the final analysis, it is a question of relating the criteria bearing on the social structure and its tensions, on situations and behaviors, to the variable constructed—the types of representations. This makes it possible to situate the constructed variable with respect to the social structure, even if this relationship is mediate and complex.

But it will not do to settle for crossing the identification data pell-mell with the constructed variable. The former must also be constructed according to the hypothetical conceptual scheme which has been adopted. This means that—outside of the classical characteristics—one must dispose of a criterion relating to the structure of the society. To be more precise, it is important to be able to bring together the types of representations of the various class fractions—although their relationship is neither simple nor unilinear. The data one may have available provide, as an indicator which approaches this criterion to a certain extent, the possibility of going ahead with aggregates of socioprofessional categories. (In this sense, Thomas et al. (1976) prove nothing when they claim to demonstrate the existence of a consensus without utilizing any criteria bearing upon the social structure, not even those drawn from aggregates of socioprofessional categories. And their celebrated criterion of occupational prestige is totally irrelevant in representation sociology.)

Methodological Principles

I do not pretend to give an exposé on methods here, simply to set down a few general principles of methodology or procedure. There are two of them and I think it is indispensable to represent them in any relevant study of social representations in the penal realm.

The first principle is that of successive approaches. It rests upon the ambition of bringing out various representation models instead of burying them forever beneath the preconceived ideas of the researcher, of those around him, or of those who hired him. Contrary to what might be thought, the application of this principle does not mean that an intensive and constant hypothetical conceptual elaboration may be dispensed with. Quite the opposite, therein resides the only protection against the risk of degrading empirical explication into pure empiricism. But this principle implies that research should in fact constitute a battery, or bunch, of investigations[13] in which the possibility of problematical, conceptual, and methodological readjustments is provided for between each of the research phases, the preceding one serving as an exploration for the following one.

The second principle consists in alternating qualitative and quantitative procedures—not by mere juxtaposition or by subordinating the qualitative to the quantitative—but by virtue of a sequential complementarity where the different modes of approach serve to discern progressively the various facets of the object under investigation.

By way of example and in order to avoid a lengthy development, we offer figure 12-1, the organization of a sequential research battery on the social representations of the penal system (Robert and Faugeron, 1973a, b, c; Faugeron and Robert, 1974; Faugeron and Poggi, 1975; Robert and Moreau, 1975; Kandel, 1972; Weinberger et al., 1976; Robert et al., 1975, 1976).

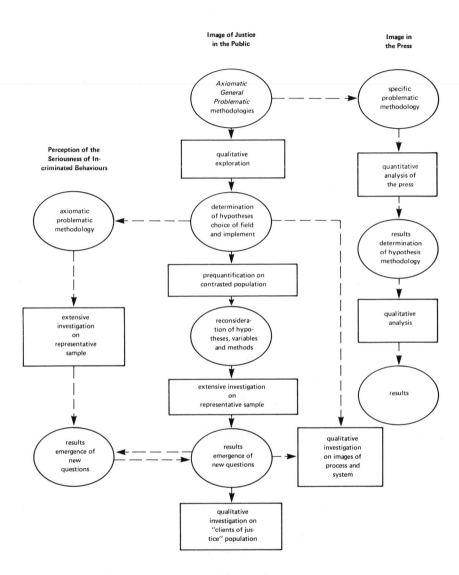

Figure 12-1. S.E.P.C. Research Studies on Social Representations of the Criminal Justice System.

Notes

1. Previous studies on judges' attitudes (Robert et al., 1975) have shown us to what extent they are concerned about remaining in agreement with the pervading state of opinion and mores, failing which they fear being "delegitimized."

2. This point has been remarkably demonstrated in a recent paper (Bottomley and Coleman, 1976) which also has the quality of striking a balance with previous studies.

3. Such infractions weigh, in fact, not on a particular individual but on whole fractions of the population; this is true for fiscal fraud which can only be accomplished on a grand scale by those who declare their incomes themselves (nonsalaried workers, companies) and which is damaging to those who might resort to similar procedures but whose incomes are declared by employers (the case of all salaried employees).

4. An ideology which, just like the public's, is far from transparent for the researcher. Such ideologies are a complex mixture of institutionalized constraints, negotiation on the level of practices, modifications in order to avoid excessive dissonance between norms, and practical reality.

5. In addition to the above-cited reasons, the reader may examine a recent case of utilization of methods of representations sociology in evaluative penology (Chang and Zastrov, 1976).

6. Not to mention those who persist in using the postal questionnaire, forgetting that the reasons for answering or not answering such a questionnaire undergo no control whatsoever, and that one has no right to call this a "representative sample" (for an example see Thomas and Cage, 1976).

7. We are supplied with some caricatured examples by Hindeland (1975) in his not very critical analysis of American polls on penal problems.

8. Take, for example, these questions from American polls (Hindelang, 1975): "The state governor has proposed that all pushers of hard drugs like heroin be sentenced to life imprisonment with no possibility of parole. Do you approve of this proposal?" (American Institute of Public Opinion, study no. 862).

9. Let us cross the Atlantic to choose our next example in a poll carried out in France in 1974 (public opinion poll done by Société française d'enquête et de sondage for the French daily *Sud-Ouest*).

The induction effect here is exemplary. The first question talks about gangsterism. The second associates it with criminality, implicitly reducing the latter to the former. It is hardly surprising then that in the third question—in which it is supposed that police action is exclusively devoted to the struggle against criminality—53 percent of the respondents ask for prolongation of custody. The next question surreptitiously reenlarges the problem ("Generally speaking . . .") while up to this point the action of the police and of justice had been restricted to gangsterism alone. In this way, it manages to get 76 percent of the interviewees to say that justice "tends not to be severe enough." Finally, in the fifth question, the social wrong resulting from violent criminality takes precedence over that created by organized crime and financial delinquency. The very disposition of the questionnaire made this a good bet; and the results provide nothing more than a methodological exercise on how to make people say what we want them to say, which amounts to manipulation.

10. One example are the answers reflecting dissatisfaction with penal justice which constitute only an apparent homology between those who deplore a weakening in the defense of the "values inherited from our forefathers" and those who accuse the penal system of overprotecting the present state of affairs and impeding a change they regard as desirable. If this question of satisfaction is treated in an isolated manner, we would put into the same barrel these two attitude structures which oppose each other on all other points. And the results would deserve no better than history's garbage pail as a final resting place.

11. Worse still when these famous majorities exist at the cost of dubious or debatable counts such as those seen in numerous commercial polls.

12. This problem has been energetically analyzed by Kandel (1972).

13. The concept of bunch research has been exposed in a report to the European Council (Robert, 1971).

13

Law, Crime, and Legal Attitudes: New Advances in Scandinavian Research on Knowledge and Opinion about Law

Berl Kutchinsky

Karl Otto Christiansen's many-faceted work includes the study of public knowledge and opinion about law and other legal phenomena. Around 1950 he initiated an interview survey of legal knowledge and attitudes among a sample of prisoners and a sample of men and women in the general population. This was in fact one of the very first studies of its kind and a model for numerous later ones (see Kutchinsky, 1972). My own interest in the study of KOL (Knowledge and opinion about law) is directly owing to Karl Otto Christiansen's influence, since in 1962 he set me to work on the completion and continuation of these early studies of his. This chapter reports on the recent progress within the Scandinavian KOL tradition which has developed under his constant attention. The chapter is dedicated to his memory with sorrow and gratitude.

In recent years there has been a continued expansion of studies on knowledge and attitudes regarding law, law breaking, law enforcement, legal institutions, and related matters (KOL). This expansion has geographical as well as quantitative and qualitative aspects.

The geographical expansion refers to the fact that scholars from countries like Japan and Brazil have added their contributions to the KOL works so far carried out in several European and North American countries (in particular: West Germany, Belgium, Poland, the Netherlands, France, the Scandinavian countries, and Canada).

Quantitatively speaking, the expansion of KOL research and publications has been steady rather than accelerating, but it is perhaps especially worth notice that the interest in KOL research among postgraduate students has resulted in some excellent studies with equal emphasis on empirical and theoretical aspects (for example, Malow, 1974).

As regards the qualitative expansion I refer in particular to the fact that KOL research has moved into a number of important, but hitherto underdeveloped, areas. In this chapter I shall present examples of such more or less innovative developments, all of them representing recent Scandinavian studies in the field of KOL. These studies will also form the point of departure for a discussion, in the concluding part, on future KOL research.

First, however, it would seem appropriate to say a few things about the term KOL. The word stands for knowledge and opinion about law and was coined, quite accidentally, in conjunction with the establishment in 1968 of the Research Group on Knowledge and Opinion about Law under the Research Committee on the Sociology of Law of the International Sociological Association. Despite this historical connection, I use the word KOL simply for practical reasons as a neutral collective designation for all sorts of research within the wide field of what—with a more adequate but unwieldy term—might be called knowledge, opinions, attitudes and other conceptions regarding legal phenomena. Legal phenomena refer to laws, law breaking and law enforcement, as well as all other concepts, institutions, and categories of persons related to these. Moreover, to the concepts of knowledge, opinions and attitudes may be added concepts such as feelings, beliefs, perceptions, images, symbolic representations, and many more. Within the boundaries of, or at least closely related to, KOL research is the study of such topics as have been termed moral convictions and beliefs, feelings of justice and injustice, prejudice and stereotypes. Finally there is a close connection and overlap between research on KOL and the public survey type of studies on victimization (reporting behavior and attitudes) and studies of so called self-reported crime and delinquency.

The great diversity of purposes and approaches to KOL research will appear in the following review of some recent studies carried out in Scandinavia.[1]

Sweden: Some Preconditions for General Prevention

One of the most comprehensive—in terms of topics covered—Scandinavian studies on KOL of recent years is a pilot survey in a Swedish town carried out in 1975 by Ulla Bondeson of the University of Lund. Four hundred men and women, a random sample of the adult population of the city of Malmö (third largest in Sweden) were interviewed or requested to fill in questionnaires sent through the mail. Since no considerable systematic differences could be observed between the results of the two types of samples, the results were lumped together. The following review of this survey and some of its most interesting results is based on a preliminary report written at an early stage of working up the computerized results (Bondeson, 1975).

The main hypotheses of this study were similar to those of the Swedish pioneer study by Segersted (1949), namely that a number of clear-cut differences exist in peoples' knowledge about and attitudes toward legal rules, and that these differences can be explained on the basis of demographic factors such as occupation, income and fortune, education, political and religious affiliation; situational factors such as level of information and earlier experience; and personality factors such as rigidity and authoritarian attitudes.

In addition to questions about these background variables, questions were asked concerning problems such as the acceptance of society and of the legitimacy of the legal system, various conceptions of justice and equality before the law and the structure of criminalization; severity in general and in relation to specific crimes; conformity and nonconformity with regard to the laws; conceptions about the causes of conformity and criminality; conceptions about the moral education and the deterrent effects of punishment as well as other preconditions for general prevention, including knowledge about the risk of detection and percentages of clearing up; conceptions related to crime and punishment, victimization, damages, and contact with the penal system.

As far as the main hypotheses are concerned, I believe that these were confirmed to a reasonable extent: for the thirty background variables, statistically significant or nearly significant relationships were found with one-third of the dependent variables. The largest number of significant correlations were obtained for the following ten factors, here listed by rank order: income, social level, religious attitude, fear of being assaulted, age, education, experience as guardians, political party affiliation, visit to a prison, and sex. Not all of these variables have been included in earlier studies, but to the extent that comparisons can be made, these findings by Bondeson appear to be in agreement with earlier experience (see Kutchinsky, 1972). A more detailed analysis of the way independent and intermediary variables influence the formation of legal attitudes has not yet been carried out.

Among many other interesting results of this study, I shall confine myself to mentioning those that are one way or another related to the concept of *general prevention*. Despite repeated calls for studies related to this important issue, Bondeson appears to be among the first to engage in a comprehensive and thorough investigation of some of the basic assumptions regarding the deterrent and moral educational effect of the penal system, namely those related to the public perception of the functioning of that system and its various institutions.[2] As Bondeson justly points out, earlier studies on general prevention have placed far too much weight on the actual threat of punishment as this can be measured in terms of detection rates, clearing-up rates, and severity of punishments as indicated in the penal code or meted out in courtrooms. What matters is, of course, not the objective risk or severity of punishments, but people's conceptions about these. People's conceptions about legal matters are to some extent influenced by the objective state of affairs, but by far not as much as most legal authorities, many legal scholars, and—incredibly—quite a few social scientists tend to believe.

Few people have a chance directly to perceive manifestations of the penal system, and if they do, this perception is likely to be rather fragmentary. To most people any influence of the penal system is transmitted through other people and the mass media—whether in the form of nonfiction or semifiction ("news") or fiction (crime novels, detective films). Very often this transmission process forms a long and complex chain, and in each link selection and distortion takes place. For instance, both news reports and fiction stories about crime deal mainly with the most serious types of offenses, which are more often cleared up. News reports, moreover, tend to give more coverage to serious crimes that are cleared up than to crimes that are not cleared up, simply because the former represent news in more stages than the latter. In crime fiction—probably the most popular and at the same time strangely respected kind of entertainment that was ever invented and, to millions of children and adults, the main source of information about the penal system—clearing-up rates are usually 100 percent.

No wonder, therefore, that Bondeson finds a highly exaggerated estimate of detection risk and clearing-up rates in her sample of the general population. There is also, as expected, a tendency toward gross overestimation of the prevalence of serious offenses (crimes of violence committed in public places and by strangers), whereas the prevalence of minor offenses, such as traffic offenses, is underestimated. From the point of view of general prevention, these two kinds of distortion of the public image of criminality and law enforcement might be expected to counteract each other. On the one hand, people generally believe that if they commit a crime they are likely to be punished for it, thus preventing many people from committing crimes. On the other hand, this idea seems to be linked with the more serious types of crimes, the ones that are dealt with in the media. It is likely, therefore, that the less serious crimes (which constitute perhaps 90 percent of all crimes reported and 99 percent of all crimes committed) are often not even thought of as being criminal by the offenders, and the general prevention effect is accordingly more or less cancelled.

Other findings in Bondeson's study which have a bearing on general prevention theory can be summarized as follows:

Only one-third of the respondents thought that "generally speaking, people know what punishment they can get if they commit a crime."

Nearly all respondents thought that "people know little about what goes on in a trial."

A majority of respondents thought it was morally objectionable to punish some people in order to deter others from committing crimes.

A heavy majority believed that people who are punished consider themselves unjustly sentenced.

Nearly all respondents considered it unjust that the family must suffer because a member of the family has committed a crime.

Less than half of the respondents believed that "the laws are in agreement with people's conceptions of right and wrong."

While the findings so far mentioned cast doubt upon the general visibility, the perceived justness, and even the perceived legitimacy of the punishments—all of which are usually, by legal scholars, considered important for the general preventive effects of punishments (Andenaes, 1975)—a series of other questions in Bondeson's fascinating study investigate another one of the pillars of the theory and practice of general prevention: the importance of punishments in general, and, in particular, the importance of imprisonment and of the progression of severity of the sentences.

In order to find out what stages of the judicial process and what consequences of punishments were considered the most important, the respondents were asked to rank order ten different alternatives according to what they thought would be considered most serious. The resulting order of items was (1) losing one's job or place of residence, (2) family and friends would get to know about the case, (3) detection of the crime, (4) the punishment itself, (5) the general publicity, (6) the sentence, (7) the trial, (8) the prosecution, (9) various other legal consequences, and (10) the police investigation.

To the extent that these results can be applied to the question of general prevention, it seems that the general public considers the detection more deterrent than the punishment itself, while the so-called latent functions of the punishment—that is, the officially unintended side effects—appear to be much more serious than the manifest functions. Also, the informal degradation and stigmatization (by friends or family) would appear to be much more important than the formal degradation and stigmatization (by the penal system).

It is interesting to note that these opinions about the suffering connected with various stages and consequences of the criminal justice procedure, opinions which are largely based on the imagination and empathy of persons who have never experienced such a situation, are in rather close agreement with the opinions of a sample of experienced persons, namely a population of institutionalized juvenile delinquents earlier interviewed with similar questions by Bondeson (1974). Less than half of these inmates thought that the worst thing was being placed in the institution, whereas a larger proportion thought the worst thing was to be caught by the police or to be put on trial.

Neither of these studies prove that the imprisonment itself is unimportant. It is possible, and indeed very likely, that the suffering connected with being detected is derived from the suffering connected with the punishment itself. If there were no punishment at all, it would hardly be such an awful thing to be detected. Similarly, the informal stigmatization, the shame and degradation felt by the offender knowing that friends and family are informed about his ill fate, is derived from the formal stigmatization. And the loss of job and home, of course, is a direct consequence of the punishment, that is, a fairly long term of imprisonment.

The significance of these findings, therefore, is not that they tell us that imprisonment is not such a serious matter, relatively speaking. The important thing is that they confirm the notion we have from other sources as well, that something has gone terribly wrong with our penal system since the unintended side effects of the punishments create more suffering than the punishment it-self. (I do not mean to say that this is a completely new development. It has probably come about gradually in the course of a hundred years or so along with the growing humanization of the penal system that partly made incarcera-tion shorter and less brutal, partly turned intended side effects (for example, loss of honor and civil rights) into unintended side effects.) Along with this disturbing fact, however, we learn something extremely positive, namely that the public is aware of the unhappy state of affairs and seems to be discontented with it. This means that there is fertile soil for penal law reforms.

That this "fertile soil" could need some cultivation would seem to appear from another finding in this Swedish study, namely that the classical KOL question "Do you consider punishments in this country to be on the whole too severe, too lenient, or just right?" gave answers similar to those found in Segerstedt's (1949) study, almost thirty years before, as well as in studies from other countries (see Kutchinsky, 1966, 1972). On this highly abstract level, most people consider punishments too lenient (54 percent) and very few con-sider them too severe (8 percent). Other sorts of answers, however, confirmed once again my own findings that at a more concrete level, people tend to be much more lenient, very often, in fact, more lenient than judges.

A very convincing example of the existence of a widespread readiness among the citizens to accept even very radical criminal law reforms (despite the apparent call for more severe punishments) is the opinion expressed in Bondeson's study about the recent proposal of the Swedish Minister of Justice to reduce the prison population of the country from today's 3,700 to less than 1,000 before 1980. The number of respondents who thought that this reduction was suitable or too small was equal to the number who thought that the reduc-tion was too large.

In several ways (and many more than I have been able to mention in this brief review) Bondeson's pilot study lends direct or indirect support to the most important penal law reform in 200 years facing at least the western European and North American countries, namely the abolition of imprisonment as the modal type of punishment for serious offenses. One rather traditional alternative to imprisonment is the use of fines. We shall now look at two Norwegian studies attempting to provide an answer to the old controversy over the deterrent effect of a fine compared to that of a prison sentence.

Norway: Time versus Money

It is well known that Norway has extremely severe legislation and judicial practice regarding drunken driving—probably the most severe in the world. A person arrested while driving a car with an alcohol concentration in the blood of 0.5 pro mille (per thousand) or more (the effect of one glass of beer) is sentenced to an unconditional prison term of at least twenty-one days even if there has been no accident or unorderly driving. This law dates back to 1936, but up to 1958 convicted "pro mille drivers" had the possibility of serving their term under qualified prison conditions—bread and water—which reduced the term by two-thirds; as a result most of the convicts spent only one week in jail. After the prison reform in 1958 which abolished qualified imprisonment, the number of prisoners serving short sentences (mostly twenty-one days) for pro mille driving began to increase rapidly—an increase which was exactly parallel to the increase in the number of cars. In 1972 no less than 5,761 persons had to go to jail for pro mille driving, that is, about one in every 650 Norwegians and one for each 221 cars. These prisoners occupy an increasingly large pro-portion of the total prison capacity of Norway (also because there is a tendency to depenalize other types of offenses), and with the present favorable prospects for economic development in Norway as a result of the oil and gas strikes in the North Sea, it is foreseen that Norway will have to build a whole series of prisons and work camps to make room for the ever growing host of pro mille drivers.[3]

No wonder that Norwegians are seeking alternative punishments. Generally speaking, fines are often not very suitable alternatives to imprisonment for the simple reason that many of those who are sentenced to prison do not have any money. In the case of pro mille driving, however, this argument against fines can be rejected. Most people who drive cars can be expected to be able to pay a reasonable fine. The opposition to replacing imprisonment by fine (in both cases accompanied by temporary suspension of the person's driver's license) is, of course, that a fine does not have a sufficient general preventive effect. This appeal to general prevention has resisted the most heavy attacks on short prison sentences in general and such sentences used for drunken driving in particular. Yet that very argument has been irreparably damaged since the first study by Bratholm and Hauge in 1966.

Bratholm and Hauge's solution to the problem (inspired by Nils Christie) was as ingenious as it was simple: if you want to know how prison and fine— time and money—compare in people's minds, why not ask them? So they hired a Norwegian public opinion poll institute (Fakta) to ask a nationwide represen-tative sample of men and women how much money they would be willing to pay in order to avoid having to go to prison for thirty days (Bratholm, 1967; Hauge, 1968). Much to their surprise, the sums mentioned were very low: 30 percent mentioned amounts of less than 400 Norwegian kroner (at the time equal to approximately $55); 25 percent mentioned sums between N.Kr. 400 and 700, whereas only 10 percent were willing to pay N.Kr. 3,000 (around $400) or more. As might be expected the amounts of money people were willing to pay were proportional to their income, but at all levels of income the proportions were low. Less than half of the respondents were prepared to pay the equivalent of two week's income, and just a tiny group would pay as much as one month's income. In addition to those who either spontaneously or after some encouragement mentioned a sum of money, a number of respondents—18 percent of all the 1,530 persons interviewed—gave various other kinds of answers or no answer; thus 108 respondents said they would prefer to serve the prison sentence under all circumstances, while 18 persons said they would pay all they had, that liberty could not be traded for money, or that the amount of money would depend on what sort of offense they were accused of.

As expected, these results were met with great skepticism. Objections of all kinds were raised, and in order to prevent the findings from being discarded on purely technical grounds, it was decided to repeat the study in 1972 with certain changes that took into account objections raised against the method and technique (Bratholm and Hauge, 1974). This time reference was made directly to the penal practice with regard to drinking and driving, and the respondent was asked to imagine that he or she had been taken for that offense and was offered the choice between twenty-one days in prison and a fine; how much would he or she be willing to pay in order to avoid going to prison?

Despite the changes, the results of the 1972 study were almost exactly the same as in 1966. True enough, the amounts of money people were willing to pay had gone up from a median sum of N.Kr. 722 in 1966 to 985 in 1972, but this increase was almost precisely the same as that of the price index. When inflation was taken into account, the result was that the median sum people would pay in 1966 was 4.2 percent higher than the median sum of 1972 (that is, 771 and 740 kroner, based on 1968 kroner). A difference in that direction was to be expected since the term of imprisonment to be traded in was thirty days in 1966 and twenty-one days in 1972.

In the 1972 study the question of suspension of the driver's license was also brought into the picture. The respondent was first informed of present practice according to which someone taken for drinking and driving has his driver's license suspended for two years in addition to the unconditional prison sentence. The respondent was then asked to imagine that he had been taken in for this offense and sentenced to prison. How much would he be willing to pay as a fine in order to avoid having his driver's license suspended for two years?

In this case, the amounts mentioned were about 50 percent higher than the amounts people were willing to pay in exchange for a prison sentence—a median of N.Kr. 1,480 for two years without driver's license as against N.Kr. 985 for twenty-one days in prison (both 1972 value). Further questioning clarified whether the respondent had a driver's license and how often the respondent would drive a car. As expected, people who had a driver's license and who drove a lot were willing to pay higher sums in order to avoid suspension than people without licenses and people who seldom drove. On the whole, however, the sums mentioned were unexpectedly low, although higher than what people were prepared to pay to avoid a prison sentence.

One should think that the simple and unambiguous results of these two very reliable and carefully executed studies ought to have immediate legislative consequences. After all, these results strongly support a kind of penal reform which would also have the best possible consequences in terms of a cost benefit analysis. Through a combined punishment of suspension of the driver's license and a fine of, say, one month's income, one would in all probability obtain a better general preventive effect than hitherto, while at the same time getting rid of serious administrative and human problems and turning an increasingly heavier economic deficit for the state into a considerable profit.

Nevertheless, there has been no change in the Norwegian laws on drunken driving. The majority of leading Norwegian politicians refuse to accept the findings of the study as a valid reflection of the realities of this issue and continue to believe that the threat of imprisonment is necessary to keep up the general preventive effects. According to Hauge and Bratholm one reason for this rigidity on the part of the politicians is their own personal position regarding the prison sentence: to them the sentence of a term of imprisonment, no matter how short, would be a social catastrophe, it would mean public humiliation and the end of their professional career. To people in general, on the other hand, this short prison sentence, which can be served during a holiday and therefore may be expected to have a minimum of unhappy side effects, does not appear to be very much of a deterrent. Also, going to jail for pro mille driving, because it happens to so many otherwise respectable people (every Norwegian personally knows somebody to whom it has happened) and because it appears to be a stroke of bad fortune rather than the result of bad conduct (many Norwegians seeing a neighbor going to jail for pro mille driving cannot help thinking that it could have been them), does not have a stigmatizing effect on ordinary people; it is not a socially degrading event. This seems to be true even to the extent that persons who are sentenced to short-term imprisonment for other, more traditional offenses are said to take advantage of the nonstigmatizing consequences of serving a pro mille sentence by pretending, if possible, that they have been convicted of pro mille driving.

The main objection against Bratholm and Hauge's studies, brought forward by those who have qualms about giving up the unconditional prison sentence, has to do with the hypothetical nature of their enquiry. They maintain that there is a long way from the purely fictitious and inconsequential choice by the survey respondent between two options, of which one (the fine) does not exist, in a purely hypothetical situation, to the actual behavior of people in the real situation. It would therefore be hazardous to take serious political steps on the basis of the findings in such a study.

This objection would be valid, to some extent, if the purpose of the study was to predict how convicted pro mille drivers would actually react if given the choice between twenty-one days in prison and a fine of a certain amount. It is likely that in such a concrete situation a number of factors would become important which did not have any influence at all in the survey situation and vice versa. That, however, was not the purpose of the Norwegian studies. The purpose was to get an estimate of the deterrent (and perhaps morally educative) effect of the threat of being punished by a fine as compared to imprisonment on potential pro mille drivers. We do not know if the deterrent effect (and the moral educative effect) works at all, but without entering into this problem we can study the prerequisite of any effect of a threat of punishment, namely the relative severity of that punishment as perceived by those who are expected to be effected by the threat. There is hardly any better way of doing that than the one used by Bratholm and Hauge, and there could be no better sample to ask than a representative sample of the general population with special regard to that part of the sample who have driver's licenses and who drive fairly often. The answers of the sample as a whole are of interest to the question of the morally educative effects of the threat of punishment, while the answers of car drivers, of course, are directly relevant to the deterrent effects of the threat.

The point is that the psychological distance between the interview situation and the real life situation to which the results of the interview are to be applied, does not seem so large that one may expect considerable discrepancies between the two. In both cases there is reference to a future, hypothetical situation (being caught in the act of pro mille driving) which neither the interview respondent nor the potential pro mille driver may be expected to consider very likely to occur.

The question of psychological distance between the test situation and the relevant real life situation, as measured along a number of dimensions such as level of abstraction and generality, degree of realism, and of ego involvement, is important for the validity of all KOL research (see Kutchinsky, 1972). The studies by Bratholm and Hauge are examples of research to which this question becomes crucial. This is not just because of the immediate and indeed very important applicability of their results. The study which we are now going to deal with is an example of research of primarily theoretical interest, to which the question of psychological distance is equally important.

Sweden Again: Delinquency and Neutralization Techniques

This concerns an exploratory study of the norm conceptions of school children carried out by Erik Lasner and Edward de Montgomery at the Institute of Criminal Science of the University of Stockholm (1974). Paper-and-pencil questionnaires were completed in April 1974 by all the pupils in seven classes in the ninth grade in two schools in Stockholm—a total of eighty-eight boys and sixty-five girls in the age group around sixteen years. The explicit purpose of this very careful study was to test some of the "classical" crime theories, in particular certain theories about juvenile delinquency. Since some of these theories are based upon certain assumptions about the legal norms or legal definitions of potential offenders, they can be put to a more or less crucial test by means of KOL research (Kutchinsky, 1972). Very conveniently, such studies do not require large representative samples of the general population; on the contrary, specific purposive samples, for example, of delinquent or nondelinquent youngsters, are required.

In studies combining questions about certain types of legal attitudes with self-reported delinquency, interesting results in this regard have been found by Clark and Wenninger (1969), Syren and Tham (1968), Waldo and Hall (1970), and Hindelang (1970).

Hindelang (1970) studied in particular the theory by Matza (1964) on delinquency and drift when trying to assess whether delinquents were indeed "committed to their misdeeds." According to Matza's theory there should be no difference between the moral attitudes of delinquents and of nondelinquents. Nevertheless, Hindelang found that juvenile delinquents were significantly more approving of acts they themselves had committed than were those who had not committed these acts. In my review of Hindelang's study (Kutchinsky, 1972), I suggested that, contrary to Hindelang's assumption, one should indeed find that delinquents looked more leniently upon the acts they themselves committed because of the so-called neutralization techniques employed.

The concept of neutralization technique (very much akin to the psychoanalytic concept of defense mechanism) refers to a more or less unconscious tendency of someone committing a criminal offense to "manipulate" his own perceptions and expressed opinions of certain matters in such a way that it permits him to break the law without considering himself "a criminal." These techniques have been pointed out and described by Sykes and Matza (1957).

Neutralization techniques are exactly what the young Swedish criminologists Lasner and de Montgomery set out to study. For this purpose Sykes and Matza's theory was split up into a number of hypotheses. Each hypothesis was put to test on the basis of one or a series of pertinent questions. I shall deal with some of their hypotheses and results which have never been published in an internationally understood language, but deserve to be known. First, it must be mentioned that a factor analysis of several items indicated that it was possible to divide the respondents into three main categories according to their "inclination to commit offenses." This was done on the basis of the respondents' answers to whether they would consider stealing a transistor radio in a department store. Half of the respondents (40 percent of the boys and 63 percent of the girls) declared that they would "definitely not" do such a thing, 35 percent (44 percent of the boys and 23 percent of the girls) thought they would "most probably not" steal the radio, and the remaining 15 percent were either uncertain or would "perhaps," "probably," or "definitely" commit the offense. In this trichotomy, therefore, we have one category of absolutely conforming (AC), one group of relatively conforming (RC), and one group of nonconforming (NC).

The first hypothesis tested is fundamental to the theory of neutralization:

nonconforming youths should more often than conforming youths be inclined
to think that committing a criminal offense does not necessarily make someone
"a criminal." This hypothesis was tested on the basis of the respondents' reactions to the statement: "Committing an offense does not necessarily mean
being a criminal." The answers are given in table 13-1. Although a large proportion of respondents in all of the three "conformity groups" agreed to this
statement, there is nevertheless such a clear tendency in the direction of supporting the basic hypothesis of the theory of neutralization that further exploration
of elements of the theory is warranted.

The first technique pointed out by Sykes and Matza has been called *denial
of responsibility*: nonconforming youths or juvenile delinquents are more often
than conforming youths inclined to waiver responsibility for the criminal act,
to assert that "delinquent acts are due to forces outside of the individual and
beyond his control such as unloving parents, bad companions, or slum neighborhood" (Sykes and Matza, 1957, p. 668). To test this hypothesis, the respondents
were asked to consider the following statement: "Persons who commit crimes
often have more trouble and problems than other people." Again, the hypothesis
was clearly supported (table 13-2) although a majority in each of the three
categories disagreed with this statement.

A further concretion of this hypothesis also yielded results in the same
direction: the statement "unfortunate home conditions make many people
commit crimes" was rejected by no less than 95 percent of the ACs and 85 percent of the RCs, as against 71 percent of the NCs.

The next hypothesis has to do with Sykes and Matza's second technique
of neutralization, which has been called *denial of injury*: "The criminal law has
long made a distinction between crimes which are *mala in se* and *mala prohibita*
—that is, between acts that are wrong in themselves and acts that are illegal but
not immoral—and the delinquent can make the same kind of distinction in
evaluating the wrongfulness of this behavior" (Sykes and Matza, 1957, p. 668).
One way of doing this is, for instance, to consider a car theft merely an act of
"borrowing." That this neutralization technique may indeed be at work among

Table 13-1
"Committing an offense does not necessarily mean being a criminal."

	Agree	Uncertain	Disagree	Total	(N)
AC (%)	46	26	28	100	(76)
RC (%)	57	29	14	100	(52)
NC (%)	74	26	0	100	(23)

Source: Lasner and de Montgomery (1974).

Table 13-2
"Persons who commit crimes often have more trouble and problems than other people."

	Agree	Uncertain	Disagree	Total	(N)
AC (%)	3	8	89	100	(76)
RC (%)	2	12	86	100	(53)
NC (%)	33	9	58	100	(24)

Source: Lasner and de Montgomery (1974).

nonconforming youths was clearly indicated in the reactions to the following statement: "To borrow a bicycle when you have to go home late one night is not a serious offense." In table 13-3 it can be seen that this question discriminates very strongly among the three groups.

The kind of neutralization technique designated as "the denial of injury" has also been studied in a more direct way, the hypothesis being that the NCs more often than ACs and RCs will tend to deny the harmful effects of criminal acts. The reactions to the following statements highly discriminate among the three conformity categories: "It is all right to break the law once in a while as long as it does not directly harm anybody." The majority of ACs and NCs have directly opposite viewpoints with the RCs in between (table 13-4).

Lasner and de Montgomery point out that the attitude of the nonconforming category to the act of stealing a bicycle can also be interpreted as being due to a lack of interest in or empathy with the victim. This leads to the third type of neutralization technique: *denial of the victim*. The basis of this technique is the idea that "the injury is not wrong in the light of the circumstances" (Sykes and Matza, 1957, p. 668). There are several ways of denying the victim; for instance, the offender may claim that the victim has only himself to blame for

Table 13-3
"To borrow a bicycle when you have to go home late one night is not a serious offence."

	Agree	Uncertain	Disagree	Total	(N)
AC (%)	14	22	64	100	(76)
RC (%)	28	15	57	100	(53)
NC (%)	50	17	33	100	(24)

Source: Lasner and de Montgomery (1974).

Table 13-4
"It is all right to break the law once in a while as long as it does not directly harm anybody."

	Agree	Uncertain	Disagree	Total	(N)
AC (%)	25	14	61	100	(76)
RC (%)	41	17	42	100	(53)
NC (%)	57	17	26	100	(23)

Source: Lasner and de Montgomery (1974).

the offense. Among two questions related to this hypothesis, one turns out to discriminate very clearly among the three categories (table 13-5).

The hypothesis was clearly supported. On the other hand, this very distinction might perhaps be expected merely on the basis of the way the three categories were selected. Someone who is prepared to steal a radio from a department store might also be expected more often to be prepared to keep a wallet found with a large sum of money.

Another angle of the "denial of the victim" technique has to do with denying that the victim exists at all. This was most clearly expressed in the following statement: "In our affluent society it really doesn't matter if you take something in a department store." Again, the connection was very clear: in the AC category only 1 percent accepted this statement as against 21 percent of the NCs (the RCs were in between with 13 percent). In all categories a majority rejected the statement; the proportions, however, were 91 percent among the ACs as against 66 percent among the NCs.

A number of other hypotheses, related to other theories of juvenile delinquency, including the importance of sex roles, have been tested in a similar way in this excellent study, which ought to be a model for similar testing of criminological theories.

Table 13-5
"If you find a wallet with several thousand Kroner in it, you certainly aught to take it."

	Agree	Uncertain	Disagree	Total	(N)
AC (%)	22	8	70	100	(76)
RC (%)	55	9	36	100	(53)
NC (%)	67	8	25	100	(24)

Source: Lasner and de Montgomery (1974).

One methodological pitfall should be pointed out in this connection. Although we tend to use the phrase, the hypothesis was confirmed, this is definitely a wrong conclusion to draw. It would be better to say that the hypothesis was supported. Strictly speaking, however, the only correct conclusion that can be drawn in a context, such as the present one, where findings are in agreement with what had been expected is that the hypothesis was not falsified or could not be rejected. This caution, which has been emphasized by Karl Popper (*The Logic of Scientific Discovery*, 1959), is not just a matter of scientific pedantism, it is a most relevant and practical fact. That findings agree with what is expected on the basis of a certain hypothesis by no means proves that the hypothesis is correct, just as the finding that the street is wet does not prove a hypothesis to the effect that it has been raining (to use an example from an old textbook on logic). The wet street may be due to the passing of a water cart. Singular concrete observations can only falsify general hypotheses. If the street is *not* wet then it could *not* have been raining just a minute ago.

The fact that findings in the study by Lasner and de Montgomery are in agreement with hypotheses derived from the neutralization theory by Sykes and Matza does not prove that this theory is correct. There may be other reasons for that agreement. Nevertheless, the fact that the theory has stood up to a whole series of crucial tests in this study has certainly served to increase the credibility of the theory. That should encourage other students of criminology to pursue problems along the same lines.

Quite apart from the interpretation, the very fact that we have found quite large and clear-cut differences between a group of supposedly nondelinquents and a group of potential delinquents is in itself very significant since it stands in glaring contrast to nearly all earlier findings in studies where criminals and noncriminals (according to many different criteria) have been compared. It is interesting to note that in the above-mentioned survey of several studies of attitudes among criminals and noncriminals (Kutchinsky, 1972), only one came up with sharply contrasting viewpoints between juvenile delinquents and nondelinquents. That was the study by Ball (1957-58). It will be recalled that Ball thought he had found that 71 percent of the delinquents held positive attitudes toward stealing, as against only 38 percent among the nondelinquents. Upon closer examination of the questionnaire technique, I concluded that rather than revealing something about attitudes toward stealing, Ball's study suggested the functioning of one of the neutralization techniques proposed by Sykes and Matza, namely the fourth technique designated *condemnation of the condemners* (one neutralization technique which Lasner and de Montgomery have not explicitly tried to assess).

In conclusion, therefore, Matza's (1964) theory of delinquency and drift does seem to have gained considerable support inasmuch as all major differences between attitudinal statements of delinquents and nondelinquents appear to be related to the working of neutralization techniques among the former to a larger extent than among the latter. That these are the only major differences so far[4] agrees with my conclusion on this subject in my Council of Europe report (1972). According to this conclusion it would be unreasonable to expect juvenile delinquents to have a delinquent norm system as opposed to a conform or law-abiding norm system of nondelinquents, simply because the majority of acts in both categories are law-abiding. Taking all acts together, a group of registered or by other criteria classified delinquents may commit more criminal acts than a group of nonregistered or by other criteria classified nondelinquents, but in both categories criminal acts are exceptional. The point in neutralization theory is exactly that the criminal act is an exception—an exception due to holes in the otherwise conventional norm system, holes which, however, are enabled by the occasional workings of what could perhaps be called an auxiliary norm system, namely the neutralization techniques.

As has been pointed out by Sykes and Matza (1957), "these techniques make up a crucial component of Sutherland's 'definitions favorable to the violation of law.' It is by learning these techniques that the juvenile becomes delinquent, rather than by learning moral imperatives, values or attitudes standing in direct contradiction to those of the dominant society" (p. 667).

I should like to add that although I do believe neutralization technique is an important component of the etiology of much criminal behavior, I also believe that it offers only one part, and not the most important part, of an explanation. It may be said that neutralization is a necessary condition for a good deal of criminal behavior, but it is certainly not a sufficient condition. The other important components of a fuller explanation of criminality—which have to do with the structure of society and of certain subsystems of society including the family, the educational and the penal systems, the distribution of wealth and power and of opportunities to attain valued goals—can only partially be studied by means of KOL research.

Denmark: The Fear of Crime

As a final example of recent Scandinavian research within the field of KOL, let me turn now to some Danish studies which represent quite a different angle of KOL research, yet an angle of great importance and topicality: *the reactions to crime*. I am not referring to the reactions of the offender, or of the specific victim, or of the authorities, but to the reactions of all the ordinary people who rarely witness crimes directly, but who hear about them from friends or colleagues or, most often, from the mass media.

During the second half of the 1960s and the first years of the 1970s most countries in the industrialized world experienced a considerable upsurge of crime rates (Japan, for some reason, seems to be the only country which has had a decrease in reported offenses). Apparently as a quite natural reaction, there has been a growing concern among the authorities as well as the ordinary person about the crime problem, and a growing fear of becoming a victim of crimes.

It is quite reasonable to expect that when the risk of victimization grows, the fear of victimization grows along with it. It is also quite natural that as the risk of victimization, and accordingly the fear of it, grows people begin to take certain precautions. These can be of a more passive, defensive nature, such as staying off the street at night or staying out of certain neighborhoods, always being accompanied by others when going out, locking doors, ignoring strangers, taking taxies (*avoidance behavior*); or they can be of a more active, counter-active nature, such as installing extra locks, floodlights, bars, electric timers or burglar alarm systems, procuring private guards or a watch dog, and purchasing a gun or another weapon presumably for self defense (*mobilization*) (Furstenberg, 1972).

Logically speaking, the relationship among the growing crime rate, growing concern about crime, growing fear of crime, and the growing frequency of avoidance behavior and of various kinds of mobilization seems to be in order (in particular if we disregard the most drastic sorts of mobilization, such as buying hand weapons, which is probably less common in Europe than in the United States).

Upon closer examination, however, this whole process turns out to be extremely complex, far from reasonable, and perhaps, if it gets out of control, extremely dangerous.

The growing amount of reported offenses may very well be an artifact which, at least in part, may be a direct consequence of the fear of crime itself. It is well known that reported offenses constitute only a very small proportion of all offenses committed. Many crimes are not at all detected (for example, minor property offenses) and when detected not recognized as crimes (for example, again minor property offenses as well as offenses against the person). Even when detected and recognized as being criminal, crimes very often are not reported for a number of reasons, but mostly because the victim does not consider the offense serious enough to warrant police action.

With a growing concern about crime, a growing awareness and fear of this phenomenon, chances are that crimes are more often detected by the victim and when detected more often recognized by the victim as being criminal acts. For example, it is very likely that the disappearance of property which was indeed due to a "natural loss" are defined and reported as crimes, partly because of the awareness of the crime problem, partly in consideration of the insurance. Moreover, such crimes are more often reported by the victim for several reasons. First, fear breeds aggression which in turn leads to a wish for retaliation, or simply to the idea that "the offender should not get away with it." Second, the victim may reason along these lines: "This act is trifling in itself, but perhaps the one who has committed this offense has committed other and more serious offenses. The police may be looking for him this very moment.

In any case, I had better do my part to get him stopped, because who knows what he will do next?" In short, the concern about crimes may "for the sake of society" encourage "good citizens" to report offenses which they would otherwise not have reported, perhaps not even noticed.

So, if growing crime rates create concern and fear, this very concern and fear in turn also create growing crime rates. We have a classical vicious circle, a "crime carrousel."[5] The motive power of this "worry-go-round" is not only inside people, it comes to a large extent from several types of agencies whose prosperity depends fully or partly on crimes, and whose growth therefore depends on a growth in crime rates. I am thinking of the police and other agents of the penal system, persons working in close relationship to the penal system (for example, lawyers, criminologists), the insurance companies, agencies who produce and sell security equipment, private police and protection agencies and the mass media. It is very likely that the profits made by these agencies by far surpass the profits made by the criminals.

Another often overlooked category of noncriminals who profit from crimes are all the good citizens who buy transistor radios, color television sets, cigarettes, liquor, and other goods at half price or less from unidentified strangers—no questions asked. The fact that these respectable receivers of goods and services from the black market are among the most important movers of the crime carrousel hardly keeps them from complaining or even worrying about the growing crime problem. The public cooperation in crime through receiving —a widely accepted short-cut to obtaining scarce goods (Kutchinsky, 1972)— is now being investigated by the United Nations Social Defence Research Institute in Rome. The UNSDRI is carrying out KOL-type studies of receiving in the United States, Brazil, the Netherlands, Tanzania, and Sweden. In Sweden a pilot study of public attitudes toward and knowledge about receiving has already been carried out and reported (Brännström and Hansson, 1975; Elmhorn, 1975).

Let us for a moment look more closely at the mass media. The following excerpts of a recent newspaper article on sex offenders may serve as an example both of the fear provoking function of the mass media and some of the components of the crime carrousel just mentioned.

"A man who constantly suppresses his sexual desires may suddenly explode into violence."

"The awful thing is that we do not know the dividing line that can make one man stop at rape and another go on to kill."

Pathologist James Cameron sees the pathetic results, but he has at least one crumb of comfort for the parents.

"I honestly do believe that in most cases where rape becomes murder the child is unconscious or dead before the real horror starts."

"The problem is that the rapist is often in the grip of uncontrollable sexual instincts. Sexual crimes are greatly increasing, and they are becoming more violent. We are finding bite marks on bodies."

"The best way to cut down the number of attacks is to bring more attackers to the court.". . .

"In homicides in Britain today, the pattern is changing. More and more murders have an underlying sexual cause. Yet we still do not know why."

The rapist is still a makeshift photofit, a fleeing figure fading into the darkness. Catch him and he is still a mystery, a man with a name and a past but no *raison d'etre*. (Italics in original)[6]

It is all there, the repeated assertions that crimes are steeply rising and becoming more violent (despite the fact that, as far as we know, sex offenses in Great Britain as in most other countries have decreased rather than increased during recent years), the appeal to report offenders more often, the reference to terrifying concrete details, the mystification surrounding the acts and the offender, the offender as a completely unknown stranger, the tendency to identify all sex offenses with rape and to suggest that all sex offenses may end up as murder, and the professional "pathologist"—who should know better—as a fear booster.

A newspaper article such as this one is totally destructive; it serves no other "positive" purpose than that of selling the newspaper (and perhaps a few more "security gadgets"). It exposes a true problem, because obviously rape represents a problem, but does so in a completely misleading way which covers up the causes of the problem and points toward no solution. It creates fear, indeed terror, but offers no constructive advice to the fearful. Psychological experiments with animals and humans have simply shown that fear is one of the strongest and most dependable of all motivational factors. It is a repulsive fact that some cynical newspapers have begun utilizing this drive (in addition to, or combined with, the classical ones: sex and aggression) for the purpose of profit.

Thousands of innocent people are victimized by serious crimes. But millions are victimized by the *fear of crime*, created or transmitted and amplified by the mass media. This is another side of the balance sheet weighing the profits of crime against the costs of crime. As has been pointed out by Biderman et al. (1967):

What economists label opportunity costs for feeling safe probably are greater economic burdens of crime for these citizens than the direct costs of victimization. With these precautions go . . . the psychic costs of living in an atmosphere of anxiety (p. 159).

I suppose that somebody who sleeps with a gun under his pillow does not sleep very soundly.

The vicious circle, "growing crime rates breed growing fear which again leads to more reported offenses," also has a more tangible and not less dangerous element. The mobilization created by the fear of crimes in terms of alarm systems and barricaded doors may stop some offenders; but others may decide to learn something about alarm systems and how to get into houses through other openings. In other words, mobilization in defense may lead to mobilization in attack. For every move in crime defense there is a countermove, and for every countermove the criminal becomes more of an expert, a professional man who is not prepared to give up his livelihood (Balvig, 1975a).

Nowhere in the world, I believe, has the crime carrousel gathered so much momentum as in the United States. One sometimes has the impression that it is one day going to get out of control (just like the merry-go-round in the famous Hitchcock movie *Strangers on a Train*). Says James Brooks (1974), Associate Professor of political science:

> The fear of crime in the United States is a fundamental social problem which has not yet received attention in proportion to its severity and which may well prove to be more difficult to treat than criminality itself (p. 241).

Yet more studies on the fear of crime, including secondary analyses of public opinion polls, have been carried out in the United States than in the rest of the world.[7]

Even a small country like Denmark has its crime carrousel, and perhaps the most interesting study so far on the fear of crime was carried out very recently by Flemming Balvig, sociologist and lecturer at the Institute of Criminal Science of the University of Copenhagen, and his associates.

What is so special about Balvig's study is the fact that it was carried out in one particular town in Denmark just after the fear of crime had created an uproar in that town, culminating with a mass meeting where 2,000 citizens gathered in a large hall in the town to express their fear and anger about what they thought was an upsurge in criminality in that town. These people accused the authorities of slackness and demanded more protection, preventive measures, and stricter punishments.

Part of the background for this outburst of public concern about crime was the fact that the area has no less than four institutions for adult criminals or juvenile delinquents, mostly open or semi-open institutions. The citizens claimed that much of the crime committed in this area was carried out by inmates of these institutions. As a matter of fact, the police district of that town, which has about 50,000 inhabitants, has the highest proportion of detainees in all of Denmark.

The angry voices of the mass rally in the town resounded all over Denmark. In all major newspapers the town was cried out as the "Chicago of the North," "a fortress" and "the town of fear"—sometimes in an ironical vein, but with a good portion of seriousness behind it.

Balvig decided to take this opportunity of studying the anatomy, the causes, and the effects of the fear of crime at the peak of an outburst of this fear. Since such a study should be carried out quickly, there was little time for preparation, and the study therefore has the nature of an exploratory pilot. The questionnaires could not be pretested, the sample of interviews had to be small, and so forth. Nevertheless, because of the topicality of the subject, the energy and efficiency put into this project, this study of fear in a provincial town turned out to be one of the most interesting and provocative studies on KOL ever carried out.

The KOL part of the study was carried out toward the end of November 1974— about two months after the big rally—when 126 persons, a representative sample of adult citizens of the town, were interviewed by 22, mainly female, students. In addition to this survey, a number of other studies were carried out: historical investigations, a content analysis of the crime reports of the local newspaper, and descriptions of the actual amount of crime committed in the town. The following is an outline of some of the major findings, based on a report with the title (translated from Danish), *The Theft of a Town —Law-and-Order Tendencies in a Danish Provincial Town* (Balvig, 1975b).

First of all, the various investigations showed that (1) the crime rate in the town was not particularly high as compared with other towns, and it was not on the increase at the time when the rally took place, although it had been going up in the town as in the rest of Denmark for several years; (2) only a negligible proportion of the crimes carried out in the town had anything to do with the penal/social institutions in the district; and (3) the anxious and repressive viewpoints expressed at the mass rally were not representative for the population in general.

As to the last point, only 37 percent of the respondents made any reference to the crime problem when directly asked to point out the negative features of the town. When asked to check the sort of problems that the respondent personally was most concerned about, the fear of the respondent and his or her family becoming victims of a criminal offense obtained a median position in the "hierarchy of fear." A clear number one in this regard was the fear of illness, while the fear of a traffic accident was a clear number two concern. Only then, as number three, came the fear of crime.

It should be mentioned that both of these questions about concern and fear of crime were rather suggestive inasmuch as it was, of course, difficult to disguise the purpose of the investigation. The figures on fear of crime are therefore probably somewhat exaggerated.

Nevertheless, the fact remains that a minority, but a significant minority, appeared to be seriously concerned about crime: 8 percent of all respondents considered the risk of victimization a matter of the most serious concern, and

12.5 percent would nearly all the time or very often think about the risk of becoming a victim. The important question therefore was: What are the factors determining fear among the fearful?

Fear was relatively high among women (although the difference between men and women was not very large), among elderly persons and very young persons, among persons who knew somebody that had been a victim of a rather seriously violent offense, among persons who were frequent readers of crime reports in the newspapers, and among persons who were rather isolated from any direct contact with either criminals or legal authorities.

On the other hand, the fear of crime was relatively low among youngish and middle-aged persons, among persons who had been victims of trifling and undramatic offenses, and among persons who knew present or former detainees, police officers, or correction officers.

Most of Balvig's findings are in line with the conclusions of earlier American studies on the fear of crime—to the extent that comparisons are possible. One unexpected difference, however, refers to the fact that whereas most of the earlier studies found little or no statistical relationship between the experience of victimization and the fear of victimization, Balvig, as mentioned, found a clear tendency in the direction that persons who had been victims of crimes were less fearful than persons who had not been victims. One plausible explanation of this fact offered by Balvig is that becoming a victim of a minor offense (the majority of all offenses, including those referred to in crime statistics) has a dedramatizing effect on the victim. The fear of the unknown is worse than the fear of that which you have only heard or read about. Unless, of course, the concrete experience is in itself fear provoking, such as was the case with those few cases where respondents had been victims of more serious crimes.

The dedramatizing effect of the concrete experience with everyday crimes and everyday criminals, as opposed to the dramatizing effect of crime reports in the mass media, dealing only with unusual crimes, is also apparent in other results and leads Balvig to suggest the following hypothesis: One important determinant of the fear of crime is the "distance to criminals as persons"; the greater this distance the greater the fear, the shorter the distance the lesser the fear of crime.

There is an interesting resemblance between Balvig's hypothesis of *distance and fear*, and my own hypothesis of *concreteness and severity* mentioned earlier in this chapter. The connection between *distance* and *concreteness* has already been touched upon, and the link between *fear* and *severity* becomes clear when the term *aggression* is placed in between.

In conclusion, Balvig makes a number of suggestions as to how the problem of the fear of crime could be treated. He points out a number of alleged solutions, which he classifies into four categories: (1) the solutions that will not help; (2) the fast, short-term solutions; (3) the long-term solutions; and (4) the radical solutions.

1. It will not help—that is, we shall not be able to influence the fear of crime and the corresponding repressive attitudes toward crimes and criminals— if we make arrangements to give restitution to victims of criminal offenses, to sharpen punishment or otherwise escalate criminalization, to increase the power or the quantity of the police force. Nor will it help, according to Balvig, to improve the level of correct information about crimes and criminals. (I am not sure that I agree altogether with this last point—a lot depends upon *how* the information is given.)

2. Short-term solutions could be based on attempts to reduce the distance between ordinary people and offenders through greater contact between inmates and outmates, while at the same time reducing the sensationalism of crime reports in the mass media.

3. Adequate long-term solutions would be an extension and institutionaliza-tion of the short-term solutions, which would otherwise wither away. The goal would be an increase in the common activities between inmates and the sur-rounding community. Prisoners should be employed by workshops and plants of the general community and should attend the general schools, while the people from outside should work in the prisons, use the leisure time activities of the prisons together with the prisoners, and so forth. Press reports should deal with these efforts rather than with the commission of crimes.

4. The radical solutions, of course, refer to complete changes of the in-equalities in society through reform or revolution: radical structural changes which remove the basic sources of tension and antagonism between criminals and the rest of society.

The order of these four solutions to the fear of crime problem is also the order of their effectiveness, according to Balvig. The first sort of measures are absolutely ineffective—as we have seen, they may in fact have quite the opposite effect: mobilization and escalation promotes rather than reduces the fear of crime. The second and the third types of solution are patch-work, whereas only the radical solution goes to the core of the problem.

If one takes a look at the prospects of carrying through any of these solu-tions—those which are politically feasible—the order is the same. Most of the Western countries are oscillating between solutions (1) and (2); that is, between the traditional, repressive, at best restitutive, but essentially ineffective kinds of solutions and the short-term attempts to open up for some sort of liberalization. The long-term solutions may be referred to at international conferences, and the radical solutions may be the goal of small left-wing associations and political parties, but the possibilities of actually implementing such reforms are close to zero. This, I might add, seems to be true not only of the Western world, but of all countries in the world of today.

The Scope and Purpose of KOL Research

When originally planning this chapter, I intended to discuss methodological problems and political implications. As I worked out these ideas, I found it difficult to separate the presentation of the Scandinavian research projects from the more fundamental discussion of methodology and policy. What is needed at this point is some sort of declaration about the purpose of KOL research.

In their recent book on *Critical Criminology*, three British criminologists, Taylor, Walton, and Young (1975) wager a rather fierce attack on KOL studies in general with a special reference to my work in this field. They claim that "the ideological thrust underlying these studies ... is one of social defence: the containment of increasingly complex social conflicts via a law constructed and operated in tune with the predominent social attitudes in a population ... KOL researchers only question their respondents on the 'seriousness' with which they view offenses as defined by *existing* law ..." (p. 36). Furthermore, "The KOL studies are ... concerned ... to specify the existence of a 'variable' (*norm acceptance*) existing invariantly as a medium between law and morality. The fundamental purpose of such studies is to engineer a balance in these relationships in the interest of the continued legitimation of existing social order" (p. 40).

It is certainly true that some KOL research and researchers are concerned with social defense within the confines of existing law (this is particularly true of most of the contributions from eastern Europe). But to claim that this is the only or the ultimate purpose of KOL research in general and of my contribution to it in particular, is not just a gross exaggeration but, in fact, nonsense.

In the comparative study of many KOL studies, referred to but, I regret to say, hardly read by Taylor et al., I concluded that "there is a great discrepancy between what acts are considered criminal, and what degree of seriousness is attributed to them by the law, the courts, and various subgroups of the people. In some societies and regarding some types of crime, these sub-culture differences and the discrepancies between the law and the people are so considerable that it hardly makes any sense to speak about a 'general concept of crime' (Kutchinsky, 1972, p. 84). In addition to the "very great variation of attitudes among individuals ... research has shown that the attitudes of one and the same individual do not necessarily form a consistent pattern—they are often vague, contradictory and subject to situational influences" (p. 85). I furthermore concluded that "empirical evidence indicates that the importance of knowledge about law and legal attitudes for the adherence to legal rules has generally been exaggerated. Broadly speaking, good knowledge about law or positive attitudes towards law enforcement are neither a necessary nor a sufficient condition for being a lawful citizen. Conversely, the lack of legal knowledge, and negative attitudes towards law enforcement, are not inevitably bound up with criminal behaviour. It is especially worth noting that only slight differences were found between the legal attitudes of registered criminals and non-criminals. The majority of criminals have very conventional attitudes towards law" (p. 85).

I should not have mentioned and repudiated the statement by the British criminologists if it were not for the fact that this statement represents a particularly tough version of a rather widespread misunderstanding of the scope and purpose of KOL research—a misunderstanding which, I regret to say, is shared also by some of those who are involved in this kind of research. The latter, of course, do not share the misunderstanding that KOL research deals *only* with public representations of criminal transgressions. Anyone who has read publications on KOL, including my own, could hardly have missed the fact that one particular topic of interest is exactly the borderline area between criminalized and noncriminalized behavior which some people consider deviant, immoral, or antisocial.

So, far from being used, as Taylor et al. (1975) have it, "as resolutions to the problems facing the ruling-groups in the regulation of highly fragile social systems they control" (p. 36), KOL research can be used, and has been used, if not to blow up systems (for that task cannot be accomplished by social sciences, not even that represented by Taylor and associates) then to make those (fragile?) systems perhaps a little (more) shaky. I believe that this point is clearly demonstrated in some of the Scandinavian research on KOL I have just described.

The study by Bondeson has cast serious doubt upon one of the central pillars of the building of the penal system, namely that of the general preventive effect of punishments. Bratholm and Hauge's study launched a crushing blow to one particular part of the pillar of general prevention: that of the deterrent effect of imprisonment. And the study by Balvig and associates clearly pointed out, among other things, the futility, at best, and the dangerousness, at worst, of the traditional crime preventive measures. In an earlier survey of KOL research I have dealt with the Finnish studies by Blom (1968) showing that most people believe there is a very great social inequality in relation to the legal system (see Kutchinsky, 1972). Distrust and lack of confidence in the penal system and its agents has also been shown in several other KOL studies (Kutchinsky, 1968). I could also mention studies indicating that certain kinds of acts which are still criminalized and punished are no longer considered criminal by most people (Kutchinsky, 1971).

Admittedly, many of these results point toward reformist solutions to the problems exposed and analyzed by the KOL research. As a matter of fact, I do think that many, perhaps most KOL researchers are blue-eyed reformists who cling to the hope that somehow, someday their findings may convince legislators of the necessity to carry out more or less radical reforms of the penal system or even of society as a whole. This attitude, however, is hardly restricted to KOL researchers for the simple reason that KOL is a method and a field of research and not a special breed of researchers. The fact is that the study of the perceptions and the conceptions of laws and legal systems, of law breaking, law breakers, and other forms of "social deviancy," of punishments and other reactions, among other people than lawyers is enormously relevant to criminology and the sociology of law. It therefore attracts the interest of social empirically oriented researchers regardless of political and meta-scientific observance. I do not mean to say that this is because KOL is a value free area of research—no area of research has that quality—but contrary to what Taylor et al. seem to think, this field of research is extremely complex and diversified, and therefore it can be used and abused for many different purposes.

This diversity, I hope, has been brought out clearly in the examples of Scandinavian research on KOL. Each of the four studies on which I have concentrated represents quite different but important *uses* of such research. Indeed, these are four interrelated areas into which future KOL research should be directed.

1. The study of the numerous elements of general prevention theories—studies which, I suspect, will hardly serve to consolidate these theories in their classical form, but, on the contrary, will pile up evidence against them and in favor of penal reforms which will remove some of the most repressive elements of our penal systems. It is a strange fact that research of this kind has only just started, although the need and appeal for this type of research has been present for at least twenty years.

2. Another large and important area for KOL research is the study of various aspects of theories of crime and delinquency such as the one reviewed here by Lasner and de Montgomery. Contrary to the situation in regard to theories of general prevention, criminological theories have not infrequently been studied by means of KOL research. But much is still left to be done in this area.

The study of socialization is an area which is covered by both of the above mentioned types of studies.

Although most KOL research may have more or less direct practical application—guidelines for criminal policy in a broad sense—the two mentioned areas are nevertheless somewhat theoretically oriented. The next two areas, on the other hand, are more directly oriented toward immediate application to criminal policy.

3. The study of reactions to crime, in particular the concern about and the fear of crime and its consequences. As already mentioned, these types of studies are extremely important, indeed vital for social life both in the short and the long run. Many more studies of this kind should be carried out. The knowledge we have at disposal for the time being is rather scanty; there is a need to go into many different details, as well as to closely study and test some of the major hypotheses.

4. Finally, research is needed on the possibilities and consequences of penal

reforms, in particular of depenalization, diversion, and decriminalization. (*Depenalization* refers to various forms of mitigation of punishments, such as shortening prison sentences, applying more often conditional sentences or less punitive alternatives to imprisonment. *Diversion* refers to the application of nonpunitive measures outside the penal system (very often in the form of counseling or treatment in liberty) to behavior which is still criminalized; such measures, as a rule, are applied at the presentence or even pretrial stage. *Decriminalization*, finally, refers in a narrow sense to a complete abolishing of penal measures or, indeed, any other type of application of force to control types of behavior which were formerly punishable. In a broader sense, decriminalization can apply also to legislative transfer of the control of behavior from the penal system to other systems such as the civil and the administrative systems.) Three different categories of KOL research related to penal reforms can be distinguished:

1. Studies of public knowledge and attitudes regarding the particular types of behavior which are contemplated for penal reforms, and of attitudes toward such measures, especially among those who are personally involved with the type of behavior in question.

2. Studies related to the possible consequences of such legislative measures.

3. Studies of what sort of communicational/educational measures can and should be taken to accompany penal law reforms in order to obtain the best possible results and avoid negative effects. Sometimes, of course, no particular measures are needed, for example when incest among consenting adults is removed from the penal law (Swedish proposal at the moment). But very often such measures are extremely important, for instance when decriminalizing or diverting various types of behavior related to the misuse of alcohol and drugs.

While these are examples of what I consider essentially important *uses* of KOL research (although they could be misused), I can also think of a number of ways of *abusing* KOL research. In my Council of Europe report (Kutchinsky, 1972) I have mentioned some examples of what I consider abuse of KOL research, namely studies which are aimed at constructing a questionnaire by which to diagnose and predict future criminal behavior of individuals. These kinds of studies are not only useless, but may in fact be dangerous because they are trying to establish a distinction between criminals and noncriminals which is artificial and which may be used to take serious measures against totally innocent people in the name of crime prevention. It is well known that these measures, in addition to being unjust and arbitrary, have a tendency to fulfill their own prophecies.

Another kind of abuse of KOL research is the use of, very often privately ordered, public opinion polls to back up repression and law-and-order tendencies within criminal policy. It is well known that public opinion polls can manipulate interviewees in such a way that nearly any kind of opinion can be produced.

Nevertheless, the danger lies not so much in the fact that these polls are carried out as in the way they are used.

Generally speaking, however, I am quite optimistic about the future of KOL research. I believe—and I think that the studies presented here clearly illustrate—that KOL research can offer valuable contributions toward the shaping of a society with less crime and less repression, better criminal justice and better social justice. I am less optimistic about the receptiveness of politicians to these contributions, but that is another story.

Notes

1. This review of some Scandinavian studies on KOL carried out and reported (mostly in a preliminary form) during the last six or seven years can be seen as an extension of an earlier similar review of studies from the 1960s (Kutchinsky, 1970). The discussion also continues and expands upon considerations in my report in "Sociological Aspects of the Perception of Deviance and Criminality" published in English and French by the Council of Europe (Kutchinsky, 1972). I wish to express my gratitude to Ulla Bondeson, Anders Bratholm, Ragnar Hauge, Erik Lasner, Erik de Montgomery and Flemming Balvig for consenting to this extensive review of their works.

2. See the review of earlier studies of this kind by Bondeson (1975), and the related discussions by Christiansen (1975), Klette, (1975), and Lindén and Similä (1975).

3. For a detailed exposition of the drinking-and-driving situation in Norway and in Scandinavia in general, see Volume 6 of *Scandinavian Studies in Criminology* (Hauge, 1978), which appeared after the completion of this manuscript.

4. In a recent study of institutionalized juvenile delinquents, Ulla Bondeson (1974) has found rather considerable differences as compared to the average population on certain attitudinal items and the knowledge of certain argot words. As far as argot is concerned, the results are hardly contradictory since neutralization is essentially a verbal process in which argot euphemisms may be helpful. This relationship is suggested by Bondeson herself (1968, p. 76).

5. I am indebted to an anonymous student of the School of Criminology in Leuven for the invention of this handy term. This in turn inspired me to produce another neologism, the "worry-go-round."

6. Reprinted with permission from London *Daily Mail*, January 21, 1976.

7. This does not mean much. See my brief exposition of this issue in Kutchinsky (1972), p. 70-71, with references, and articles by Block (1971), Poveda (1972), Furstenberg (1971, 1972), Gibbons et al. (1972), and Erskine (1974).

Bibliography

Adorno, T.W. Soziologie und empirische Forschung. In T.W. Adorno, R. Dahrendorf, and H. Pilot (eds.), *Der Positivismusstreit in der deutschen Soziologie.* Neuwied: Luchterhand Verlag, 1969.

Alexander, F., and Staub, H. *The Criminal, the Judge and the Public.* Rev. ed. Springfield, Ill.: Charles C. Thomas, 1956.

Allen, F.A. Criminal justice, legal values, and the rehabilitative ideal. *Journal of Criminal Law, Criminology and Police Science*, 1959, 50:226-230.

Alonso, W. Beyond the interdisciplinary approach to planning. *AIP's Fifty-fourth Annual Conference.* Washington, D.C., October 1971, pp. 24-28, offprint.

Andenaes, J. General prevention revisited: Research and policy implications. *Journal of Criminal Law and Criminology*, 1975, 66:338-365.

Anttila, I. *The Cumulation of Sanctions Following a Crime.* Ius humanum, Studia in honorem Otto Brusiin, Annales Universitatis Turkuensis, series B, Tom 101, Turku 1966.

Anttila, I., and Jaakkola, R. *Unrecorded Criminality in Finland.* Institute of Criminology, publications series A:2, Helsinki, 1966.

Aron, R. Macchiavel et Marx. *Contrepoint*, 1971, 4:9-23.

Aubert, V. *Likhet og rett: Essays om forbrytelse og straff* (Equality and law: Essays on crime and punishment). Oslo: Pax Forlag, 1964.

Bader-Bartfai, A., and Schalling, D. *Recovery Times of Skin Conductance Responses as Related to Some Personality and Physiological Variables.* Stockholm: Psychological Institute, University of Stockholm, 1974.

Baechler, J. De quelques principes généraux du libéralisme. *Contrepoint*, 1975, 17:125-147.

_____. *Qu'est-ce que l'idéologie?* Paris: Gallimard, 1976.

Bailey, W.C. Correctional outcome: An evaluation of 100 reports. *Journal of Criminal Law, Criminology and Police Science*, 1966, 57:153-160.

Bainton, M.A. Problèmes fondamentaux de la recherche pénologique. *Orientations actuelles de la recherche criminologique, Etudes relatives à la recherche criminologique.* Conseil de l'Europe, 1970, pp. 38-51.

Baldassini-Faini, G. Criminalitá della strada? *Abstracts on Criminology and Penology*, 1970, 10:519-520.

Ball, D.W. Self and identity in the context of deviance: The case of criminal abortion. In R.L. Henschel and R.A. Silverman (eds.), *Perception in Criminology.* New York: Columbia University Press, 1975.

Balvig, F. Af angst for kriminalitet (For the fear of crime). *Socialrådgiveren*, 1975a, pp. 195-205.

_____. Tyveriet af en by. Lov-og-orden tendenser i en Dansk provinsby. Kriminalistisk Institut, Københavns Universitet, 1975b (stencil).

Banks, A. *Cross-polity Time Series Data.* Cambridge: MIT Press, 1971.

Becker, H. *Systematic Sociology on the Basis of the Beziehungslehre and Gebildelehre of Leopold von Wiese.* New York: Wiley, 1932.

————. (ed.). *The Other Side: Perspectives on Deviance.* London: Free Press of Glencoe, 1964.

Bell, B., Mednick, S.A., Gottesman, I.I., and Sergeant, J. Electrodermal parameters in young, normal male twins. In S.A. Mednick and K.O. Christiansen (eds.), *Biosocial Bases of Criminal Behavior.* New York: Gardner Press, 1977.

Bell, D. *The Coming of Post-Industrial Society. A Venture in Social Forecasting.* New York: Basic Books, 1973.

Berglund, E., and Johansson, K. *Rattfyllerister, Rapport nr. 8* (Drivers under Influence of Alcohol, Report No. 8). Stockholm: Kriminalvårdstyrelsen, 1974.

Biderman, A.D., Johnson, L.A., McIntyre, J., and Weir, A.W. *Report on a Pilot Study in the District of Columbia on Victimization and Attitudes Toward Law Enforcement.* U.S. President's Commission on Law Enforcement and Administration of Justice, Field Survey I. Washington D.C.: U.S. Government Printing Office, 1967.

Black, D.J., and Reiss, A.J. Jr. Police control of juveniles. *American Sociological Review,* 1970, 35:63-77.

Blackburn, R. An empirical classification of psychopathic personality. *British Journal of Psychiatry,* 1975, 127:456-460.

Block, R.L. Fear of crime and fear of the police. *Social Problems, 1971,* 19:91-101.

Blom, R. Contentual differentiation of penalty demands and expectations with regard to justice. University of Tempere, Institute of Sociology, 1968 (mimeographed).

Bondeson, U. Argot knowledge as an indicator of criminal socialization. In N. Christie (ed.), *Scandinavian Studies in Criminology.* Vol. 2. Oslo: Universitetsforlaget, 1968, pp. 73-107.

————. *Fången i Fånesamhället* (The prisoner in prison society). Malmö: Norstedt, 1974.

————. Det allmänna rättsmedvetandet (The general sense of justice). Paper presented at the Nordic Conference for Young Researchers in Law, August, 1975a (mimeographed).

————. Survey research as a means to explore general deterrence. In The National Swedish Council for Crime Prevention (eds.), *General Deterrence—A Conference on Current Research and Standpoints.* Stockholm, 1975b.

Borgström, C.A. Eine serie von kriminellen zwillingen. *Archiv für Rassenbiologie,* 1939.

Börjeson, B. *Om påföljders verkningar.* Uppsala: Almquist & Wiksell, 1966.

Bottomley, A.K., and Coleman, C.A. Criminal statistics: The police role in the discovery and detection of crime. *International Journal of Crime and Penology,* 1976, 4(1):33-58.

Brännström, G., and Hansson, M. Inställning till och kunskaper om häleri—en interviewundersökning i Stockholm. C:1 Uppsats, Stockholms Universitet, Sociologiska Institutionen, 1975 (stencil).

Bratholm, A. Bør adgangen til å anvende bøtestraff utvides? Lov og Rett, 1974, 24-38.

Bratholm, A., and Hauge, R. Reahtionene mot promillehjørere (Reactions against pro mille drivers). Lov og Rett, 1974, 24-38.

Brooks, J. The fear of crime in the United States. Crime and Delinquency, 1974, 20:241-244.

Buikhuisen, W. Research on teenage riots. In P. Meadows and E.H. Mizruchi (eds.), Urbanism, Urbanization and Change: Comparative Perspectives. Reading, Mass.: Addison-Wesley, 1969.

Buikhuisen, W., and Jongman, R.W. A legalistic classification of juvenile delinquents. British Journal of Criminology, 1970a, 10:109-123.

_____. Druggebruik en de relatie leeftijd/kriminaliteit bij studenten. Nederlands Tijdschrift voor Kriminologie, 1970b, 12:1-11.

Bursten, B., and D'esopo, R. The obligation to remain sick. In T.J. Scheff (ed.), Mental Illness and Social Processes. New York: Harper and Row, 1967, pp. 206-219.

Burt, C. The Young Delinquent. London: University of London Press, 1938.

Cameron, M.O. The Booster and the Snitch. Glencoe, Ill.: The Free Press, 1964.

Cannel, C.F., and Kahn, R.L. L'interview comme méthode de collecte. In L. Festinger and D. Katz (eds.), Les méthodes de recherche dans les sciences sociales. Paris: Presses Universitaires de France, 1959.

Census of population: 1970, General population characteristics, Final Report PC(1)-B1, U.S. Summary. Washington, D.C.: Bureau of the Census, 1972.

Chambliss, W.J., and Seidman, R.B. Law, Order and Power. Don Mills, Ontario, Canada, 1971.

Chamboredon, J.C. La délinquance juvénile, essai de construction d'objet. Revue Francaise de Sociologie, 1971, 12(3):335-377.

Chang, D.H., and Zastrow, C.H. Inmates' and security guards' perceptions of themselves and of each other: A comparative study. International Journal of Crime and Penology, 1976, 4:89-98.

Chapman, D. Sociology and the Stereotype of the Criminal. London: Tavistock Publications, 1968.

Christiansen, K.O. Mandlige landssvigere i Danmark. Copenhagen: Direktoratet for Faengselsvaesenet, 1950.

_____. Landssvigerkriminaliteten i sociologisk belysning. Dissertation. University of Copenhagen, 1955.

_____. Threshold of tolerance in various population groups illustrated by results from the Danish criminologic twin study. In A.V.S. de Rueck and R. Porter (eds.), The Mentally Abnormal Offender. Boston: Little, Brown, 1968.

_____. Identification des problèmes clés de la recherche sociologique dans le domaine de la criminologie. Orientations actuelles de la recherche *criminologique, Etudes relatives à la recherche criminologique.* Conseil de l'Europe, 1970, pp. 81-101.

————. The genesis of aggressive criminality: Implications of a study of crime in a Danish twin study. In J. Dewit and W.W. Hartup (eds.), *Determinants and Origins of Aggressive Behavior.* The Hague: Mouton, 1974.

————. On general prevention from an empirical viewpoint. In the National Swedish Council for Crime Prevention (eds.), *General Deterrence.* Stockholm, 1975, pp. 60-74.

————. A preliminary study of criminality among twins. In S.A. Mednick and K.O. Christiansen (eds.), *Biosocial Bases of Criminal Behavior.* New York: Gardner Press, 1977a.

————. A review of studies of criminality among twins. In S.A. Mednick and K.O. Christiansen (eds.), *Biosocial Bases of Criminal Behavior.* New York: Gardner Press, 1977b.

Christiansen, K.O., and Nielsen, A. Nulevende straffede maend i Danmark (Punished men in Denmark today). *Nordisk Tidsskrift for Kriminalvidenskab,* 1959, 47:18-28.

Christie, M.J., Andenaes, J., and Skerbaekk, S. A study of self-reported crime. *Scandinavian Studies in Criminology,* 1965, 1:86-116.

Christie, N. *Tvangsarbeid og alkoholbruk.* Oslo: Universitetsforlaget, 1960.

Cicourel, A.V. *The Social Organisation of Juvenile Justice.* New York: Wiley, 1968.

————. Delinquency and the attribution of responsibility. In R.A. Scott and J. Douglas (eds.), *Theoretical Perspectives on Deviance.* New York: Basic Books, 1972.

Clark, J.P., and Wenninger, E.P. The attitude of juveniles toward the legal institution. *Journal of Criminal Law, Criminology and Police Science,* 1964, 55:482-489.

Cleckley, H. *The Mask of Sanity.* St. Louis: C.V. Mosby, 1964.

Clinard, B.M. *Sociology of Deviant Behavior.* New York: Holt, Rinehart & Winston, 1963.

Clinard, B.M., and Quinney, R. *Criminal Behavior Systems: A Typology.* New York: Holt, Rinehart & Winston, 1959.

Cloward, R.A., and Ohlin, L.B. *Delinquency and Opportunity: A Theory of Delinquent Gangs.* Glencoe, Ill.: Free Press, 1960.

Cohen, A. *Delinquent Boys: The Culture of the Gang.* Glencoe, Ill.: Free Press, 1955.

————. *Deviance and Control.* Englewood Cliffs, N.J.: Prentice-Hall, 1966.

Cormier. Quoted from H. Mannheim. *Comparative Criminology.* London: Routledge & Kegan Paul, 1965, p. 689.

Coser, L.A. *Continuities in the Study of Social Conflict.* New York: Free Press, 1967.

————. Presidential address: Two methods in search of a substance. *American Sociological Review,* 1975, 40(6):691-700.

Council of Europe. *Crime on the Roads*. Council of Europe's Fourth European Conference of Directors of Criminological Research Institute. November 22-25, 1966, Strasbourg.

Cusson, M. Les theóries de l'échange et al délinquance. Unpublished manuscript, University of Montréal, 1976.

Debuyst, C. Les nouveaux courants dans la criminologie contemporaine—La mise en cause de la psychologie criminelle et de son objet. *Revue de Droit Pénal et de Criminologie*, 1974-1975, pp. 845-870.

De Greef, E. *Introduction à la criminologie*. Bruxelles: Van der Plas, 1946.

Devlin, I. Drug talk makes sixth formers queasy. *Times Educational Supplement*, January 30, 1970.

Dickens, C. *American Notes for General Circulation*. London: Chapman and Hall, 1842. Cited by T. Eriksson, *The Reformers: A Historical Survey of Pioneer Experiments in the Treatment of Criminals*. New York: Elsevier, 1976, p. 70.

Dollard, J., Doob, L.W., Miller, N.E., et al. *Frustration and Aggression*. New Haven: Yale University Press, 1950.

Douglas, J.W.B., and Blomfield, J.M. *Children under Five*. London: Allen & Unwin, 1958.

Downes, D.M. *The Delinquent Solution: A Study in Subcultural Theory*. London: Routledge & Kegan Paul, 1966.

Durkheim, E. *The Rules of Sociological Method*. Chicago: University of Chicago Press, 1938, pp. 67-71.

_____. *Suicide*, translated by J.A. Spaulding and G. Simpson. Glencoe, Ill.: Free Press, 1951.

Elmhorn, K. Receiving and receivers. A pilot study in Sweden. UNSDRI: August, 1975.

Empey, T., Lubeck, S.G., and Laporte, R.L. *Explaining Delinquency. Construction, Test and Reformulation of a Sociological Theory*. Lexington, Mass.: Lexington Books, D.C. Heath, 1971.

Erickson, E. The problem of identity. *Journal of the American Psychoanalytical Association*, 1956, 4:56-121.

Erikson, K.T. Notes on the sociology of deviance. *Social Problems*, 1962, 9:308.

Erskine, H. The polls: Fear of violence and crime. *Public Opinion Quarterly*, 1974, 38:131-145.

Eysenck, H.J. *Crime and Personality*. London: Routledge & Kegan Paul, 1964.

_____. *The Biological Basis of Personality*. Springfield, Ill.: Charles C. Thomas, 1967.

Faugeron, C., and Poggi, D. Les femmes, les infractions, la justice pénale: Une analyse d'attitudes. *Revue de l'Institut de Sociologie*, Université Libre de Bruxelles, 1975, 3-4:375-384.

Faugeron, C., and Robert, P. Un problème de représentation sociale: Les attitudes de punitivité. *Déviance, Cahiers de l'Institut de Criminologie de Paris*, 1974, 1:23-48.

———. Les représentations sociales de la justice pénale. *Cahiers Internationaux de Sociologie,* 1976, 61:341-366.

Fabrega, H., Jr., and Manning, P.K. Disease, illness and deviant careers. In R.A. Scott and J. Douglas (eds.), *Theoretical Perspectives on Deviance.* New York: Basic Books, 1972.

Ferracuti, F., Dinitz, S., and de Brenes, E.A. *Delinquents and nondelinquents in the Puerto Rican Slum Culture.* Columbus: Ohio State University Press, 1975.

Ferrero, G. *Pouvoir, les génies invisibles de la cité.* Plon, 1945.

Filipović, V. *Filozofijski rječnik.* Zagreb: Matica Hrvatska, 1965.

Fishman, G. Can labeling be useful? In P.C. Friday and V.L. Stewart (eds.), *Youth, Crime and Juvenile Justice.* New York: Praeger, 1977.

Fox, J.A. *Forecasting Crime Data.* Lexington, Mass.: Lexington Books, D.C. Heath, 1978.

Fromm, E. *The Anatomy of Human Destructiveness.* New York: Holt, Rinehart & Winston, 1973.

Furstenberg, F.F., Jr. Public reaction to crime in the streets. *The American Scholar,* 1971, 40:601-610.

———. Fear of crime and its effects on citizen behavior. Presented at the Symposium on Studies of Public Experience, Knowledge and Opinion of Crime and Justice. Bureau of Social Science Research, Washington, D.C., March 1972.

Galtung, J. *Fengselssamfunnet.* Oslo: Universitetsforlaget, 1959.

Garfinkel, H. Conditions of successful degradation ceremonies. *American Journal of Sociology,* 1956, 61:421-422.

Gibbons, D.C., Jones, J.F., and Garabedian, P.G. Gauging public opinion about the crime problem. *Crime and Delinquency,* 1972, 18:134-145.

Gibbs, J.P. Conceptions of deviant behavior: The old and the new. *Pacific Sociological Review,* 1966, 9(Spring):9-14.

———. Issues in defining deviant behaviour. In R.A. Scott and J.D. Douglas (eds.), *Theoretical Perspectives on Deviance.* New York: Basic Books, 1972.

Gillin, J.L. *Criminology and Penology.* New York: Appleton-Century Company, 1945.

Glueck, S., and Glueck, E. *Unraveling Juvenile Delinquency.* Cambridge: Harvard University Press, 1950.

Goffman, E. *Stigma.* Englewood Cliffs, N.J.: Prentice-Hall, 1963.

Goode, E. On behalf of labeling theory. *Social Problems,* 1975, 22(5).

Gouldner, A.W. *The Coming Crisis of Western Sociology.* New York: Basic Books, 1970.

Gove, W.R. Societal reaction as an explanation of mental illness: An evaluation. *American Sociological Review,* 1970, 35:873-874.

Gray, W.J. The English prison medical service. In Ciba Foundation Symposium 16, *Medical Care of Prisoners and Detainees.* Amsterdam: Elsevier, 1973, p. 133.

Greve, V. *Kriminalitet som normalitet*. Copenhagen: Juristforbundets Forlag, 1972.

Gruenberg, E.M. The failures of success. *Health and Society*, 1977(Winter):3-24.

Hare, R.D. *Psychopathy: Theory and Research*. New York: Wiley, 1970.

———. Talk presented at NATO meeting on Psychopathic Behavior, September 1975.

Hauge, R. Tid eller penger. *Nordisk Tidsskrift for Kriminalvidenskab*, 1968, 56:137-140.

———. (ed.). Drinking-and-driving in Scandinavia. *Scandinavian Studies in Criminology*. Vol. 6. Oslo: Universitetsforlaget, 1978.

Healey, W. *The Individual Delinquent*. Boston: Little, Brown, 1915.

———, and Bonner, A. *New Light on Delinquency and its Treatment*. New Haven: Yale University Press, 1936.

Henderson, D. *Psychopathic States*. New York: Norton, 1947.

Henshel, R.L., and Silverman, R.A. (eds.). *Perception in Criminology*. New York: Columbia University Press, 1975.

Hindelang, M.J. The commitment of delinquents to their misdeeds: Do delinquents drift?, *Social Problems*, 1970, 17:502-509.

———. *Public Opinion regarding Crime, Criminal Justice and Related Topics*. Washington, D.C.: Law Enforcement Assistance Administration, 1975.

Hirschi, T. *Causes of Delinquency*. Berkeley: University of California Press, 1969.

Hjort, P. Statement in the daily newspaper *Politiken*. January 10, 1970, p. 3, and January 11, 1970, p. 3.

Høgh, E., and Wolf, P. Project Metropolitan: A longitudinal study of 12,270 boys from the Metropolitan area of Copenhagen, Denmark 1953-1977. In S.A. Mednick (ed.), *Prospective Longitudinal Research in Europe*. London: Oxford University Press, in press.

Hood, R.G. Research on the effectiveness of punishments and treatments. In Council of Europe, European Committee on Crime Problems (eds.), *Collected Studies in Criminological Research*. Vol. 1. Stroudsburg: Council of Europe, 1967, pp. 74-102.

Hurwitz, St., and Christiansen, K.O. *Kriminologi I* (Criminology I). Copenhagen: Gyldendal, 1968.

Hutchings, B., and Mednick, S.A. Criminality in adoptees and their adoptive and biological parents: A pilot study. In S.A. Mednick and K.O. Christiansen (eds.), *Biosocial Bases of Criminal Behavior*. New York: Gardner Press, 1977.

Jensen, E.P. Feature article in *Berlingske Aftenavis*. August 4, 1956, p. 7.

Jessor, R., Graves, T.D., Hanson, R.C., and Jessor, S.L. *Society, Personality and Deviant Behavior*. New York: Holt, Rinehart & Winston, 1968.

Joutsen, M. *Young offenders in the Criminal Justice System of Finland*. Research Institute of Legal Policy Publications No. 14, Helsinki, 1976.

Kahn, E. *Psychopathic Personalities*. New Haven: Yale University Press, 1931.

Kaiser, G. *Kriminologie* (Criminology). Uni-Taschenbücher 594. Heidelberg-Karlsruhe: C.F. Müller Verlag, 1976.

Kallestrup, L.R. Straffefrekvensen i forskellige sociale grupper (The frequency of punishment in various social groups). *Nordisk Tidsskrift for Kriminalvidenskab*, 1954, 42:30-34.

Kandel, L. Reflexions sur l'usage de l'entretien, notamment non directif, et sur les études d'opinion. *Epistémologie Sociologique*, 1972, 13:25-46.

Klein, G.S., and Schlesinger, H.J. Perceptual attitudes of form boundedness and form-liablity in Rorschach responses. Abstract. *American Psychologist*, 1950, 5:321.

Klette, H. Some minimum requirements for legal sanctioning systems with special emphasis on detection. In the National Swedish Council for Crime Prevention (eds.), *General Deterrence*. Stockholm, 1975.

Kolakowski, L. *Alienation of Reason: A History of Positivist Thought*. New York: Doubleday, 1969.

———. Le diable peut-il etre sauve? *Contrepoint*, Paris, 1976, 20:151-164.

Korn, R.R., and McCorkel, L.W. *Criminology and Penology*. New York: Holt, Rinehart & Winston, 1959.

Kosik, K. *Dialektika konkretnega*. Translated and edited by F.Jerman. Ljubljana: Cankarjeva založoa, 1967.

Kranz, H. Discordant soziales verhalten eineuger zqillinge. *Monatschrift für Kriminalpsychologie und Strafrechtsreform*, 1935, 26:511-516.

Kriminaalihuoltokomitean mietintö (Report of the Committee on Probation and Parole), Committee Report 1972: A 1 (in Finnish only). Helsinki: Government Printing Centre, 1972.

Kriminalstatistik 1974 og 1975 (Crime statistics 1974 and 1975). Statistiske Meddelelser 1976, 3, and 1977, 5. Copenhagen: Danmarks Statistik, 1976, 1977.

Kutchinsky, B. Law and education: Some aspects of Scandinavian studies on "the general sense of justice." *Acta Sociologica*, 1966, 10:21-41.

———. Knowledge and attitudes regarding legal phenomena in Denmark. In N. Christie (ed.), *Scandinavian Studies in Criminology*. Vol. 2. Oslo: Universitetsforlaget, 1968, pp. 125-259.

———. Advances in Scandinavian studies on knowledge and opinion about law. In J.M.M. Maeijer et al. (eds.), *Rechtssociologie en jurimetrie*. Deventer, Holland: Kluwer, 1970.

———. Towards an explanation of the decrease in registered sex crimes in Copenhagen. *Technical Report of the Commission on Obscenity and Pornography*. Vol. 7. Washington, D.C.: Government Printing Office, 1971, pp. 263-310.

———. Sociological aspects of the perception of deviance and criminality. In European Committee in Crime Problems (eds.), *Collected Studies in Criminological Research*. Vol. 9. Strasbourg: Council of Europe, 1972.

LaGache, D. *Psycho-Criminogenese: Tenth General Report*. Paris: 2nd International Congress of Criminology, 1950.

Lange, J. *Verbrechen als schiskal.* Leipzig: Georg Thieme, 1929. English ed. London: Unwin Brothers, 1931.

Lascoumes, P., and Moreau-Capdevielle, G. Presse et justice pénale, un cas de diffusion idéologique. *Revue Francaise de Science Politique*, 1976, 16(1):41-68.

Lasner, E., and Montgomery, E. de. En explorativ studie av skolungdomars normuppfattning. (An exploratory study of the norm conceptions of youth of the schools). Stockholm: Kriminalvetenskapliga Institutet vid Stockholms Universitet, Afdelningen för allmän kriminalvetenskap och kriminalpolitik, 1974 (stencil Nr. 36).

Legras, A.M. *Psychese en criminaliteit bij twellingen.* Utrecht: Kemink en Zoon N.V. 1932. A summary in German can be found in Psychosen und kriminalitat bei zwillingen. *Zeitschrift fur die gesamte Neurologie und Psychiatrie*, 1933, 198-228.

Lemert, E.M. *Human Deviance, Social Problems and Social Control.* Englewood Cliffs, N.J.: Prentice-Hall, 1967.

Linden, P.A., and Similä, M. General deterrence and the general sense of justice. In the National Swedish Council for Crime Prevention (eds.), *General Deterrence.* Stockholm, 1975.

Lipton, D., Martinson, R., and Wilks, J. *The Effectiveness of Correctional Treatment: A Survey of Treatment Evaluation Studies.* New York: Praeger, 1975.

Loeb, J., and Mednick, S.A. A prospective study of predictors of criminality: 3. Electrodermal response patterns. In S.A. Mednick and K.O. Christiansen (eds.), *Biosocial Bases of Criminal Behavior.* New York: Gardner Press, 1977.

Lofland, J. *Deviance and Identity.* Englewood Cliffs, N.J.: Prentice-Hall, 1969.

Lombroso, C. *Crime: Its Causes and Remedies.* Boston: Little, Brown, 1912, pp. 34-35.

Lykken, D.T. A study of anxiety in the sociopathic personality. *Journal of Abnormal and Social Psychology*, 1957, 55:6-10.

McFarland, R., and Moseley, A.L. *Human Factor in Highway Transport Safety.* Boston: Harvard School of Public Health, 1954.

Maestro, M. Benjamin Franklin and the penal law. *A Journal of Ideas*, 1975, 36:551-562.

Malow, U. Die einstellung der bevölkerung zum strafvollzug: Ein kritischer vergleich empirischer untersuchungen. Unpublished dissertation, Hamburg, 1974.

Martinson, R. What works?—Questions and answers about prison reform. *Journal of Public Interest*, June 1974, 6:22-54.

Marx, K. Bevölkerung, Verbrechen und Pauperismus. *New York Daily Tribune*, September 16, 1859. In *Marx-Engels Werke* Bd. 13. Institut für Marxismus-Leninismus beim ZK der SED. Berlin: Dietz Verlag, 1961.

Mathiesen, T. *The Defences of the Weak.* London: Tavistock Publications, 1965.

Matza, D. *Delinquency and Drift.* New York: Wiley, 1964.

Mead, G.H. *Mind, Self and Society from the Standpoint of a Social Behaviorist.* Edited by Charles W. Morris. Chicago: University of Chicago Press, 1934.

Mednick, S.A. *Proceedings of the Second International Symposium: The Biological Model, Part 2.* Sao Paulo, Brasil, 1975.

———. Kirkegaard-Sorensen, L., Hutchings, B., Knop, J., Rosenberg, R., and Schulsinger, F. An example of bio-social interaction research: The interplay of socioenvironmental and individual factors in the eitology of criminal behavior. In S.A. Mednick and K.O. Christiansen (eds.), *Biosocial Bases of Criminal Behavior.* New York: Gardner Press, 1977.

———, and Schulsinger, F. Some premorbid characteristics related to breakdown in children with schizophrenic mothers. *Journal of Psychiatric Research,* 1968, 6:267-291.

———, Schulsinger, F., Higgins, J., and Bell, B. *Genetics, Environment and Psychopathology.* Amsterdam: North-Holland/American Elsevier, 1974.

Merton, R. *Social Theory and Social Structure.* Glencoe, Ill.: Free Press, 1957.

Merton, R.K., Fiske, M., and Kendall, P.L. *The Focused Interview: A Manual of Problems and Procedures.* Glencoe, Ill.: Free Press, 1956.

Michelat, G. Sur l'utilisation de l'entretien non directif en sociologie. *Revue Francaise de Sociologie,* 1975, 16:229-247.

Mike, B. Willem Adriaan Bonger's "Criminality and economic conditions": A critical appraisal. *International Journal of Criminology and Penology,* 1976, 3:211-238.

Miller, W.B. Lower class culture as a generating milieu of gang delinquency. *Journal of Social Issues,* 1958, 14:5-19.

Miller, W.C., and Conger, J.J. *Personality, Social Class and Delinquency.* New York: Wiley, 1966.

Moedikdo, P. Criminology and politicization. In G.W.G. Jasperse, K.A. van Leeuwen-Burow, and L.G. Toornvliet (eds.), *Criminology between the Rule of Law and the Outlaws.* Netherlands: Kluwer and Deventer, 1976, pp. 99-131.

Morris, T. *The Criminal Area. A Study in Social Ecology.* London: Routledge & Kegan Paul, 1957.

Mortensson, G. Psykiatrisk undersøgelse af mandlige landssvigere i Danmark. *Nordisk Tidsskrift for Kriminalvidenskab,* 1953, 41:2.

Mulvihill, D.J., Tumin, M.M., and Curtis, L.A. *Crimes of Violence.* Vol. 2. The staff report submitted to the National Commission on the Causes and Prevention of Violence. Washington, D.C.: U.S. Government Printing Office, 1969.

Nielsen, K. *Resumé af arresthusundersogelsen* (Summary of the study of local prisons in Denmark). Research Report No. 2. Copenhagen: The Research Group of the Directorate of Prisons and Probation, 1974.

Nordisk Råd. *Straffesystemer i Norden* (Penal systems in the Nordic countries: A conference report). NU 1977, 25, Stockholm: Nordisk Råd, 1977.

Nunnally, J. *Popular Conceptions of Mental Health.* New York: Holt, Rinehart & Winston, 1961.

Nuorisorikollisuustoimikunnan mietintö (Report of the Commission on Juvenile Delinquency). Committee Report 1966: A 2 (in Finnish only). Helsinki: Government Printing Centre, 1966.

Nuorisorikollisuuskomitean mietintö (Report of the Committee on Juvenile Delinquency). Committee Report 1970: A 9 (in Finnish only). Helsinki. Government Printing Centre, 1970.

Nye, J.E., and Short, J.F. Scaling delinquent behavior. *American Sociological Review*, 1957, 22:326-331.

Nyqvist, O. *Juvenile Justice*. Uppsala: Almqvist & Wiksell, 1960.

Packer, H.L. *The Limits of Criminal Sanction*. Stanford: Stanford University Press, 1968.

Pareto, V. *Mind and Society*. Translated and edited by A. Livingston. New York: Harcourt, Brace, 1935.

Parsons, T. *The Structure of Social Action*. Glencoe, Ill.: Free Press, 1949.

_____. *The Social System*, Glencoe, Ill.: Free Press, 1951.

Pečuljić, M. *Metodologija društvenih nauka*. Beograd: Službeni list SFRJ, 1976.

Petrie, A. Collins, W., and Solomon, P. The tolerance of pain and sensory deprivation. *American Journal of Psychology*, 1960, 73(1):80-90.

Phillipson, M. *Sociological Aspects of Crime and Delinquency*. London: Routledge & Kegan Paul, 1971.

Pinatel, J. *Etienne De Greeff*, Paris: Cujas, 1967.

_____. Aperçu général de la recherche criminologique en France. *Orientations actuelles de la recherche criminologique: Etudes relatives à la recherche criminologique*. Conseil de l'Europe, 1970, pp. 161-194.

_____. *La société criminogène*. Paris: Calmann-Lévy, 1971.

_____. *Criminologie*. 3d ed. Paris: Dalloz, 1975.

_____. Criminologie et pathologie sociale. *Revue de Science Criminelle*, 1976, pp. 181-189.

Platt, A.M. *The Child Savers: The Invention of Delinquency*. Chicago: University of Chicago Press, 1969.

Pollner, M. Sociological and common-sense models of the labeling process. In R. Turner (ed.), *Ethnomethodology*. Harmonsworth: Penguin Books, 1974.

Popper, K.R. *The Logic of Scientific Discovery*. London: Hutchinson, 1959.

Poveda, T.G. The fear of crime in a small town. *Crime and Delinquency*, 1972, 18:147-153.

Quinney, R. *The Social Reality of Crime*. Boston: Little, Brown, 1970.

_____. *Criminal Justice in America: A Critical Understanding*. Boston: Little, Brown, 1974.

Ray, I. *A Treatise on the Medical Jurisprudence of Insanity*. Boston: Little, Brown, 1838.

Raymondis, L.M., and Le Guern, M. *Le langage de la justice pénale*. Paris: Centre National de la Recherche Scientifique, 1977.

Reasons, C.E. Images of crime and the criminal, the dope fiend mythology. *Journal of Research in Crime and Delinquency*, 1976, 13(2):133-144.

Reckless, W.C. *American Criminology: New Directions*. New York: Appleton-Century-Crofts, 1973.

Reiss, A.J., Jr. The social integration of queers and peers. *Social Problems*, 1961, 9:102-120.

Rikosoikeuskomitean mietintö (Report of the Penal Law Committee). Committee Report 1976:72 (in Finnish with a Swedish summary). Helsinki: Government Printing Centre, 1977.

Robert, P. La recherche opérationnelle dans le système de justice criminelle. In European Committee on Crime Problems (eds.), *Etudes relatives à la recherche criminologique*. Strasbourg: Conseil de l'Europe, 1971, 8:55.

_____. La sociologie entre une criminologie du passage à l'acte et une criminologie de la réaction sociale. *Année Sociologique*, 1973, 24:441-504.

_____. Recherches en criminologie de la reaction sociale. In *Neue Perspektiven in der Kriminologie*. Zurich: Verlag der Fachvereine an den Schweizerischem Hochschulen und Techniken, 1975, pp. 55-83.

_____. Les statistiques criminelles et la recherche: Réflexions conceptuelles. *Déviance et Societe*, 1977, 1(1):3-28.

_____, and Faugeron, C. Analyse d'une représentation sociale, les images de la justice pénale. *Revue de l'Institut de Sociologie*, Université Libre de Bruxelles, 1973a, 1:31-85.

_____. L'image de la justice criminelle dans la société. *Revue de Droit Pénal et de Criminologie*, 1973b, 53(7):665-719.

_____. Représentation du système de justice criminelle, essai de typologie. *Acta Criminologica*, 1973c, 6:13-65.

_____, Faugeron, C., and Kellens, G. Les attitudes des juges à propos des prises de décision. *Annales de la Faculté de Droit de Liège*, 1975, 20:23-152.

_____, P., and Laffargue, B. *L'image de la justice dans la société: Le système pénal vu par ses clients*. Paris: Service d'Etudes Penales et Criminologiques, 1977.

_____, P., Lambert, T., and Faugeron, C. *Image du viol collectif et reconstruction d'objet*. Geneva, Paris, Médecine and Hygiène: Masson, 1976.

_____, P., and Moreau, G. La presse française et la justice pénale. *Sociologia del Diritto*, 1975, 2(2):359-395.

Rosanoff, A.J., Handy, L.M., and Rosanoff, F.A. Criminality and delinquency in twins. *Journal of Criminal Law and Criminology*, 1934, 24:923-934.

Rothman, D. *The Discovery of the Asylum: Social Order and Disorder in the New Republic*. Boston: Little, Brown, 1971.

Rubington, E., and Weinberg, M.S. *Deviance: The Interactionist Perspective*. New York: Macmillan, 1968.

Sagarin, E. *Deviants and Deviance*. New York: Praeger, 1975.

Schachter, S., and Latane, B. Crime, cognition and the autonomic nervous system. *Nebraska Symposium on Motivation*, 1964, 12:221-275.

Scheff, T. *Being Mentally Ill*. Chicago: Aldine, 1966.

_____. (ed.). *Mental Illness and Social Processes*. New York: Harper and Row, 1967.

_____. Negotiating reality: Notes on power in the assessment of responsibility. *Social Problems*, 1968, 16:3-17.

Schneider, K. *Die psychopatischen persönlichkeiten*. 4th ed. Vienna: Franz Deuticke, 1940.

Schulsinger, F. Psychopathy: Heredity and environment. *International Journal of Mental Health*, 1972, 1:199-206.

Schur, E. *Labeling Deviant Behaviour*. New York: Harper and Row, 1971.

_____. A critical assessment of labeling. In R.L. Henshel and R.A. Silverman (eds.), *Perception in Criminology*. New York: Columbia University Press, 1975.

Schwartz, R.D., and Skolnick, J. Two studies of legal stigma. *Social Problems*, 1962, 10:133-142.

Segerstedt, T., Karlsson, G., and Rundblad, B. A research into the general sense of justice. *Theoria*, 1949, 15:321-338.

Sellin, T. *Culture, Conflict and Crime*. New York: Social Science Research Council, 1938.

_____, and Wolfgang, M.E. *Delinquency: Selected Studies*. New York: Wiley, 1969.

Separovic, Z. Criminological analysis of the personality of traffic offenders. *Abstracts on Criminology and Penology*, 1972, 12:51.

Shah, S.A., and Roth, L.H. Biological and psychophysiological factors in criminality. In D. Glaser (ed.), *Handbook of Criminology*, Chicago: Rand McNally, 1974.

Shaw, C.R., and McKay, H.B. *Social Factors in Juvenile Delinquency*. Vol. 2. The National Committee on Law Observance and Law Enforcement, Report on the Causes of Crime. Washington, D.C.: U.S. Government Printing Office, 1931.

_____, *Juvenile Delinquency in Urban Areas*. Chicago: University of Chicago Press, 1942.

Shoham, S.G. *Crime and Social Deviation*. Chicago: Henry Regnery, 1966.

_____. *The Mark of Cain*. St. Lucia: Queensland University Press, 1970.

_____. *Social Deviance*. New York: Gardner Press, 1976.

_____. *Salvation through the Gutters*. Washington: Hemisphere Publications, 1978a, in press.

_____. *The Myth of Tantalus*. St. Lucia: Queensland University Press, 1978b, in press.

_____. Weissbrod, L., Markowsky, R., and Stein, J. The differential pressures toward schizophrenia and delinquency. In P. Friday and V.L. Stewart (eds.), *Youth, Crime and Juvenile Justice*. New York: Praeger, 1977.

Siddle, D.A.T. Electrodermal activity and psychopathy. In S.A. Mednick and K.O. Christiansen (eds.), *Biosocial Bases of Criminal Behavior*. New York: Gardner Press, 1977.

_____, Mednick S.A., Nicol, A.R., and Foggitt, R.H. Skin conductance recovery in anti-social adolescents. In S.A. Mednick and K.O. Christiansen (eds.), *Biosocial Bases of Criminal Behavoir*. New York: Gardner Press, 1977.

———, Nicol, A.R., and Foggitt, R.H. Habituation and overextinction of the GSR component of the orienting response in anti-social adolescents. *British Journal of Social and Clinical Psychology*, 1973, 12:303-308.

Sigsgård, T. *Psykologisk undersøgelse af mandlige landssvigere i Danmark under besaettelsen.* Copenhagen: Direktoratet for Faengselsvaesenet, 1954.

Simmons, J.L., and Chambers, H. Public stereotypes of deviants. *Social Problems,* 1965, 13.

Sjöbring, H. Strucktur och utvickling. Personlig information, 1954.

Skinner, B.F. *Par delà la liberté et la dignité* (Beyond freedom and dignity). Paris: HMH-Laffont, 1972.

Sorel, G. *Reflexions sur la violence.* Paris: M. Riviere, 1936.

Sorokin, P.A. *Sociological Theories of Today.* New York: Harper and Row, 1926.

Stang Dahl, T. The emergence of the Norwegian Child Welfare Law. *Scandinavian Studies in Criminology,* 1974, 5, 83-98.

Stangeland, P., and Hauge, R. *Nyanser i grått.* En undersokelse av selvraportert kriminalitet bland norsk ungdom. Oslo: Universitetsforlaget, 1974.

Statistical Yearbook. *Statistisk Årbog.* Danmarks Statistik. Copenhagen: Danmarks Statistik, 1977.

Steer, D.J., and Carr-Hill, A. The motoring offender—Who is he? *The Criminal Law Review,* April 1967, pp. 214-224.

Straffelovrådet. *Straffelovrådets betaenkning om spirituspavirkede motorforere. No. 588* (Report no. 588 of the Permanent Committee on Penal Reform on Drivers under the Influence of Alcohol). Copenhagen: Statens Trykningskontor, 1970.

Struggle for justice. A report on crime and punishment in America, prepared for the American Friends Service Committee. New York: Hill and Wang, 1971.

Stumpfl, F. *Die ursprunge des verbrechens. Dargestellt am lebenslauf von zwillingen.* Leipzig: Georg Thieme, 1936.

Stürup, G.K. *Psykiatrisk journalskrivning.* Copenhagen: Nyt nordisk Forlag, 1948.

———. *Treating the "Untreatable".* Baltimore: The Johns Hopkins Press, 1968.

———. Therapeutic attitudes to treatment of behavior-disordered criminals. *San Diego Law Review,* 1978, in press.

Stürup, G.K., and Berntsen, K. Tilbagefaldet i ny kriminalitet hos danske statsfaengselsfanger. *Menneske og Miljø.* Copenhagen, 1948, pp. 1-12.

Stürup, G.K., and Christiansen, K.O. 335 statsfaengselsfanger. Unpublished manuscript, Copenhagen, 1946.

Sutherland, E.H. *Principles of Criminology.* Philadelphia: Lippincott, 1934.

———, and Cressey, D. *Criminology.* 9th ed. Philadelphia: Lippincott, 1974.

Svalastoga, K. *Prestige, Class and Mobility.* Copenhagen: Gyldendal, 1959.

———, Differential rates of change and road accidents in Western Europe and North America. *Acta Sociologica,* 1970, 13(2):73-95.

Sveri, K. Trafiknykterhetsbrottsklientelet (The offending clientele of intoxicated persons in the traffic). *SOU*, 1970, 61:57-72.

Sykes, G.M. *The Society of Captives: A Study of a Maximum Security Prison.* Princeton: Princeton University Press, 1958.

_____, and Matza, D. Techniques of neutralisation: A theory of delinquency. *American Sociological Review*, 1957, 22: 664-670.

Syrén, S., and Tham, H. Brottslighet, normer och sanktioner (Delinquency, norm, and sanctions). Uppsala Universitet, Sociologiska Institutionen, 1968 (stencil).

Szabo, D. *Crimes et villes. Étude statistique comparée de la crimalité urbaine et rurale en France et en Belgique.* Paris: Cujas, 1960.

_____. *Criminologie sociologique et modèles en délinquance et inadaptation juvéniles.* Montréal: Centre international de criminologie comparée, 1976.

_____, Gagne, D., and Parizeau, A. *L'adolescent et la société* (étude comparative). Bruxelles: Charles Dessart, 1972.

Tarde, G. *La criminalité compareé.* Paris: Feliz Alcan, 1924.

Taylor, I., Walton, P., and Young J. *The New Crimonology: For a Social Theory of Deviance.* London: Routledge & Kegan Paul, 1973.

_____. *Critical Criminology.* London: Routledge & Kegan Paul, 1975.

Thomas, C.W., and Cage, R.J. Correlates of public attitudes towards legal sanctions. *International Journal of Criminology and Penology,* 1976, 4(3):239-255.

_____, Cage, R.J., and Fosters, S.C. Public opinion on criminal and legal sanctions: An examination of two conceptual models. *The Journal of Criminal Law Criminology,* 1976, 67(1):110-116.

Thomas, W.I. *The Unadjusted Girl.* Boston: Little, Brown, 1923.

_____. The relation of the individual to the group. *American Journal of Sociology,* 1927, 33:814.

Tienari, P. *Psychiatric Illness in Identical Twins.* Copenhagen: Munksgaard, 1963.

Tillman, W.A., and Hobbes, G.E. The accident prone automobile driver. *American Journal of Psychiatry,* 1949, 106:321-331.

Törnudd, P. *Deterrence Research and the Needs for Legislative Planning.* The National Swedish Council for Crime Prevention, Report No. 2, Stockholm, 1975.

Trasler, G. Criminal behavior, In H.J. Eysenck (ed.), *Handbook of Abnormal Psychology.* London: Putnam, 1972.

Uniform Crime Reports. Washington, D.C.: Federal Bureau of Investigation, 1975.

Verhaegen, B. *Introduction à l'histoire immédiate: essai de méthodologie qualitative.* Gembloux: Editions J. Duculot, 1974.

Vodopivec, K. O društvenim prilikama koje pogoduju soijalnoj patologiji dece i omladine. In *Socijalna patologija dece i omladine*, Simposium Zlatibor 27-29 Oct. 1971. Beograd: Institut za kriminoloska i kriminalistička istraživanja, 1971.

――――. (ed.). *Maladjusted Youth—An Experiment in Rehabilitation*. Westmead: Lexington Books, 1974.

Vold, G.B. *Theoretical Criminology*. New York: Oxford University Press, 1958.

von Hirsch, A. *Doing Justice: The Choice of Punishments*. New York: Hill & Wang, 1976.

Vranicki, P. *Historija marksizma*. Vol. 1. Zagreb: Naprijed, 1971.

Waben, K. *The Danish Criminal Code*. Copenhagen: G.E.C. Gad, 1958.

Wadsworth, M.E.J. Delinquency, pulse rates and early emotional deprivation. *British Journal of Criminology*, 1976, 16(3):245-256.

Waldo, G.P., and Hall, N.E. Delinquency and attitudes toward the criminal justice system. *Social Forces*, 1970, 49:291-298.

Ward, D.A. Evaluations of correctional treatment: Some implications of negative findings. In S.A. Yefsky (ed.), *Law Enforcement, Science and Technology*. Washington, D.C.: Thompson, 1967, pp. 201-208.

Warren, C.A.B., and Johnson, J.M. A critique of labeling theory from the phenomenological perspective. In R.A. Scott and J.D. Douglas (eds.), *Theoretical Perspectives on Deviance*. New York: Basic Books, 1972.

Weinberger, J.C., Jakubowicz, P., and Robert P. Il declino del diritto . . . como strumento du controllo sociale. *Questione Criminale*, 1976, 2(1):73-96.

――――. Société et gravité des infractions. *Revue de Science Criminelle et de Droit Pénal Comparé*, 1976, 4:915-930

Werner, B. Den faktiska brottsligheten. *Nordisk Tidsskrift for Kriminalvidenskab*, 1971, 1-2:106-141.

Westheuss, K.W. Class and organisation as paradigms in social science. *The American Sociologist*, 1976, 2(1):38-49.

Whiteside, T. Annals of crime: Dead souls in the computer. *The New Yorker*, August 22, 1977, pp. 35-65; August 29, 1977, pp. 34-64.

Willett, T. *Criminal on the Road: A Study of Serious Motoring Offences and Those Who Commit Them*. London: Tavistock Publications, 1964.

Wilson, J.Q. *Thinking about Crime*. New York: Basic Books, 1975.

Wing, J.K. Institutionalism in mental hospitals. In T.J. Scheff (eds.), *Mental Illness and Social Processes*. New York: Harper & Row, 1967, pp. 219-242.

Witkin, H.A., Dyk, R.B., Faterson, H.F., Goodenough, D.R., and Karp, S.A. *Psychological Differentiation*. New York: Wiley, 1962.

Witkin, H.A., Faterson, H.F., Goodenough, D.R., and Birnbaum, S. Cognitive patterning in mildly retarded boys. *Child Development*, 1966, 37:301-316.

Witkin, H.A., Mednick, S.A., Schulsinger, F., Bakkestrom, E., Christiansen, K.O., Goodenough, D.R., Hirschhorn, K., Lundsteen, C., Owen, D.R., Philip, J., Rubin, D.B., and Stocking, M. Criminality, aggression and intelligence among XYY and XXY men. In S.A. Mednick and K.O. Christiansen (eds.), *Biosocial Bases of Criminal Behavior*. New York: Gardner Press, 1977.

Wolf, P. Crime and social class in Denmark. *The British Journal of Criminology*, 1962, 3:5-17.

———. Forskningsnote angående myten om den paene faerdselssynder (Research note concerning the myth of the respectable traffic offender). *Sociologiske Meddelelser*, 1964, 9(1):73-77.

———. A contribution to the topology of crime in Denmark. In K.O. Christiansen (ed.), *Scandinavian Studies in Criminology*. Vol.1. Oslo: Universitetsforlaget; London: Tavistock Publications, 1965.

———. *Kriminalitet i velfaerdssamfundet—20 år efter I* (Crime in a welfare society—20 years after I). Serie M, 29. Metropolitgruppen, Sociologisk Institut, University of Copenhagen, 1976.

———. Unpublished victimization study carried out for and financed by the local government of the community of Fredensborg-Humlebaek, Denmark, 1977.

———, and Høgh, E. *Kriminalitet i velfaerdassamfundet* (Crime in a welfare society). Copenhagen: Jorgen Paludans Forlag, 1975.

———, Kaarsen, J., Høgh, E. Kriminalitetshppighenden i Danmark (The frequency of crime in Denmark). *Nordisk Tidsskrift for Kriminalvidenskab*, 1958, 46:113-119.

Wolfgang, M.E. A preface to violence. *The Annals of the American Academy of Political and Social Science*, 1966, 364:1-3.

———. The viable future of criminology. *Criminology in Action*. Montreal: University of Montreal, 1968, pp. 109-134.

———, and Ferracuti, F. *The Subculture of Violence: Towards an Integrated Theory in Criminology*. London: Tavistock Publications, 1967.

———, Figlio, R.M., and Sellin, T. *Delinquency in a Birth Cohort*. Chicago: University of Chicago Press, 1972.

Yablowski, L. *The Violent Gang*. Baltimore: Penguin, 1970.

Yinger, M. Contractulture and subculture. *American Sociological Review*, 1960, 25:625-636.

Yoshimasu, S. Crime and heredity, studies on criminal twins. *Japanese Journal on Race Hygiene*, 1947.

Young, J. The role of the police as amplifiers of deviancy. In S. Cohen (ed.), *Images of Deviance*. Harmondsworth: Penguin Books, 1971.

About the Contributors

Inkeri Anttila is professor of criminal law, and director of the Research Institute of Legal Policy, University of Helsinki, Helsinki, Finland.

Karen Berntsen is clinical director at Ungdomskliniken (Youth Clinic) in Copenhagen, Denmark.

Wouter Buikhuisen is professor of criminology at the Ministerie van Justitie, The Hague, The Netherlands.

Berl Kutchinsky is senior lecturer of criminology at the Institute of Criminal Science, University of Copenhagen, Copenhagen, Denmark.

Sarnoff A. Mednick, Ph.D., Dr. Med., is director of the Psykologisk Institut, Copenhagen, Denmark, and professor of psychology at the University of Southern California, Social Science Research Institute, Los Angeles, California.

Jean Pinatel is professor of criminology, and president of the International Society for Criminology, Paris, France.

Phillippe Robert, Ph.D., is director of Service d'Etudes Pénales et Criminologiques (E.R.A.–C.N.R.S.), Paris, France.

S. Giora Shoham is professor of law at Tel Aviv University, Ramat Aviv, Israel.

Georg K. Stürup, M.D., is a forensic psychiatrist in Randers, Denmark.

Denis Szabo is professor of criminology at the International Centre for Comparative Criminology, Université de Montréal, Montreal, Canada.

Katja Vodopivec, LL.D, is professor of criminology, Pravna fakulteta, Ljubljana, Yugoslavia.

Preben Wolf, LL.M., is associate professor of sociology at the Sociological Institute, University of Copenhagen, Copenhagen, Denmark.

Marvin E. Wolfgang is professor of sociology and law, and director of the Center for Studies in Criminology and Criminal Law, University of Pennsylvania, Philadelphia, Pennsylvania.

About the Editors

Sarnoff A. Mednick received the Ph.D. in psychology at Northwestern University in 1954, and the Dr. Med. at the University of Copenhagen in 1976. His research has emphasized the primary prevention of the mental and social illnesses of man. As director of the Psykologisk Institut in Copenhagen, he has initiated longitudinal studies of children at risk for antisocial behavior and mental illness. He is a consultant in mental health for the European Regional office of the World Health Organization with special responsibility for the ascertainment and description of longitudinal research in Europe. He is currently research associate and professor of psychology at the Social Science Research Institute at the University of Southern California.

S. Giora Shoham is currently a professor on the Faculty of Law at Tel Aviv University. He studied at the University of London and Cambridge University and received the LL.M. and LL.D. from Hebrew University in Jerusalem. He was formerly director of the Institute of Criminology and Criminal Law at Tel Aviv University and a visiting associate professor in the Department of Sociology at the University of Pennsylvania. He has published numerous books and articles in the field of criminology, and was awarded the presidential citation for outstanding achievement in the field of criminology from the American Society of Criminology in 1975.

Barbara Phillips received the masters degree in clinical psychology from the California School of Professional Psychology in 1977. In collaboration with Dr. Mednick she was the assistant editor of a World Health Organization publication entitled *An empirical basis for primary prevention: Prospective longitudinal research in Europe* (forthcoming, Oxford University Press).